Dennis Acott retired to Norfolk in July 2018, with his wife Cathy, after several years of lay ministry involving using and teaching about spiritual gifts, especially the gifts of healing. This accelerated after Dennis was dramatically set free from M.E. in May 2008, following which they founded their 'Eagles 4031' ministry, receiving invitations from churches in the UK and France as well as opportunities for memorable trips to India and Colombia as part of other teams. The itinerant aspect of their ministry has reduced considerably in recent years after accepting an offer to join the leadership team of The Way Christian Fellowship in Hunstanton for a season, but their passion for this ministry is unabated.

To Catthy with love, for your unfailing support and encouragement.

Dennis Acott

BLESSED

Enabled to BE,
Empowered to DO

AUSTIN MACAULEY PUBLISHERS®
LONDON * CAMBRIDGE * NEW YORK * SHARJAH

Copyright © Dennis Acott 2025

The right of Dennis Acott to be identified as the author of this work has been asserted by the author in accordance with sections 77 and 78 of the Copyright, Designs and Patents Act 1988.

All rights reserved. No part of this publication may be reproduced, stored in a retrieval system, or transmitted in any form or by any means, electronic, mechanical, photocopying, recording, or otherwise, without the prior permission of the publishers.

Any person who commits any unauthorised act in relation to this publication may be liable to criminal prosecution and civil claims for damages.

A CIP catalogue record for this title is available from the British Library.

ISBN 9781035874880 (Paperback)
ISBN 9781035874897 (ePub e-book)

www.austinmacauley.com

First Published 2025
Austin Macauley Publishers Ltd®
1 Canada Square
Canary Wharf
London
E14 5AA

Friends and colleagues from St. Luke's, Maidstone; Eastgate Church & School of Supernatural Life; Bethel Sozo (UK); The Way Christian Fellowship.

Table of Contents

Foreword—Daniel Holland, Lead Evangelist with T.F.M. — 11

Part One: Blessed—Enabled to BE — 13

  Introduction (1) — 15

  1. Blessed Are... — 19

  2. Blessed Are the Poor in Spirit, for Theirs is the Kingdom of Heaven — 24

  3. Blessed Are Those Who Mourn, for They Shall Be Comforted — 33

  4. Blessed Are the Meek for They Shall Inherit the Earth — 45

  5. Blessed Are Those Who Hunger and Thirst for Righteousness for They Shall Be Filled — 54

  6. Blessed Are the Merciful for They Shall Obtain Mercy — 64

  7. Blessed Are the Pure in Heart for They Shall See God — 75

  8. Blessed Are the Peacemakers for They Shall Be Called Sons of God — 88

  9. Blessed Are Those Who Are Persecuted for Righteousness' Sake for Theirs Is the Kingdom of Heaven — 98

  Enabled to Be Postscript ! — 111

Part Two: Blessed—Empowered to Do — 115

  Introduction (2) — 117

  1. Blessed by His Perfect Example — 124

  2. Blessed by Spiritual Gifts — 133

  3. Blessed by Spiritual Fruit — 151

4. Blessed by Abundant Life	*180*
5. Blessed by Freedom	*192*
6. Blessed by Healing	*201*
7. Blessed by Sonship	*211*
8. Blessed by Seeds Sown	*218*
9. Blessed by the Five-fold Ministries	*227*
10. Blessed by Metamorphosis	*245*
Empowered to Do Postscript 2	*255*

Foreword—Daniel Holland, Lead Evangelist with T.F.M.

As disciples of Jesus, we live in the tension of an expansionist Kingdom that has come *(at times violently Matthew 11v 12)*, is now here, and will fully manifest when its King, Jesus, returns. Ministering in the battleground between D-day and VE day is by no means easy, with relentless psychological warfare employed by the dominion of darkness.

Especially needed for this reason, Dennis's second book blows away the fog of war, with a timely and clear reminder of how blessed we truly are. What a privilege it is to live in this day with the return of Jesus on the horizon and the harvest of souls so plentiful. We can breathe the fresh air of truth again.

Blessed is edifying, refreshing and convicting. I was reminded of just how blessed I am in Christ. Dennis celebrates this reality, but not just in the future sense (as is so often presented), it is for Now. The book helpfully reminds us also of how futile it is to attempt to live a blessed life in our own strength.

A supernatural manifestation cannot emanate from a natural source.

The book's progression through the be-attitudes peels back the onion's layers of discipleship. It strikes a lovely balance between God's transformative work in us through His Spirit and our submission to, and cooperation with, Him.

Sometimes we feel overwhelmed by the need we see in ourselves, the church and the world. This book shows us the abundant spiritual supply so readily available to us and in us. In fact, 'Blessed carefully reveals to us that our provision is actually a person—Jesus! Hallelujah!'

The second part of the book enlarges on our blessedness in Christ, stripping away more lies that so often attack our position in Christ. Much practical empowering is given to live out this high and blessed calling. If you are walking through a difficult season, feeling battered by spiritual attack, or experiencing spiritual dryness for any reason, this book will supercharge your faith and restore to you the joy of your salvation *(Psalm 51v 12)*. It is after all in being blessed that we become a blessing *(Gen 12v 1-3)*.

I heartily recommend this book to you, confident that it will impart joy, hope and of course, blessing! Be blessed, as you read.

(www.throughfaithmissions.org)

Part One
Blessed—Enabled to BE

Introduction (1)

BLESSED…(Greek: Μακάριοι—Makarioi)
are the poor in spirit, for theirs is the Kingdom of Heaven
are those who mourn, for they shall be comforted
are the meek, for they shall inherit the Earth
are those who hunger and thirst for righteousness, for they shall be filled
are the merciful, for they shall obtain mercy
are the pure in heart, for they shall see God
are the peacemakers, for they shall be called sons of God
are those who are persecuted for righteousness' sake, for theirs is the Kingdom of Heaven.

(Matthew 5:1-10)

(Strong's Greek 3107): Happy, blessed, to be envied. A prolonged form of the poetical makar; *supremely blessed; by extension, fortunate, well off.*

What a privilege, what a glorious product of God's grace, it is to be blessed. To be favoured by Him. To be enriched, fortunate, delighted, privileged, select, happy, content, joyful, joyous, blissful, glad and enviable. Yes, even to be congratulated!

That is the true breadth of meaning of the words translated blessed. It is the position every Christian occupies on being called out of darkness into His wonderful light. The more we appreciate our standing in Him, the more we rejoice in Him. The more we begin to understand all that His grace has wrought for us, the more this realisation genuinely humbles us.

The questions to ask ourselves are, How much do we understand this privilege? Do we fully appreciate it? How much does our knowledge of who we are gain expression in what we do? Are we progressively living an abundant life of awesome potential that we have been born again into? Are we continually moving forward through the process of sanctification that is God's purpose for us individually and collectively—for His glory?

The essence of my chosen subject matter is our new identity *in Christ*. A growing appreciation of who we are now, achieved by His grace and our cooperation with Him. We Christians have an awesome position, in Jesus, that seems almost too good to be true.

In fact, it is only in the more recent of my 50-plus years of knowing Him as my Lord and Saviour that my eyes have been increasingly opened to realise just how blessed I am. And this is through no merit of my own.

The more limited my understanding of my identity in Christ, the more limited my capacity to live out all that Jesus, the Son of Man and the Son of God, has graciously invested in me through His incarnation, death, resurrection, ascension and outpouring of His Spirit.

My ever-grateful awareness that my sins are forgiven has been there from the beginning, from when I was born again (in May 1971). I know that this rich blessing opened the way for a precious relationship with God, the Three in One, to be experienced forever.

What I did not adequately appreciate, for too long a time, was that this restored relationship was the Father's primary purpose in sending His Son. That the forgiveness of sins is a glorious means to that end, not simply an end in itself. I say this because, in some church circles, forgiveness of sins seems to be seen as the (only) goal of the Christian life, rather than the starting point.

Which means that the rest of this life is spent twiddling our thumbs in Heaven's waiting room! Heaven is our final destination, but Kingdom of Heaven life begins here on Earth.

This apparent disparity serves as an illustration of the difference there can be between our position in Christ and our daily experience of living out of that glorious position. It can be so easy to be a hearer of the word but not also a doer of it *(James 1:22)*. Especially if what we hear comes through leaders with an apparently restricted appreciation and experience of doing that consequently has a limiting influence on what they teach and preach.

So, in Part One, I am going to look closely at the Beatitudes of Matthew 5, the beginning of the Sermon on the Mount. Matthew's Gospel conveys to us the truth, the reality of God's heavenly domain invading Earth and its potential impact on human lives.

He refers to the Kingdom almost 40 times and to the Kingship of Jesus Christ some 14 times. However, this Kingdom is not the one that the Jews expected and, sadly, not always the reality that we, His Christian followers, have fully embraced.

The Beatitudes describe very important characteristics of the true Christian position, an essential prerequisite to Christian experience. For me, they are the attitudes of the Christian being (the be-attitudes), intended by the Father to be the foundation for Christian doing.

In Part Two, I will be focussing more on the doing side of being Christian, the empowering for service. This is ours, by grace, because of who we are in Christ.

To be, we must be born again *(John 3:3)*. It is possible to do Kingdom works *(Ephesians 2:10)* effectively only in cooperation with Holy Spirit *(John 15:5)*.

As you journey with me through the following pages, I hope to convey to you accurately my own understanding and appreciation of being truly blessed. I don't claim to be doing this as an expert but as a fellow disciple. Still learning, still discovering, still finding new layers of revelatory and experiential onion to be peeled back, so as to go ever deeper into all He has prepared for me to be and to do.

This is the journey of a lifetime that will last my whole lifetime. I will continually look forward to discovering more of Christ in me, the hope of glory *(Colossians 1:27)* as I press on towards the goal *(Philippians 3:14)*. I invite you to join me, praying that you will go even further than I will manage to do in the remaining time He has reserved for me on Earth.

To be or not to be? That is the question.(William Shakespeare)

Bibliography for Part One

'Studies in the Sermon on the Mount'—D. Martyn Lloyd-Jones
(Inter-Varsity Press & Wm B Eerdmans Publishing Company, 1959-60)
'The Plain Man Looks at the Beatitudes'—William Barclay
(Fontana Books, 1963)
'The Sermon on the Mount'—R. T. Kendall*(Monarch Books, 2013)*

ADDENDUM

Word	Version	Testament	Totals	(Gospels)
Bless	NKJV	Old	**124**	N/A
Blessed	NKJV	Old	**218**	N/A
Blessing	NKJV	Old	**66**	N/A
Blessings	NKJV	Old	**15**	N/A
Bless	NKJV	New	**10**	(2)
Blessed	NKJV	New	**89**	(56)
Blessing	NKJV	New	**23**	(1)
Blessings	NKJV	New	**0**	(0)
Blessings	NIV	New	**6**	(1)

(Source: Olive Tree Bible App)

1
Blessed Are...

Enabled to Be

For most people the Sermon on the Mount is the essence of the Christian faith and life, and equally for most people, the Beatitudes are the essence of the Sermon on the Mount. It is therefore not too much to say that the Beatitudes are the essence of the essence of the Christian way of life.

(William Barclay)

It has also been said that the Beatitudes are the text for Jesus' sermon on the Mount. And that the remainder of Matthew 5, plus chapters 6 and 7, contain the application of that text. This sermon shows us how the Christian life is meant to be lived. It is only possible to do that with the empowering of Holy Spirit. He is the One who enables us to be all that God intends us to be; and to do all that God has planned (in advance) for us to do *(Ephesians 2:10)*.

It sets out what is required of us, going deeper than the requirements of the Old Testament Law of Moses. It points us to the only source of power by which we are enabled to meet these more demanding requirements. In effect, Jesus is teaching how it is possible to keep or, more accurately, to fulfil the Law.

He had demonstrated this by His own Life here on Earth. He is not emphasising an outward duty but an inward transformation, or transfiguration. Life in the spirit is made possible by His grace alone. He calls, equips, and enables us.

For what the law could not do in that it was weak through the flesh, God did by sending His own Son in the likeness of sinful flesh, on account of sin: He condemned sin in the flesh, that the righteous requirement of the law might be fulfilled in us who do not walk according to the flesh but according to the Spirit.

(Romans 8:3-4)

As Christians, we understand that we are *not under law but under grace (Romans 6:14)*. But, as I have already said, I believe that God enables us to fulfil the Law, just as Jesus did, by the working of His Spirit within us. The Sermon on the Mount is not meant to be a code of ethics, rules, or morals (as it can sometimes be presented).

It is a description of the lifestyle standards that Christian character, or characteristics, in action, are capable of. All made possible by the gracious gift of His divine power at work within us *(2 Peter 1:3)*.

As Doctor Martyn Loyd-Jones wrote, "The Christian view of the Law is one that is concerned about the spirit and is interested in the details only as they are an expression of the spirit."

It is important to appreciate that Jesus is describing here what is possible for every single Christian. It is not reserved for an elite few, those in responsible positions of leadership. It is not a case of, living *like this to become a Christian but* you can *live like this because you are a Christian* (Loyd-Jones again).

For the grace of God that brings salvation has appeared to all men, teaching us that, denying ungodliness and worldly lusts, we should live soberly, righteously, and godly in the present age, looking for the blessed hope and glorious appearing of our great God and Saviour Jesus Christ, who gave Himself for us, that He might redeem us from every lawless deed and purify for Himself His own special people, zealous for good works.

(Titus 2:11-14)

I agree with the view that the Beatitudes are the firm foundation of the Sermon on the Mount. They are essential to every illustration or application that follows from them. We must be the blessed ones to do what is expected of us by *the power that works in us (Ephesians 3:20)*. This is not a gospel of works but a radical inward transformation being given outward expression through our spirit-prompted actions.

Therefore, before we look at the features of individual Beatitudes, we would do well to consider a general overview of them all. Whether we believe that there are seven, eight or nine in total, I think it is important to look at them first as a whole. Even so, each one is inseparable from the others. For my purposes, I am going to settle for eight, enabling us to begin and end with, *for theirs is the Kingdom of Heaven.*

This is because I believe the Kingdom of Heaven is central to the Beatitudes and what follows in the Sermon on the Mount. It is fundamental to the whole matter of being blessed. Of being both enabled to be and equipped to do. All Christians, whether we are currently living or asleep *(1 Corinthians 15:20)*, are citizens of the Kingdom of Heaven. We are born again into it. We are called and equipped to serve in it, on Earth, as sons and daughters of the King. It is our ultimate destiny to meet Him face to face in Heaven, but after we have fulfilled His purpose for us here on Earth.

The bliss of the blessed ones is nothing less than eternal life, a sharing in the Life of God *(2 Peter 1:4)*. This is independent of our outward circumstances, the chances, and changes of natural life. In the Kingdom of God, we invariably find that perceptions of the world are turned upside down.

No worldview could ever understand how the poor in spirit, those who mourn, the hungry and thirsty or the persecuted could possibly be blessed. Let alone to be congratulated!

Therefore, the first hearers of these words of Jesus would have been shocked and amazed as they gathered around Him. They were hearing what amounts to His ministry manifesto. The natural man would conclude that the Beatitudes are very confusing, expecting to find blessings in all the wrong places.

But the born-again, supernaturally blessed ones find that, both in fact and experience, they hit the spot perfectly. Who could expect anything less from the plans and purposes of God?

I have already shared a detailed definition of what it means to be blessed. We could also say that to be *blessed* is to be *anointed* by Holy Spirit, as unimpeded carriers of His Presence. Provided, of course, we neither *quench (1 Thessalonians 5:19)* nor *grieve (Ephesians 4:30)* Him.

This is the only way by which it is possible to *be* enabled both to inwardly possess and outwardly express all the characteristics described in the Beatitudes. And indeed, in the whole Sermon on the Mount. This is the type of person who is truly *happy* and *to be congratulated*, in God's Kingdom on *Earth*.

William Barclay points out that there is no verb *(are)* in the original Greek text. He contends that the Beatitudes are not statements, as we would tend to see them in English, but exclamations!

Rather than saying, "Blessed are—", he says Jesus is exclaiming, "O, the bliss of…!"

This means that they are not statements containing prophetic promises of a future blessed state. They are present gifts available to Christians here and now. This view is consistent with the, *now and not yet* teaching about the Kingdom of God, conveying both present and future realities.

As already mentioned, the lifestyle characteristics shown in the Beatitudes are impossible for the natural man to attain. Certainly, on a consistent 24/7 basis. But the impossible is always possible with God the Holy Spirit resident and free to be active within and through us. We should never underestimate what is achievable through His Holy Presence. The blessed ones have recognised their deepest needs and discovered how, and in whom, those needs can, and will, be met.

The blessed ones have entered the blessed, blissful discovery of:

- their own natural poverty.
- a sorrowful awareness of the sinful state in which they had lived; and
- a hunger and thirst for a righteousness unattainable by self-effort.

They have found it in the Christian life. In the One who, during His time ministering on Earth, exemplified this blessed Life through mercy, meekness, purity of heart and peace-making. They have discovered that there is no better way than to follow in the footsteps of Jesus. To embark on an amazing adventure, by the grace of God and in the power of Holy Spirit within them.

They now possess the type of character that can express, as *fruit (Galatians 5:22)*, the conduct that is exemplified in the remainder of the Sermon on the Mount. That explains why these qualities are highlighted at the beginning of the sermon. As I pointed out earlier, the general comes before the particular. The horse always precedes the cart.

It is not wise to home in on any specific injunction from the remainder of the sermon without first considering the Beatitudes. Everything derives from those 10 verses. All of us Christians are meant to give expression to all of these characteristics. They are not intended to be isolated expressions either but to be unified in every single believer.

Again, none of these qualities can be identified as natural tendencies. Each one is dependent upon grace alone. They are impossible to produce without full cooperation with Holy Spirit activity from within us. They are neither products of our birth, nor nature, nor temperament. Even though this may appear to be so with some people—at least some of the time. A supernatural manifestation cannot emanate from a natural source.

The born-again Christian life is distinguishable from the natural, Adamic, life. So, the essential identity and conduct of the Christian are distinguishable from that of the non-Christian. Even if aspects of the outward appearance can sometimes be similar. A church that is distinctly different from the world is more likely to prove attractive to the world than one which employs outreach programmes and initiatives which blur the lines in an attempt to widen the appeal of the gospel. The potential drawbacks of the *seeker-friendly* concept are a watered-down gospel and a presentation of *religious entertainment.*

The Lord's intention is that the process called sanctification will make us more like Jesus. He, who attracted *sinners* to Himself precisely because He was so different from the religious authority figures of the time. Religiosity and compromise are no substitutes for authentic Christian spirituality. Can we expect this to attract the lost and make disciples of them *(Matthew 28:19-20)?*

Yes, the blessed ones, the happy ones, the ones to be congratulated are those who are born again, empowered by Holy Spirit, seeking to hear from Him and then to be obedient to what He says. This is the potent combination of words and actions, hearing and doing.

2
Blessed Are the Poor in Spirit, for Theirs is the Kingdom of Heaven

Blessed are the poor in spirit

> *For thus says the High and Lofty One*
> *Who inhabits eternity, whose name is Holy:*
> *I dwell in the high and holy place,*
> *With him who has a contrite and humble spirit,*
> *To revive the spirit of the humble,*
> *and to revive the heart of the contrite ones.*

(Isaiah 57:15)

I believe it is important to begin by pointing out that those who are *poor in spirit* should not be confused with those who are *poor* in terms of financial means or what could be termed their *social status*. I suggest it is possible for a rich man to be *poor in spirit* and for a poor man not to be.

The same Greek word for *poor (ptóchos)* is also used in *Luke 6:20* and, according to *Strong 4434*, it describes *one who crouches and cowers; hence beggarly, poor* and it can be used in relation to the *poor, destitute, spiritually poor, either in a good sense (humble, devout persons) or bad.*

Therefore, in Luke's Gospel, it is possible to interpret the *poor* in both a spiritual and a natural context. However, there can be no confusion about Matthew's meaning because he refers specifically to the *poor in spirit*. Then he goes on to describe them as blessed ones (a term I will be using a lot).

Blessed, in this context, is not a description one would apply automatically to a person who is poor in financial and/or social terms. I am taking the liberty of labouring the point a bit simply in order to make the distinction very clear.

The description applied to the blessed ones by Matthew refers to their spiritual position, a position attained by the grace of God alone.

For the sake of clarity, I suppose it should also be noted that being *poor in spirit* has nothing to do with what is known as the *poverty spirit*. I do not want to dwell on this, as it is not my subject, but Stephen de Silva has taught that *the fingerprints of a poverty spirit are a) things are always going to fail; b) I won't be enough; c) I'm not smart enough; d) I am not handsome enough or beautiful enough.* This describes low self-esteem.

There is no indication of any spiritual quality derived from the Kingdom of Heaven. Indeed, the natural processes which produce such thoughts can be hijacked by the enemy and become a (negative) spiritual stronghold in a person's life. This will hold them back from the purposes of God.

Being *poor in spirit* is the quality brought to our attention in the first Beatitude, the first of the *being-attitudes*. Simply because this is where each one of us must begin. The other Beatitudes are progressions from, or additions of equal merit to, first becoming *poor in spirit* and thereby gaining admission to the Kingdom of Heaven. There is no one in the Kingdom of Heaven who was not, is not, or is not wanting to remain, *poor in spirit*.

It is not possible to mourn, to be meek, to hunger and thirst for righteousness, to be merciful, to be pure in heart, to be a peacemaker, and certainly not to be persecuted for righteousness's sake, authentically, unless one is first, and seeking to continue to be, *poor in spirit*. Each of these characteristics is a product of the grace of God at work in our lives. None of them are qualities we acquire by natural means, by our own efforts.

Being *poor in spirit* indicates an emptying. The necessary precursor to the fullness becomes apparent as the other blessed characteristics begin to be manifested. If we are to be filled then, first, we need to be emptied. Emptied of self-reliance or dependence upon our own effort and attainment to gain admittance to the Kingdom of Heaven. We need to come into a *healthy brokenness* as R. T. Kendall describes it. The only effective remedy for such brokenness is God's gracious mercy.

When we reach this point, when we are humble and totally dependent upon God for everything, we have reached the stage at which God can reach us. He would have already been reaching out to us to bring us to this crucial turning point, of course. Probably without us necessarily being aware of it. We can begin with Him only when we have reached the end of ourselves. When we acknowledge our state of spiritual bankruptcy.

There was a time when there was a widely held view that all that was necessary to change the world for good was for people to live by the standards set out in the Sermon on the Mount. However, the problem was that they expected these standards to be attained by human desire and effort, or *works*. This ignores the inescapable fact that such perfect standards are beyond each one of us.

You say, I am rich, have become wealthy, and have need of nothing—and do not know that you are wretched, miserable, poor, blind, and naked.

(Revelation 3:17)

Fundamental to the doctrine of justification by faith is the fact that conviction must precede conversion. This conviction is brought about by the work of Holy Spirit upon us. Just as our conversion, being *born again*, is the work of Holy Spirit—with our cooperation. In the same way, being *poor in spirit* precedes the other qualities of the blessed ones. They all develop from this first one.

Self-confidence, self-assurance, self-reliance, self-righteousness, indeed self-anything, are the antithesis of being *poor in spirit*, which is a healthy form of humility. Of course, there is such a thing as false humility, as typified by Dicken's character, Uriah Heep.

He was proud of his humility, which was only an affectation anyway. Being *poor in spirit* should not be confused with that! No, true humility is a *biblical virtue*, and humility always comes before honour in the Kingdom.

Therefore, humble yourselves under the mighty hand of God, that He may exalt you in due time.

(1 Peter 5:6)

When an honest person comes face to face with a Holy God, how can such a confrontation fail to produce a healthy kind of poverty of spirit? We are not born with that quality. We could, though, be born with a weak character, diffidence, nervousness and lacking in courage. Such characteristics could give the appearance of being *poor in spirit* but they are not the genuine article.

Being *poor in spirit* is not a suppression of natural personality either. That is not a healthy kind of self-denial. We are who we are. We do not have to create a false self in order to be *poor in spirit*.

Neither do we need to put every (natural) effort into creating a good impression in front of others. It is more likely that the *poor in spirit* will create a good impression without consciously trying to do so. Through being focussed on others rather than themselves.

From among the many characters in the Bible, the Apostle Peter provides an interesting example for us. He was naturally a bold, aggressive type of person. My wife, Cathy, would probably describe him as one who *uses gob before brain*. There are several examples of his habit of *getting it wrong* in the gospels.

Probably the trait that particularly endears him to most of us. Reading about him in Acts and learning about him from his epistles we can see that, although his essential personality does not change, he became *poor in spirit*.

Going back into the Old Testament, we find the example of David. That most *Christian* of men in the pre-Christian era. He was a *man after God's own heart (1 Samuel 13:14, Acts 13:22)* but he was not without his failings. For example, the situation with Bathsheba and Uriah clearly illustrates that.

But, after God's intervention through the prophet, Nathan, David came under conviction. This led him first into repentance and then into restoration of his relationship with God.

The sacrifices of God are a broken spirit, a broken and a contrite heart—these, O God, You, will not despise.

(Psalm 51:17)

The Apostle Paul is another great example to encourage us here. He had many natural gifts and advantages that he was fully aware of *(2 Corinthians 11:22-29)*. He must have constantly been fighting against the temptation of pride. Yet all of these gains were counted as losses to one who was included among the blessed ones who are were *poor in spirit*.

But what things were gain to me, these I have counted loss for Christ. Yet indeed I also count all things loss for the excellence of the knowledge of Christ Jesus my Lord, for whom, I have suffered the loss of all things, and count them as rubbish, that I may gain Christ and be found in Him, not having my own righteousness, which is from the law, but that which is through faith in Christ, the righteousness which is from God by faith; that I may know Him and the power of His resurrection, and the fellowship of His sufferings, being conformed to His death, if, by any means, I may attain to the resurrection from the dead.

(Philippians 3:7-11)

Then there is the prime example of Jesus, the Son of Man, of course. Just look at John 14:10 or Philippians 2:5-8, for example. We see there was a complete absence of pride, self-assurance, and self-reliance about His human personality. He lived and ministered in total dependence upon the Father.

He said only what He *heard* Him say and did only what He *saw* Him do. Yes, He was, is and always will be the Son of God, the second Person of the Holy Trinity. But He lived and ministered on Earth as the Son of Man. As such, He modelled for us all the potential of the normal Christian life.

The *poor in spirit* are blessed because God says they are. It really does not matter what a worldly view of humility or brokenness might be. God has a habit of turning many worldly expectations upside down. For example, He exalts the humble *(Matthew 23:12)*.

And you He made alive, who were dead in trespasses and sins…and raised us up together, and made us sit together in the heavenly places in Christ Jesus.

(Ephesians 2:1, 6)

Therefore, a consciousness of the total inadequacy of the natural man in the Presence of God is a must for us. We cannot produce it. We cannot work it up. We cannot put our trust in any our own natural gifts or advantages.

Just as Paul did, we should see our own effort and attainment as *rubbish* (a polite translation from the original Greek!) when we come before our Holy God. We are totally dependent upon His grace and mercy, which He freely gives us in Christ.

When we come before Him to whom we must give account *(Hebrews 4:13)*, what do we have in and of our natural selves that has any worth or merit in the Kingdom of Heaven? We have no effective defence, no reasonable excuse, no acceptable self-justification with which to plead our case. The natural man is a sinner, period and the wage, the outcome of sin, is death *(Romans 3:23)*.

It is impossible for us to make ourselves *poor in spirit*. This is simply the supernatural outcome of an encounter with God that leads us into conviction, confession, and total dependence upon Him for salvation and sanctification. And for a fruitful life that is pleasing to Him, an acceptable sacrifice.

We need to look at our God. To focus all our attention on Him. We cannot do this without coming into an awareness of our own, natural, absolute poverty and emptiness before him. It is His life in us, that matters *(Colossians 1:27)* if we want to enter into and live from the Kingdom of Heaven.

We could summarise by saying, *"Oh, the bliss of those who have surrendered completely to God trusting only in Him and depending fully upon Him."*

For theirs is the Kingdom of Heaven

Most assuredly, I say to you, unless one is born again,
he cannot see the Kingdom of God.

(John 3:3)

How wonderful it is that we Christians are in the Kingdom of Heaven and the Kingdom of Heaven is in us.

It came, it is present and is yet to come is the essence of the *now and not yet* of the Kingdom of God. Whilst the *not yet* is vitally important, the *now* should never be undervalued and is the primary focus of this book.

I believe that *the Kingdom of Heaven* and *the Kingdom of God* are two interchangeable phrases. They both describe the same entity. If you agree, then there can be no better place for us to find a *definition* of that phrase than within the Bible itself. We are much less likely to run into difficulty when we allow the Word of God to interpret itself, under the guidance of Holy Spirit.

The Kingdom of God is…righteousness and peace and joy in the Holy Spirit.

(Romans 14:17)

The Kingdom of God (or of Heaven) is righteousness, peace, and joy—in the Holy Spirit. It is where He is. It is found in His Presence, under His anointing. His Kingdom is where the Spirit of God has free rein. Unimpeded by sinful man or the interference of our enemy's forces *(2 Corinthians 3:17)*. If there is any opposition, the power of God is more than sufficient to deal with it.

But if I cast out demons by the Spirit of God, surely the Kingdom of God has come upon you.

(Matthew 12:28)

This is a very powerful illustration of the sovereignty of God prevailing over circumstances. Just as when Jesus commanded the storm to cease by taking Kingdom authority over it *(Mark 4:35-39)*.

The righteousness spoken of is, of course, the righteousness of Jesus. This becomes ours, by the free gift of God's grace, when we are born again.

For He made Him who knew no sin to be sin for us, that we might become the righteousness *of God in Him.*

(2 Corinthians 5:21)

The *peace* referred to is the peace of God, which it is possible for the Christian to embrace. Yes, even in seemingly impossible situations. Because it comes from a superior reality to the one in which our circumstances exist.

And the peace of God, which surpasses all understanding, will guard your hearts and minds through Christ Jesus.

(Philippians 4:7)

For the same reason *joy*, which is another fruit of the Spirit, can also triumph against all odds that would prompt the opposite emotion. This is not simple happiness, which can be fleeting and governed purely by circumstances. It is something much deeper and more lasting. Heavenly joy flows from the Spirit of God within us. He is the source of our strength *(Nehemiah 8:10)*.

In a great trial of affliction, the abundance of their joy and their deep poverty abounded in the riches of their liberality.

(2 Corinthians 8:2)

I also love R. T. Kendall's definition of the Kingdom of Heaven: *the rule of the un-grieved Spirit in the believer*. It follows that, if we grieve Him *(Ephesians 4:30)*, then *we forfeit His un-grieved Presence, although He never leaves us (John 14:16)*. We will take that matter further in a later chapter.

Having looked briefly at what the Kingdom of Heaven *is*, perhaps we should now consider *where* it is to be found.

The Kingdom of Heaven is at hand is a phrase which appears several times in the gospels Matthew 10:7 for example. In this context, it is not a reference to a *place* to which we are to go when we die.

This Kingdom is God's domain. It refers to wherever God is. Christians believe He is omnipresent, so He is everywhere at the same time! According to Psalm 24:1, which is quoted in 1 Corinthians 10:26, *The Earth is the Lord's, and everything in it*. He is Creator, Sovereign, Lord, the Supreme Ruler of (Heaven and) Earth.

The Kingdom of Heaven was present wherever Jesus went and exercised Kingdom authority. Wherever He went, and wherever *we* go, in obedience to His call and prompting, the Kingdom is and will be present. It will be manifested through Holy Spirit-empowered expressions (e.g., prophecy or healing).

Hallelujah! For our Lord God Almighty reigns, writes John in Revelation 19:6. And so He does. Always and at all times. But we live in a world where His reign is not universally acknowledged or welcomed. Whilst God's domain does embrace everything, everywhere, there are certain lives, places, situations, and circumstances in which His reign is more obvious than in others. This illustrates when the Kingdom of Heaven is both present and at hand. Where His reign is not embraced, His Kingdom is still at hand and always within reach, but not experientially present.

The Kingdom of Heaven that is promised to the blessed ones is a Kingdom reign in which righteousness, peace and joy, the gracious products of Heaven, are manifest in the lives and circumstances of those who willingly embrace the reign of God. And I am talking about *now* remember, not simply when we get to Heaven (the place) upon departing this present life.

The Christian and the non-Christian belong to totally different realms. *For theirs is the Kingdom of Heaven* is a statement referring solely to the Christian. It is a spiritual Kingdom, not a political or military domain. That was what the majority of the Jews, to whom Jesus was speaking and Matthew was writing, were expecting.

The brokenness and humility of a poor spirit bring us into the Kingdom of Heaven—and keep us there. If and when we fail, as Christians, the only way back into the Kingdom, as we know it, is the way in which we first entered it. To come before God under conviction and with confession, totally dependent upon His love, compassion, grace and mercy for His forgiveness and total acceptance in the beloved 1 John 1:8.

David understood this many years before Jesus of Nazareth came to Earth:

Create in me a clean heart, O God, and renew a steadfast spirit within me. Do not cast me away from Your presence, and do not take Your Holy Spirit from me. Restore to me the joy of Your salvation and uphold me by Your generous Spirit.

(Psalm 51:10-12)

The Kingdom of God belongs not only to those blessed ones who are poor in spirit but, as we shall remind ourselves later, also to those blessed ones who are persecuted for righteousness' sake. Humility and faithfulness lived out to the point of persecution, bring the same reward. A sobering thought on which to end this chapter!

3

Blessed Are Those Who Mourn, for They Shall Be Comforted

Blessed are those who mourn

> *O wretched man that I am!*
> *Who will deliver me from this body of death?*
> *I thank God—through Jesus Christ our Lord!*
>
> (Romans 7:24-25a)

We have discovered that being *poor in spirit* has nothing to do with a lack of financial resources. It will come as no surprise then, that *those who mourn* should not be confused with the bereaved. We may be *happy* for the one who has passed away because we know their ultimate destiny.

But to suggest that we will feel blessed, happy, lucky or to be congratulated ourselves, as a result of our loss of a loved one, is more than a little unrealistic. Again, we are dealing here with the spiritual, not with the natural.

Therefore, I contend that to take this phrase at face value would be a mistake. We must dig deeper if we are to uncover what Holy Spirit is saying to us. The blessed ones are commended because they mourn in *spirit*. To be blessed in that context is, once again, to be under the anointing of Holy Spirit. But what kind of anointing would be associated with mourning?

The Spirit of the Lord God is upon Me because the Lord has anointed Me to preach good tidings to the poor; He has sent Me to heal the broken-hearted, to proclaim liberty to the captives, and the opening of the prison to those who are bound; to proclaim the acceptable year of the Lord, and the day of vengeance of our God; to comfort all who mourn, to console those who mourn in Zion, to give them beauty for ashes, the oil of joy for mourning, the garment of praise for the spirit of heaviness; that they may be called trees of righteousness, the planting of the Lord, that He may be glorified.

(Isaiah 61:1-3)

The Greek word translated as *mourn*[1] in (*Matthew 5:4*) is *pentheō*. It refers to grief, to a sorrowful heart expressed by weeping. It can be found 10 times in the New Testament, including the (almost) *parallel* passage in *(Luke 6:21)*. The mourning we are dealing with here results from a true appreciation of sin, of suffering and of joy.

It is also a progression from being *poor in spirit*, to developing out of brokenness and humility. From seeing see ourselves as we were naturally, and would have remained, but for the gracious intervention of God. He has taken us from the old *flesh* life into the *new creation's* spiritual life.

When we are poor in spirit and become conscious of sin in our lives, part of a positive response is to mourn. We grieve over our failing. We regret our part in letting down our heavenly Father. This is the godly sorrow which leads to repentance *(2 Corinthians 7:10)*. To the forgiveness that brings us comfort and the blessing of both joy and peace because our relationship, our connection, with Him is restored *(Romans 5:1)*.

We need to look at the Beatitudes both as a whole and as a progression. For example, when Isaiah first encountered the holy Presence of God, he immediately came under conviction *(Isaiah 6:5)*. He was conscious of his poverty (of spirit) and was moved to mourn over his sinful condition.

He was forgiven and came into a special relationship with God. As a result, he received the abundant blessing from which we also benefit today as we read of his experiences and his Holy Spirit-inspired prophetic words.

The proper response to sin or suffering will come from within, from the spirit, if we are to be truly blessed. We have seen already that the *poor in spirit* are truly humble and have an accurate awareness of what their natural selves were really like before the intervention and influence of Holy Spirit.

A real sense of sin and of the positive potential of suffering will always precede the true joy of salvation. How can we have a genuine appreciation of the gospel of grace if we do not have a true awareness of our desperate need for its benefits and its blessings?

We need Holy Spirit to expose our sins and to convict us if we are to come into a spiritually healthy condition of mourning. This begins at conversion, of course, but it does not end there. We all have our weak spots. We can all make mistakes. The flesh and the spirit are in conflict, so John's reminder to the Christian, when he or she falls, is timeless.

If we say that we have no sin, we deceive ourselves, and the truth is not in us. If we say that we have not sinned, we make Him a liar, and His Word is not in us.

(1 John 1:8, 10)

But our God is so gracious that, if we respond to His prompting, to His pricking of our conscience, all is not lost. If we are humble enough to admit our error, to regret it, to confess it and to mourn over it, then we will be forgiven.

Comforted by the one who has made provision for every sin by the shedding of His blood on the cross. Paul tells us, in Romans 2:4, that the goodness, the kindness, of God leads us to repentance—not to a big stick!

If we confess our sins, He is faithful and just to forgive us our sins and to cleanse us from all unrighteousness.

(1 John 1:9)

It is basic human nature to want to avoid mourning (or suffering) if we possibly can. But, enabled by grace to see ourselves from God's perspective, knowing that He is only ever motivated by love, we have the facility to rise above the typical reactions of fallen human nature.

The old has gone and the new has come *(2 Corinthians 5:17)*. We can hold our hands up and apologise to whoever we have offended. We can put things right, both with God and man. How blessed, comforting and freeing is that?

The Lord disciplines those He loves (*Hebrews 12:6*). Notice, that it doesn't say that He punishes them. Jesus has already taken all of the punishment due to us upon Himself. The Greek word which has been translated as *discipline* can also mean *enforced learning*.

This is when God teaches us a lesson. The emphasis is on learning, not punishment. This is ultimately to bless the true disciple (i.e., one who learns). We tend to learn more from our mistakes than from our successes!

Being enabled to see our own sin is a blessing in itself because it stops us from focussing instead on the sins of others. You will know, I'm sure, that when we point the finger at someone else there are three other fingers pointing back at us! This humbles us, in a healthy way, and enables us to see ourselves objectively, with the blinkers removed. There is never any place for *Uriah Heep's* false humility.

John 11:35 is famously the shortest verse in the Bible (*Jesus wept*). Jesus mourned over the sins of others. He had no sin of his own to dwell upon, of course (*Hebrews 4:15*). He mourned over the death of Lazarus and its effect upon his family, friends and loved ones. Death is the ultimate consequence of sin coming into the world (*see Romans 6:23*).

He also mourned over Jerusalem, over the sin of His people and its inevitable consequence *(Luke 19:41-44)*. His compassion was such that He wept even though He knew what was to come. Both for Lazarus and also through the provision He would make by His own imminent death (and resurrection) for those who believe.

When we are interceding for others, we may often find ourselves mourning over sin. Especially its effects on a person's life, their family, the community, the country and even the world.

We are identifying with God's hatred of sin, not of sinners, and the harm it has done to His creation. It makes us appreciate even more the extraordinarily gracious lengths He went to in order to put things right, to redeem us, to set us free.

Mourning over sin and the trail of destruction and disruption it can leave in its wake is a necessary precursor to the comfort provided by our salvation and the joy this produces within us.

What about our response to suffering, trials or temptations that may come our way? How do we react in such difficult situations or circumstances? I suggest that our reaction if we are *poor in spirit*, is going to be quite different to what it might be if we were not under that anointing.

My brethren count it all joy when you fall into various trials…Blessed is the man who endures temptation; for when he has been approved, he will receive the crown of life which the Lord has promised to those who love Him.

(James 1:2, 12)

A natural reaction to trial or suffering is to desire instant relief. To get out of the unwelcome situation fast. To leave it far behind. Sometimes God will allow, but not cause, such circumstances to befall us to help us to grow to a new level of maturity in Christ. Escape too soon and we will not learn the lesson He can teach us through it. We will also miss the blessing of His comfort in the pain.

Christian maturity does not come with the passage of time, but by the right responses to the dealings of God.

(Paul Cain)

We can suffer for doing the right thing just as we can also suffer for doing the wrong thing. This is a simple fact of life. Which is better in God's eyes? Which is more pleasing to Him *(1 Peter 3:17)*?

(In this, you greatly rejoice), though now for a little while, if need be, you have been grieved by various trials, that the genuineness of your faith, being much more precious than gold that perishes, though it is tested by fire, may be found to praise, honour, and glory at the revelation of Jesus Christ.

(1 Peter 1:6-7)

There are times when our faith is tested, as Abraham's was *(Hebrews 11:17.)* God only allows this for our ultimate benefit. Satan may instigate something to damage us, to disadvantage us, to lead us astray. God can always turn things around for good if we look to Him (*Romans 8:28*). He can change potential defeat into glorious victory because nothing is impossible for Him.

When everything is going well, we may be inclined to become a little blasé or complacent. To lower our guard against the wiles of the enemy. Or we could just drift back into the *flesh*, the *old man*, and become vulnerable to his schemes *(2 Corinthians 2:11)*.

We need to discern the purpose of a trial, a temptation, or a period of suffering. Is it something to pray against, for instant relief, or is it to be endured for the benefit of a great blessing to follow when we have passed through it *(Romans 8:28 again)*?

Too often we ask God to deliver us from situations that He wants to equip us to endure, grow in and walk through.

(David West)

As always, Jesus is our perfect example in showing that suffering with a *purpose* leads to blessing. He did countless amazing and good things to bless His countrymen. Nevertheless, the innocent Son of Man was condemned to die the most excruciating of deaths on a cross after a mockery of a trial.

(Jesus) *who, in the days of His flesh, when He had offered up prayers and supplications, with vehement cries and tears to Him who was able to save Him from death and was heard because of His godly fear, though He was a Son, yet He learned obedience by the things which He suffered. And having been perfected, He became the author of eternal salvation to all who obey Him.*

(Hebrews 5:7-9)

The writer of Hebrews *(see chapter 12)* also refers to God disciplining us as a loving father who disciplines his sons. He does it for our own good. It should be remembered that such discipline is invariably in the context of learning. The basic meaning of *disciple* is *one who learns*. I am saying this simply to emphasise the distinction between the generally accepted understanding of discipline being to do with punishment only. Education and rehabilitation are the positive aspects of the discipline.

Coming back to suffering, let's consider Joseph. He made the right choice, but he suffered for it *(Genesis 39:7-20)*. And there are many more characters from the Bible I could use as examples, including the apostle Paul:

Are they ministers of Christ?—I speak as a fool—I am more: in labours more abundant, in stripes above measure, in prisons more frequently, in deaths often. From the Jews five times I received 40 stripes minus one. Three times I was beaten with rods; once I was stoned; three times I was shipwrecked; a night and a day I have been in the deep: in journeys often, in perils of waters, in perils of robbers, in perils of my own countrymen, in perils of the Gentiles, in perils in the city, in perils in the wilderness, in perils in the sea, in perils among false brethren; in weariness and toil, in sleeplessness often, in hunger and thirst, in fasting often, in cold and nakedness—

(2 Corinthians 11:23-27)

If we were rescued immediately from every difficult situation we encounter, how much would we learn? How much would we be enabled to grow in experience and maturity? How much would we appreciate the problems others experience so that we can really help them? (*2 Corinthians 1:3-4*).

Yes, we would mourn over the difficulties. But what if we could count this as a time of *pure joy* because we experience His comfort and the ability to endure before relief comes? And if it doesn't, consider the apostles who, having been beaten at the instigation of the Jewish leaders, *departed from the presence of the council, rejoicing that they were counted worthy to suffer shame* for His Name. (Acts 5:41)

God got Job's attention through suffering. God didn't cause the suffering. Satan did, but God allowed it. He did this so that He could reach out to Job when Job, under conviction, reached out to Him. Job had become a little self-righteous and complacent. He was not helped by his friends, who thought they were saying all the right things. Then God stepped in (*Job 40:4, 42:5-6*).

When we experience difficulties, if we are wise, we will turn to God. He will either deliver us immediately or give us the grace to endure, for a time, and to grow. He did just that with Paul and his *thorn in the flesh*, didn't He?

Concerning this thing I pleaded with the Lord three times that it might depart from me. And He said to me, "My grace is sufficient for you, for My strength is made perfect in weakness." Therefore, most gladly I will rather boast in my infirmities, that the power of Christ may rest upon me.

(2 Corinthians 12:8-9)

Suffering can actually do us good, in the long run. Nevertheless, it is very hard to welcome it. It is even harder to accept that there is an inevitability about it (*John 16:33, Philippians 1:29*). But, just as God provides a way out of every temptation if we choose to follow it (*1 Corinthians 10:13*), so He provides sufficient grace for us to bear suffering (*2 Corinthians 12:7*).

When a trial leads to a positive outcome, God is pleased, and we are blessed. He has got our attention by means that might have been less likely when all was going smoothly. We cannot deny that there is a degree of mourning with every trial or difficulty that comes our way, or when we become aware of being overtaken by some sin. Still, for the blessed ones, the outcome will be good. They will be comforted, and their joy will be restored.

It is one thing to suffer the consequences of our own folly but quite another when something has been permitted by God for our ultimate benefit.

In the former instance, if He gets our attention by stopping us short and bringing us under conviction, we will mourn over our failure and turn back to Him in confession to receive the blessing of forgiveness. The turnaround will have been worth it. The negative will have been turned into a positive. Our poverty of spirit and genuine mourning will result in comfort from the Comforter. We will know the blessing of His peace (*Romans 5:1*).

In the latter instance, it is the blessing of His gracious presence that comforts us as we endure through to the end and grow in the process. If God chooses to utilise a difficult circumstance to gain our attention, and we respond well, we are going to end up in a position of being thankful to Him.

The reason why testing can be counted as *pure joy* is because God can bring comfort. He can turn it into *the best thing that ever happened to me*. It is not necessarily going to feel like that when we are in the midst of it all. It will do, though, when we have come through it and into the benefit of 20/20 hindsight.

Our light and momentary troubles are achieving for us an eternal glory that far outweighs them all.

(2 Corinthians 4:17t)

For they shall be comforted

This is my comfort, in my affliction, for, Your word, has given me life.

(Psalm 119:50)

Whatever negative experience we are going through now that causes us to mourn, we can be assured that we *will be comforted*[1] in due course. Ultimately, our comfort will be everlasting. What a blessing! For there is always the *now and not yet* aspect of the Kingdom of God and of our Christian faith. We will fully know comfort (and joy) when we meet Him face to face. We can taste of the Kingdom here and now. Then, we will be seated with Him at His banqueting table in Heaven.

For I reckon that the sufferings of this present time are not worthy to be compared with the glory which shall be revealed in us.

(Romans 8:18)

Once again, Jesus Himself is our model and our inspiration, *who for the joy that was set before him endured the cross, despising the shame, and has sat down at the right hand of the throne of God.*

(Hebrews 12:2)

He is the One who forgives us, who delivers us, who sets us free. He brings us comfort and joy, when a period of conviction, confession and mourning, has led us to repentance. Repentance is prompted by His kindness and goodness.

O wretched man that I am! Who shall deliver me from the body of this death? Thanks be to God, who delivers me through Jesus Christ our Lord!

(Romans 7:24)

God's love for us is both unconditional and unceasing (*Lamentations 3:22*). This is true no matter what we may think, say or do either to grieve (*Ephesians 4:30*) or to quench (*1 Thessalonians 5:19*) Holy Spirit. The *poor in spirit* have humbled themselves before Him and put their faith and trust in His amazing grace. When sin or suffering overtakes them, they respond positively to the conviction, correction, and lessons He brings. Their mourning results in blessing and comfort from the Comforter Himself (*2 Corinthians 7:10*).

Count it all joy (*James 1:2*) is something the blessed ones who mourn learn to do. Whatever it feels like at the time, *count it, reckon it*, joy. Especially when you know you are in the will, or purposes, of God. It is about faith, not feelings. When we exercise (positive) faith, despite our circumstances, our feelings will come into line with what our faith has clung on to.

Joy carries great significance in the Kingdom of God. Indeed, it is a primary source of strength for us (*Nehemiah 8:10*), and much more.

For the Kingdom of God is…righteousness and peace and joy in the Holy Spirit.

(Romans 14:17)

Blessed are you who weep now, for you shall laugh.

(Luke 6:21)

To give them beauty for ashes, the oil of joy for mourning, the garment of praise for the spirit of heaviness.

(Isaiah 61:3)

For you shall go out with joy and be led out with peace; the mountains and the hills shall break forth into singing before you, and all the trees of the field shall clap their hands.

(Isaiah 55:12)

It is the joy of the Lord, a fruit of the Spirit (*Galatians 5:22*) that we are focussing on here. This is what strengthens and comforts us. Our faith increases as does our sense of His Presence. Our relationship with Him deepens in intimacy and, by association, we change for the better.

But we all, with unveiled faces, beholding as in a mirror the glory of the Lord, are being transformed into the same image from glory to glory, just as by the Spirit of the Lord.

(2 Corinthians 3:18)

It is a different story, in fact, quite the reverse, for those who are, or choose to remain, in and of the world.

Woe to you who laugh now, for you shall mourn and weep.

(Luke 6:25)

The blessed ones may mourn now, for a season, but they will be comforted. Their joy will return. A further blessing comes when God prompts us to use our own experience of His dealings with us to help someone else who is going through the same kind of situation. Nothing is wasted in Heaven's economy.

Blessed be the God and Father of our Lord Jesus Christ, the Father of mercies and God of all comfort, who comforts us in all our tribulation, that we may be able to comfort those who are in any trouble, with the comfort with which we ourselves are comforted by God.

(2 Corinthians 1:3-4)

Mourning is the product of true conviction, inspired by Holy Spirit. It leads us through godly sorrow into repentance. Ultimately to the comfort and joy that comes from knowing we are forgiven and reconciled to Him. By His amazing grace, we attain *peace through our Lord Jesus Christ.*

1. I find it interesting that 'The Passion Translation' comes at this verse from a different angle, based upon the interpretation of original texts in Hebrew and Aramaic. It uses *wait* instead of *mourn*, citing that the Hebrew words for *wait* and for *mourn* are almost identical, then referring their readers to *(Psalm 27:14).*

2. Instead of *comforted* TPT prefers *For you will find what you are looking for*. This is taken from Aramaic originals, and I would not want to dispute either issue. However, I am satisfied with the sources I have used to help with what I have chosen for this writing.

4
Blessed Are the Meek for They Shall Inherit the Earth

Blessed are the meek

> *But the meek shall inherit the Earth,*
> *And shall delight themselves in the abundance of peace.*

> (Psalm 37:11)

I believe there is a once-and-forever change of *position* for each one of us when we are born again and first enter into the Kingdom of God. Thereafter we should find ourselves in a progression, during which our life *experience* moves towards alignment with our new position in Christ (*1 John 4:17*).

There will be a gradual change in our character, attitude, and expression as we submit to the work of God within us. Indeed, He is transforming us from one degree of glory to another (*2 Corinthians 3:18*).

Having humbled ourselves so that we, and others, begin to recognise the poverty of spirit within our natural selves, consequently mourning over our inherent inadequacies, we find ourselves embracing sanctification (*1 Thessalonians 5:23*). In meekness, therefore, we submit to Him and all He seeks to do in changing us into the likeness of Jesus, enabling us to share His Kingdom blessings with others.

When the blessed ones have truly experienced poverty of spirit, mourning and meekness, there is a complete absence of ego. Our identity in Christ, which is ours by grace alone, has been recognised and accepted by us. There is no place now for pride. A meek person is not proud of himself. He has no need for self-promotion. There is no hint of self-glorification. No reliance on natural abilities. Never anything to boast about that is not received by grace alone.

When the poor in spirit have mourned over their natural failings, following genuine repentance, they understand how ridiculous self-righteousness is. How unnecessary it is to be always on the defensive whenever criticised. This is true meekness, which should never be confused with weakness.

It is probably fair to say that the poverty of spirit and mourning of the blessed ones are largely the result of (old) self-awareness. Whilst it is acceptable to see our faults and failings for ourselves, it is naturally far less palatable to see them through the eyes of others. Allowing others to examine me, rather than only doing it myself, without erecting defensive barriers, calls for meekness.

The Christian belongs to an entirely different Kingdom and a radically different mindset to the natural, or carnal, person. The blessed ones are a problem, an enigma even, to those with a worldly view and mindset. Those who see everything according to the *flesh (2 Corinthians 5:16)*.

All the Beatitudes are expressed both within us and through us to the degree that we do not grieve Holy Spirit (*Ephesians 4:30*). So far, we have seen the progression from poverty of spirit through mourning into meekness. In so doing, and as we move on to the others in due course, we need to remember that we do not leave behind those we have already encountered. We are to embrace the whole of this progression in Christian character development.

According to the Cambridge English Dictionary to be meek is, to be *quiet, gentle, not willing to argue or express your opinions in a forceful way; to be quiet and unwilling to disagree or fight or to strongly support personal ideas and opinions.*

The Oxford Learners' Dictionary says it is, to be *quiet, gentle and always ready to do what other people want without expressing your own opinion.* That comes across, to me at least, as someone wet and wimpy!

Matthew 11:29 tells us that, Jesus was meek (some translations say *gentle* but *meek* is probably more accurate). It is interesting to consider how the Son of Man fits in with these definitions. We will do that in a moment. We will also look at meekness in the characteristics of other people featured in the scriptures. First, let's examine what meekness *is* in more detail before making some comparisons with what it is *not*.

In 1 Peter 2:23, the apostle speaks of Jesus as one, *who, when He was reviled, did not revile in return; when He suffered, He did not threaten but committed Himself to Him who judges righteously.* This is an example of His meekness in denying His flesh and fulfilling His mission for our blessing.

This same quality of meekness is expressed through our demeanour, through our behaviour towards others. It embodies both patience and longsuffering (*Galatians 5:22-23*) with no inclination towards any retaliation when we are wronged or made to suffer unjustly. It is essentially a reactive quality. It also means that a person is teachable, whether that is in the context of learning or of correction (*Hebrews 5:8*).

True meekness *contrasts* with self-righteousness, arrogance, haughtiness, smugness, or defensiveness. It is unpretentious, gentle, and self-effacing. These qualities enable us to accept criticism without sulking, retaliating or resorting to self-justification. In my days as a more immature Christian, I remember a work colleague challenging me.

He said, "You have a great line in self-righteousness!"

Ouch! I trust I have moved on from that stage.

A meek person is not overly sensitive about himself. Not absorbed in self-interest. Not prone to self-defence or self-protection. He is secure in his new identity in Christ. He has come to terms with the fact that nothing of his natural self is worth such effort. He no longer puts a great store in what others think of or say about him. He knows the truth about himself and the blessing of the grace of God in his life, so he wastes no time in self-pity.

Meekness is essentially a true view of oneself, expressing itself in attitude and conduct towards others. It is my attitude toward myself, and it is an expression of that in my relationship to others.

(Dr Martyn Lloyd-Jones)

There is no limit to how far a person can go as long as he does not care who gets the credit.

(Ronald Reagan)

There is no grasping to feed one's ego. I can let others turn the searchlight on me without rushing to put up defensive barriers. I have learned the truth about myself and know that, by the grace of God, I am saved. I am free to be the unique individual He has called and enabled me to be. There is no need to compare myself with others.

A meek person does not make unreasonable demands. He does not stand upon his rights, position, privileges, possessions, or status in life. Jesus was equal with God, the second Person of the Trinity. But He did not deliberately assert His right to equality with God so as to compromise His mission as the Son of Man *(Philippians 2:5-8)*.

Following Jesus' example, we can leave everything in the hands of God, in both good circumstances and bad. We rarely see the complete picture, of what the future holds. Still, we confidently entrust ourselves to the One who knows the end from the beginning. To the One who loves us unconditionally, with everlasting love. This is true faith *(Hebrews 11:1)*.

Meekness is entirely compatible with great strength of character. Also, with authority and power that is correctly exercised for the benefit of others. Meekness will enable someone to stand for the truth, even to the point of death. There have been many martyrs down through church history, each one meek but none of them weak.

Meekness is effectively an anointing, received by the grace of God. Yet it is not something one is consciously aware of possessing. You may be aware of a brokenness before God in a personal encounter with His holiness. You may be aware of enduring a trial without resorting to complaining about it to others or to God.

But will you be conscious of displaying meekness? Others will see it in you, even if they do not recognise it for what it is. But you are most unlikely to be aware of being taken up a level by the grace of God.

The moment one becomes conscious of a quality like this within oneself or begins to look around in search of what others may think of us, meekness has been superseded. It has dissipated. When God calls us to something for His purposes, we will look to Him to equip us, not to our own natural gifts or abilities.

We are His co-workers *(2 Corinthians 6:1, for example)*. Although He is Sovereign, God invariably chooses to do His works through us. This calls for willing cooperation and submission on our part, for His glory and not our own.

The deeds of the spirit and of the flesh are in marked contrast. Look at Gideon. God chose this most unlikely general to carry out His will. Then He reduced the size of the army under Gideon's command until they were nothing more than a remnant.

They even lacked conventional weapons. This demonstrates that it is all about Him. Yet we have the privilege of being called to work alongside Him. Not because He needs us, but because He wants us there.

Meekness is not a quality that the world appreciates. In fact, meekness is not likely to achieve for us any positive recognition in the world. Some degree of self-promotion will always be required, regardless of our level of ability. Consider what happens when there is a General Election in the offing here in the UK.

How many parliamentary candidates will attract sufficient votes to win a seat without parading their apparent virtues whilst disparaging their rivals? This could be equally true of many highflyers at the top in business, sport, or entertainment.

Meekness would seem to be a distinct disadvantage. The meek will not pull strings to advance, neither in the world nor in the Kingdom of God. On the contrary, those who humble themselves will be exalted (*Luke 14:11, 1 Peter 5:6*). The meek will not manipulate in order to gain any kind of advantage.

Meekness is not a natural quality but one all Christians are meant to have. When we look at some examples of people in the Bible who demonstrated meekness, we see that none of them would be considered meek by nature. It was never their natural disposition. True meekness is the product of the Spirit of God at work in a blessed one.

Many in the world may be naturally modest, polite, and unassuming, not the least bit assertive. But that is not necessarily meekness. Although perhaps it would be considered so by the dictionary definitions, we looked at earlier! No, these natural things are invariably a product of the fear of man. A sign of weakness but not of meekness.

A meek person is not simply nice, not just easy-going, or even laid-back. He is not weak in personality or character either. It takes a strong person, or a person graced by God with strength, to be meek. It is not something that is compatible with compromise. Certainly not a passive *anything for a quiet life* attitude. Indeed, it is not an aversion to healthy disagreement or confrontation.

Have you come across the old saying, "If you think it is weak to be meek, then try being meek for a week?"

Our old nature likes nothing more than to receive attention and praise from others. To subtly draw attention to our good deeds. To receive full credit for every achievement. A meek person will win the struggles with the temptation to boast about themselves.

The Jewish expectation of the Messiah restoring the kingdom of Israel to them anticipated one who would be materialistic and militaristic by nature. He would bring about restoration by force, conquering the occupying armies.

We know that this was a false expectation because Jesus was quite different and accomplished His mission by very different means. He submitted to execution by the Romans with the connivance of the Jewish leaders (*Hebrews 12:2*).

Meekness is also not simply a matter of outward manner or appearance. Of what is on the surface to be seen by others. It is a deep, spiritual quality that can only have its origin in the indwelling Spirit of God.

Although it is not one of the nine examples listed in Galatians 5, I think it is fair to describe meekness as an authentic *fruit of the Spirit*. Surely any godly qualities displayed in and through us must be, by definition, examples of spiritual fruit.

Counterfeit meekness is, as already mentioned, usually motivated by a spirit of fear. As Paul reminds Timothy, this does not come from God (*2 Timothy 1:7*). The natural man and/or the old nature will produce false humility in order to be liked and accepted so that people will not have a negative view of us.

But this Uriah Heep characteristic is actually rooted in pride. It is used by someone as a way to impress others by disparaging himself and his achievements rather than letting these things speak for themselves without resorting to drawing attention to them (*Luke 6:5*).

No, we cannot produce this quality ourselves. Only Holy Spirit can lead us into and bless us with genuine humility. Thus, we become poor in spirit, enabled to mourn over our natural failings, producing in us a truly accurate view of self that will exemplify meekness.

Now we come to a brief look at how meekness was demonstrated in the lives of characters found in the Bible. These are just a few by way of example.

In Genesis 13 we read how **Abram** (not yet Abraham) allowed his nephew to have the first choice of the land they were to occupy. He meekly and graciously submitted to Lot's choice of the best area for himself and his entourage, without murmur or complaint.

Moses is described as *humble* in most translations of Numbers 12:3 but, in the Septuagint version, we find the same Greek word that is translated as *meek* in Matthew 5:5. Therefore, he was known as *the most meek man on the face of the Earth*. And yet, we marvel at what he achieved (under God) and know how much he is revered, especially by the Jewish people.

He had all the tempting possibilities of Egyptian royalty open to him, but he chose to humble himself before God and submit to His will (*Hebrews 11:24-27*). Even to obscurity for a period of 40 years between his departure from Egypt and the call of God into his destiny.

He was to lead the Israelites out of slavery in Egypt to the Promised Land. He also had a remarkably close relationship with God. It was so unlike that of his contemporaries and was distinguished by meekness not weakness (*e.g., Numbers 14:11-20*).

Jeremiah the prophet was charged by God to deliver a very unpopular message at a time when false prophets were telling the people only what they wanted to hear. He stuck firmly to the truth in the face of strong opposition, without fighting back. Such a great example of meekness.

Although he was anointed to be king of Israel at a very young age, **David** first had to live through difficult times of opposition and persecution. This was particularly experienced at the hands of a jealous Saul, who sought to take his life on several occasions.

David did not retaliate, because of his healthy fear of, and submission to, the Lord (*e.g., 1 Samuel 24:10*). There were similar examples of his meekness before the Lord even after he became king. For example, when his son, Absolom, conspired to seize the throne (*e.g., 2 Samuel 15:25-26, 16:7,12*).

We know that the **Apostle Paul** was originally a fervent persecutor of the church. He eventually became a selfless disciple of the Lord who suffered many things for his faith (*Acts 9:16*) without complaint. He bravely stuck to his calling, whatever happened to him *(2 Corinthians 11:23-27)*. He displayed quite extraordinary meekness, seemingly in complete contrast to the natural characteristics he probably lived out in his younger days.

Jesus is our primary example, as always. He is our perfect model for living an authentic Christian lifestyle

Come to Me, all you who labour and are heavy laden, and I will give you rest. Take My yoke upon you and learn from Me, for I am gentle (i.e., meek) and lowly in heart, and you will find rest for your souls.

(Matthew 11:28-29)

He suffered many misunderstandings, sarcasm, derision, and persecution but pressed on selflessly with His mission. He showed meekness in both His endurance of ill-treatment and His total submission to Father God (*Luke 22:42, John 4:34, 14:10, James 3:13*).

He was the One who, knowing His true identity, had the humility and meekness to wash his disciples' feet (*John 13:14*). Paul's description of Jesus in Philippians 2:5-8 probably sums up the Son of God and the Son of Man better than any other in scripture. He is seen as meekness, lowliness and humility personified.

Jesus was totally free. He had nothing to prove to anyone. He knew who He was but did not need to claim His *rights* at the expense of others. Indeed, he laid aside His Majesty (as the old worship song goes) for the benefit of others. He was always approachable. The common people loved Him in complete contrast to their inability to warm to the arrogant and hypocritical religious authority figures of the day.

Jesus, the Son of Man, perfectly exemplified the words of Bill Johnson, *"Faith is not effort but surrender."*

That is not a bad definition of meekness, either!

For they shall inherit the Earth

He who did not spare His own Son, but delivered Him up for us all, how shall He not with Him also freely give us all things?

(Romans 8:32)

God (literally) promises us (i.e., the meek) the Earth! The whole planet that was originally put under the care and authority of Adam (*Genesis 1:27-28*). Adam's reign was usurped by the deceitfulness of the serpent (*Luke 4:5-6*). It was restored by the total victory of Jesus *(Matthew 28:18b)*.

That the meek should inherit the Earth is an idea very much at odds with the typical worldview. This would expect strength, power, ability, aggression, ruthlessness, and self-assurance to be absolutely essential requisites for commercial dominance or world conquest. But the meek achieve the same end by totally opposite means.

By being humble, selfless, both committed and submitted to God and His ways. Such an inheritance is obtained by becoming more like Jesus than the natural man. Something that is only possible by the grace, anointing and equipping of God (*2 Corinthians 6:10b*).

To inherit this Kingdom is to share in the inheritance of Jesus. We get the whole world, which belongs to the Creator God because we are joint heirs with His Son (*Romans 8:16-17*).

It is promised to the blessed ones who are meek. We have a taste of it now (the anointing and equipping). The fullness will be revealed later, in Heaven (*Romans 8:18*).

In 1 Corinthians 6:2-3 Paul writes that we Christians will judge the world, even angels, when we come into our inheritance. This will be after Jesus has returned and reconciled all things to Himself (*Colossians 1:20*). Paul writes in 2 Timothy 2:12; *If we endure, we shall also reign with Him.*

Ah, but Romans 8:17 reminds us that a prerequisite of reigning with Him is to *suffer with Him*. This calls for meekness on our part. To put His Kingdom and His purposes for us before self-interest, self-protection and self-preservation. Remember, in the Kingdom, it is the humble who will be exalted (*Luke 14:11*).

The coming of the Son of Man was not announced in a palace to a powerful king, but in a field to poor shepherds. They were thought by some to be the lowest of the low in that society. He was crucified as a criminal. Even then, Pilate saw fit to have Him described as the *King of the Jews* (*John 19:22*).

Pilate recognised that Jesus' failure to defend Himself was not a sign of weakness but of great strength, and he feared Him. Pilate displayed his own weakness in not having the courage of his convictions to set free a man he knew in his heart to be innocent. His weakness contrasted with Jesus' meekness and served to accomplish the purposes of God (*2 Corinthians 13:4*).

It can be painful to be meek because this quality goes right against the grain of fallen, human nature. It is unnatural to be like this. It is supernatural, in fact. A sign of Holy Spirit at work, a fruit of the Spirit indeed.

R. T. Kendall has written, *Meekness is its own reward. Achieve this and you're there. You have arrived*!

That is a statement to meditate on, isn't it?

God has literally promised the Earth to the meek, and He always keeps His promises!

5
Blessed Are Those Who Hunger and Thirst for Righteousness for They Shall Be Filled

Blessed are those who hunger and thirst...for righteousness

Ho! Everyone who thirsts, come to the waters; and you who have no money, come, buy, and eat. Yes, come, buy wine and milk without money and without price. Why do you spend money for what is not bread, and your wages for what does not satisfy? Listen carefully to Me, and eat what is good, and let your soul delight itself in abundance.

(Isaiah 55:1-2)

As the deer pants for the water brooks, so pants my soul for You, O God. My soul thirsts for God, for the living God.

(Psalm 42:1-2a)

O God, You, are my God; early will I seek You; my soul thirsts for You; my flesh longs for You in a dry and thirsty land where there is no water.

(Psalm 63:1)

The Psalmist had a hunger and thirst for the things of God. Through the prophet Isaiah God invites His people to come to Him for food and drink that will satisfy—in a way that no natural, earthly produce ever can. When we come to the New Testament, we find that God is calling them the blessed ones who are moved by His Spirit to do the same *(John 4:13-14)*. But how urgent is this need within us? How important is it for us to seek Him with all our hearts?

A W Tozer has said, "You can have as much of God as you want."

In this Beatitude, I think we find a way in which we can almost measure just how much of God we really want. It seems that any limitation on *quantity* must be on our side alone. For, in seeking after righteousness, we are effectively desiring the Righteous One, Himself *(1 Corinthians 1:30).*

Have we experienced true physical hunger? Have we had to cope with real thirst? If not, we cannot easily identify with the depth of longing which is conveyed in this text. Sadly, there are too many people in this world today who would not have such difficulty.

We need, somehow, to be able to see ourselves in the position of such people if we are to appreciate how desperate the hunger and thirst for righteousness described here is expected to be. That level of desire that Jesus is looking for in us. A more telling translation might be:

Blessed is the man who longs for righteousness as a starving man longs for food, and as a man perishing of thirst longs for water.

(William Barclay)

The idea of people who are hungering and thirsting may not automatically suggest to us someone who is greatly blessed and happy. That would certainly be true of a worldly mindset. Therefore, we are looking again at supernatural, rather than natural, qualities as we study this Beatitude and how it describes the blessed ones.

The world tends to be focussed on natural desires, some good but not all by any means. The advertisements we see, hear, and read on television, radio, in magazines or in the street are designed to create a need and make us hungry for some product or other in the natural. Invariably quite the opposite goal to promoting a desire for godliness.

It is not a matter of simply feeling *peckish* but of being really, very hungry. Having an inner hunger that defies natural explanation. The intensity of this hunger and thirst the blessed ones have is for righteousness. Although this righteousness may be given outward expression in a variety of ways, it is essentially an inner quality emanating from the spirit.

To hunger and thirst for righteousness is only possible if we have Holy Spirit within us. His Presence promotes a desire for a greater connection with the triune Godhead.

This inner quality is again the product of the progression from becoming poor in spirit. Of seeing nothing good in our natural selves. Through mourning over the sin and inadequacy of the flesh. And on into a meekness which is devoid of any of the self-centredness of the natural self.

The paradox here is that the blessed ones are hungering and thirsting after something they have already received as a free gift of grace! How can this be?

Well, we need only to go back to what I described in the first paragraph of the previous chapter. When we were born again, we were each imputed righteousness that is by faith. This is our permanent *positional* status in Christ. However, we have not attained sinless perfection through our own life *experience* to date and are not likely to this side of Heaven *(1 John 1:8)*.

The blessing here is not for the one who has already achieved righteousness (experientially). It is for the one who is continually hungering and thirsting to be filled with it. Yes, it has already been freely given to us, by amazing grace through faith (positionally).

But the great desire of our hearts now is to pursue His righteousness experientially. To be changed from one degree of glory to another *(2 Corinthians 3:18)*. This is, of course, the ongoing process that is called sanctification *(1 Thessalonians 5:23)*.

In the 'parallel' passage in Luke 6:25, the gospel writer turns this Beatitude around. Jesus says, *"Woe to you who are full, for you shall hunger."* Here He is addressing a person who is fully satisfied with what they already have. Someone smugly content with the status quo. There is an absence of desire for what they sadly lack.

A growing relationship to and with God. Right now, they have sufficient food to eat not to be hungry and sufficient liquid to drink not to be thirsty. They think they have everything they need. But, if nothing ever changes, a day will come when such a person will discover that they have missed the greatest thing of all. The pearl of great price *(Matthew 13:46)*.

William Barclay points out that there are three possible meanings for the word that is translated as *righteousness* in our English text. The Greek word *dikaiosune* can mean, (a) *justice*, (b) *righteousness* (as in right living) and (c) *justification* (as in justification by faith). Each of these has relevance and is worth looking at. But none is adequate, in isolation, to describe accurately the righteousness spoken of in this Beatitude. With God, there is always more!

We can have a passion for *justice* for ourselves, in a personal situation. Also for others in their individual or collective difficulties. Justice is important to God. We see that clearly in the Old Testament Law and also in Jesus' strong denunciation of the hypocrisy of the Pharisees in the New Testament.

Woe to you, scribes and Pharisees, hypocrites! For you pay tithe of mint and anise and cumin and have neglected the weightier matters of the law: justice and mercy and faith. These you ought to have done, without leaving the others undone. Blind guides, who strain out a gnat and swallow a camel!

(Matthew 23:23-24)

The righteousness of the Pharisees was outward. Not only was it visible, but they were also desperate for others to see what they were doing *(Matthew 6:1-2, 23:5)*. This *Look at me!* attitude runs contrary to the complete lack of self-promotion that we discussed in the last chapter as a sign of meekness.

The outward expression of righteousness by a meek person lacks any hint of pretension. It goes beyond the requirements of the Moral Law. It is ultimately a product of grace that can only be expressed through a born-again, spirit-filled Christian responding to the inner prompting of Holy Spirit.

The Old Testament book of Amos has been dubbed, 'A Cry for Social Justice'. Inspired by Holy Spirit, this book is a record of the prophet's cries for justice for the oppressed of his time. There have been many blessed ones down the years who have hungered and thirsted for justice in many areas. For example, slavery, racial prejudice and the gulf between rich and poor.

They have fought for these things. Many Christians have been at the forefront of breakthroughs in social justice down the years. William Wilberforce is just one of those who have given their lives to overcoming a wide variety of social injustices. You can, no doubt, call to mind many more examples.

To hunger and thirst for justice is commendable. The truly blessed ones would be willing to trust God for His justice to prevail even if they did not receive vindication in their lifetimes.

The Apostle Paul suffered all manner of injustices as he went about his ministry over many years. He trusted God for justice and vindication, whether during his lifetime or not. And, of course, both he and many others have been martyred for their faith.

For this reason, I also suffer these things; nevertheless, I am not ashamed, for I know whom I have believed and am persuaded that He is able to keep what I have committed to Him until that Day.

(2 Timothy 1:12)

Righteousness, in the sense of *right living*, is the product of a love for God manifested in complete trust and obedience towards Him. In love for mankind too, revealed through selfless service and genuine forgiveness. This is not just a matter of keeping rules. It is a heart response to guidance and direction from Him. Naturally, this reflects His love and compassion towards those around us.

To live with a passionate desire to love God and mankind in such a manner is a mark of the blessed ones. When Holy Spirit has His way in us, we have more than a righteousness that is imputed to us. Of course, we have received that blessing, but the full reality goes deeper than that. Perhaps it can best be described as a righteousness that is planted in us. It changes the heart and prompts some form of outward expression. It enables us to do the things that Jesus did as, again, we are moved by the influence of his heart of compassion both upon us and within us.

As already mentioned, the Kingdom of God has been described as the domain of the unhindered, un-grieved Holy Spirit. If Holy Spirit within us is neither grieved nor quenched, it means that we are living for the things of God. For both His Presence and His purposes. Your kingdom come; your will be done on Earth as it is in heaven *(Matthew 6:10)*.

In a very real sense, we are considering here an **un**conscious righteousness. Something that *just happens* as Holy Spirit flows in us and through us. We are not looking for the approval of men but responding to the promptings of God. No thought is entertained about the positive acknowledgement of mankind.

On the other hand, the righteousness of the legalist is always a conscious thing. It is brazenly outward. It is designed to be seen. Always seeking man's approval for keeping the rules. Luke's gospel contains a prime example:

The Pharisee stood and prayed thus with himself, God, I thank You that I am not like other men—extortioners, unjust, adulterers, or even this tax collector. I fast twice a week; I give tithes of all that I possess.

(Luke 18:11-12)

The interesting thing about *justification*, in the present context, is what the original Greek verb does *not* mean. To most people, in English, it means to find reasons *why* a person is right, or even to *make* someone just. It means to *treat* and *accept* someone *as* a just person. When God justifies a person, through His grace and mercy, He treats and accepts them as a just and good person. He forgives and accepts a repentant sinner as if he or she was always a good person.

This justification by faith creates a new relationship between God and mankind. He is no longer the distant, angry judge with a big stick. One whose holiness would be a cause of permanent separation. He is now seen as the God Who *is* Love, Compassion, and Mercy. The One who is ready and willing to forgive the repentant sinner. To exchange their fear, distance and estrangement for friendship, intimacy, and trust.

To be justified, biblically, is to be in the right relationship with God. This Beatitude could therefore be restated as, *Blessed are those whose passionate desire is to be in the right relationship with God.*

However, as I said before, we do not have to choose between the three meanings of the original Greek word. Rather we can embrace all of them, whilst appreciating that the reality is even greater than the sum of these parts. But such righteousness is not popular, in a worldly context, as Jesus made very clear to His disciples.

If the world hates you, you know that it hated Me before it hated you. If you were of the world, the world would love its own. Yet because you are not of the world, but I chose you out of the world, therefore the world hates you.

(John 15:18-19)

The Apostle Paul draws our attention to an interesting difference between what the world would consider to be a good person and a righteous person. An observation that certainly provides food for thought.

For scarcely for a righteous man will one die; yet perhaps for a good man someone would even dare to die.

(Romans 5:7)

Yet it is the one who hungers and thirsts for His righteousness to whom God's promise is given, as we shall now see.

For they shall be filled

*And try Me now in this, says the Lord of hosts,
If I will not open for you the windows of heaven
And pour out for you such blessing
That there will not be room enough to receive it.*

(Malachi 3:10)

There is a purpose, in God's plan for our lives, to this hungering and thirsting. It is to be filled, to be satisfied, and to be blessed. The Bible is adamant that the one who seeks, in such a way, *will* find.

And you will seek Me and find Me when you search for Me with all your heart.

(Jeremiah 29:13)

Ask, and it will be given to you; seek, and you will find; knock, and it will be opened to you. For everyone who asks receives, and he who seeks finds, and to him who knocks it will be opened.

(Matthew 7:7-8)

You probably know that the verbs in the above text are in the present continuous tense, e.g., *ask and keep on asking*. As we embark on a never-ending pursuit of God, the Righteous One, we do so with the knowledge and certainty that we will be filled, satisfied, and rewarded. Simply because that is what He has promised.

His promises are brighter than the stars in the firmament, oh they're permanent. Yes, they are!

(*from a song by* Neil Mathieson)

The Greek word translated into English as *filled* is *chortazesthai*. In our present context, it would mean being completely satiated. Or, to put it more colloquially, to be *stuffed*! What God is offering to the blessed ones is not merely enough, but more than enough. Just as he does not make us simply conquerors but *more than conquerors (Romans 8:37)*!

The Christian, the blessed one, does not say, "I am interested in Jesus."

He says, "For to me, to live is Christ", *(Philippians 1:21a)*.

For him or her, the desire is for full commitment to the Saviour. A longing for an increasing intimacy of relationship with Father, Son, and Holy Spirit.

A deep spiritual hunger and thirst that only knowing Him in ever greater measure will satisfy. To be filled, in this context, is nothing less than, *to know the love of Christ which passes knowledge; that you may be filled with all the fullness of God (Ephesians 3:19).*

How does one come to know this love that surpasses knowledge? How does one become filled with the fullness of God? Such concepts are probably beyond the rational thought processes of most of us. However, *With men this is impossible, but with God all things are possible (Matthew 19:26).*

Heaven's realities will always surpass earthly realities. After all, what has Jesus taught us to pray for expectantly? *On Earth as it is in heaven (Matthew 6:10b).*

Being filled with this righteousness means that we will be more sensitive to Holy Spirit. More aware of how we may grieve Him. More conscious of the possibility of quenching Him. We will be equipped to emulate Jesus, our model and template for the Christian life.

He who only said what He heard the Father saying *(John 14:10)*, and only did what He saw the Father doing *(John 5:19)*. All this will come from within us, in a naturally supernatural way, as we are changed from one degree of glory to another *(2 Corinthians 3:18).*

If we never reach the stage of achieving experientially the total righteousness that has always been ours positionally, it is not as if all is lost. Our God is a God of grace who looks first upon the heart.

We may truly hunger and thirst for His righteousness in our hearts without ever hitting the bullseye in our daily life experience. But we have not missed the mark if our hearts are right towards Him.

When my children were at school they came home with their annual reports. I always pointed out to them that I was more interested in the number in the *effort* column than the letter in the *attainment* column. Of course, I wanted them to do as well as possible academically.

But, for me, the most important thing was how hard they had *tried* to do their best. If their hearts were set on getting as close to an A as their very best efforts could achieve, that was enough for me. I would value 'F1' above 'A4' every time! Good character is more important than *brains*!

God is good and, as He loves each one of us unconditionally, we are never without hope. David wanted to build a temple for the worship of God. It was his highly commendable, heartfelt desire, but it did not happen in his lifetime. God said the building of the temple would be entrusted to Solomon.

God was fully satisfied with David that it was *in his heart* to do this. He confirmed it by saying to him, *Whereas it was in your heart to build a temple for My name, you did well that it was in your heart (1 Kings 8:18).*

In other words, the genuine desire in our hearts to achieve is more important than the actual level of achievement we attain. For the Christian, Jesus has already hit the *bullseye* of that target for us. We can rejoice because He is our righteousness *(1 Corinthians 1:30)*, the essence of justification by faith.

In our final report, we will find that the *attainment* column was filled in, with an *A*, from the moment we first entered the Kingdom of God. The *effort* column entry would be governed by the degree to which we have each hungered and thirsted for the Righteous One.[1]

And what about the headmaster's comment at the bottom of the report?

Well done, good and faithful servant; you have been faithful over a few things, I will make you ruler over many things. Enter into the joy of your Lord.

(Matthew 25:23)

1. *Please don't confuse what I am calling effort with sanctification by works. My intention here is to focus on our cooperation with all Holy Spirit is doing within us to bring about His desired changes in our character, not self-effort that we can boast about.*

6
Blessed Are the Merciful for They Shall Obtain Mercy

Blessed are the merciful

> *But You are God, ready to pardon, gracious and merciful,*
> *Slow to anger, abundant in kindness, and did not forsake them.*

> (Nehemiah 9:17b)

We have now reached a crossroads, a turning point, maybe even a yardstick, in what we have discovered to be the progression within the Beatitudes. Here we find what is essentially a test which follows on from the previous Beatitudes.

But, perhaps, more specifically from the previous one. This *test* will examine not only how much we have progressed generally but also if we are truly hungry and thirsting after righteousness.

Often, it is only by being put to the test that we gain a true understanding of how far we have advanced in our education (or progression). A very real test comes to us, in everyday life, when someone hurts us, offends us, or badly lets us down. How we react in such circumstances can be very telling indeed.

We always have a *choice* when we are hurt or offended by someone. The *old man*, the *flesh*, the natural self, will desire revenge. This is so even if such revenge actually takes the form of legitimate justice, of the process of law.

The supernatural, Holy Spirit-inspired choice we *can* make is to show mercy, to forgive. To be merciful is to demonstrate true godliness, even if it costs us to do so. Jesus exemplified, to an unimaginable extent on the cross, someone experiencing the cost of being merciful and forgiving.

As the truly poor in spirit, we have come to the end of ourselves. We have recognised and accepted all the many inadequacies of the natural self in the presence of a Holy God. We are therefore better able to identify with and make allowances for others who, perhaps to our own detriment, have fallen short of the glory of God *(Romans 3:23)*.

If we have acknowledged and mourned over our own natural tendency to sin *(Romans 3:23 again)*, sometimes even despite our best intentions, we can more easily take encouragement from this when dealing with the failings of those who have sinned against us.

If we have somehow attained a level of meekness, effectively realising the futility of self-righteousness and self-justification under any circumstances, we will more readily take the initiative towards being reconciled with one who we consider has failed us in some way.

When we have gratefully received, through the gracious gift of God, all these benefits that are freely given to us when we are born again into His Kingdom, we will eagerly hunger and thirst for more of Him. The righteousness of the Righteous One is ours by faith *(Philippians 3:9, 1 Corinthians 1:30)*.

In all these things we have indeed come to the end of ourselves. We have realised the total inadequacy before God of what can be achieved only by natural endeavours. We look instead to the Righteous One. Our desire is for more of His characteristics to be manifested in and through us now that we are, by grace, partakers of the divine nature *(2 Peter 1:4)*.

In embracing the teaching about the progressive quality of the Beatitudes, we must conclude that the sequence in Jesus' teaching is not accidental but deliberate. For, when we have reached the point at which we are enabled truly to show mercy, we have made a significant breakthrough in our lives as Christians. We reflect the nature of God, which means exhibiting godliness.

It has been said that Matthew 5:7 describes true godliness, and our God is lavishly merciful. If mercy is Godlikeness, we become more like Him as we practise mercy. Again, becoming more and more like Him is the essence of the process called sanctification *(1 Thessalonians 5:23)*.

Being merciful is to hold back from obtaining justice, i.e., what the person deserves by law or custom because of what they have done to us. Instead, we choose to be merciful, i.e., what the person does not deserve. Being merciful is therefore an outward expression of godliness that comes from the heart.

Embracing this truth means our inner spiritual reality (courtesy of the Spirit of God) triumphs over what would be our natural response. The mask is removed and mercy triumphs over justice *(James 2:13)*. Especially when such justice involves a desire to punish.

Our view of godliness can be distorted by a religious perspective that is more concerned with externals. More with keeping up appearances, usually fuelled by the fear of man (not God). Some people, when they are hurt, are able to conceal their true feelings by displaying the good old British stiff upper lip. But that is simply internal effort producing an outward appearance that disguises the truth of what they really feel inside.

True godliness leads to true graciousness. A healthy way of dealing with the initial pain inside. Not by masking it but by overwhelming it to the point of replacing it with love. For love will cover a multitude of sins *(1 Peter 4:8)*.

If you have ever read 'The Sacred Diary of Adrian Plass' then you may well remember the Flushpools. This married couple headed up a radically legalistic little group whose aim was to *spot it and stop it*.

Outwardly, they seemed to champion what was right, but theirs was a form of pseudo-godliness that was devoid of grace and mercy. They were motivated more by religiosity than love.

Perhaps falling within Paul's description in *2 Timothy 3:5* of those having a form of godliness but denying its power. For true godly power derives from unconditional love, a fundamental expression of which is mercy.

The blessed ones are merciful because they have undergone a fundamental change in their nature, from old to new. They have moved from natural to supernatural empowerment.

Therefore, if anyone is in Christ, he is a new creation; old things have passed away; behold, all things have become new.

(2 Corinthians 5:17).

This is why *in Christ* we should not fear the tests that the Beatitudes bring to us, both here in Matthew 5:7 and throughout the Sermon on the Mount. They provide an opportunity to evaluate our attitudes and responses in light of all that God has done in and through us by grace.

Can my reactive thoughts, motivations and actions be considered genuine expressions of godliness? Being merciful, from the heart, is as good an indication as any of whether or not Holy Spirit is welcomed as my life source at any given moment *(Romans 8:11)*.

The Greek word for *mercy* is *eleos* and, in Greek thought, it was deemed to be an emotion. However, the New Testament takes it further than that. It also becomes a gracious *action*. Let us recap for a moment.

If we choose to give people who have hurt us what they deserve, we pursue justice with punishment. If, on the other hand, we choose to give them what they don't deserve, we are being merciful.

Now it is time for a quick look at what mercy is or means. The Hebrew word *chesedh* is translated as both *mercy* and *kindness*. It occurs more than 150 times in the Old Testament, 90% of these references being to God and His *actions*.

His mercy comes from the essential kindness of his heart. It is fundamental to the relationship He wants to re-establish with sinful mankind. Indeed, it is this *kindness* or *goodness* that leads us to repentance *(Romans 2:4)*.

These qualities are the motivation for the incarnation of Jesus who gave His life for us on the cross to facilitate the forgiveness of sins which results in the restoration of the relationship that was broken at the fall.

Genesis 24:27 brings *mercy* and *truth* together. A truth which provides for full commitment to a promise. It reflects the unchanging nature of our loving and compassionate Father God throughout human history.

In Deuteronomy 7:9 we find *mercy* and *covenant* combined. We know that the Old Testament is the setting for the special covenant relationship between God and His chosen people, Israel. He instigated it and it was to be maintained by His people through their commitment to obey the Law *(Exodus 24:7)*.

Furthermore, it was always His intention that the whole *nation* should become *holy* and a *kingdom of priests (Exodus 19:6)*, not just one tribe (Levi). Peter shows us that this promise was carried over into the new covenant for fulfilment in *all* believers *(1 Peter 2:5)*.

In the Old Testament, within that covenant relationship, God's mercy is extended to those who love Him and keep His commandments. We can see, through both the requirements of the law and many other examples in the Old Testament scriptures, that God was looking for that same quality to be expressed in mankind's relationships with one another *(e.g., Micah 6:8)*.

Moving on to the New Testament, we find that it embodies the mercy of God in complete contrast to the cultures of the pagan world (both then and now). The Jews themselves were merciless towards the sinner, as were the Greeks. They believed that *the doer shall suffer*, so every offender was to be crushed and destroyed.

They had no concept of mercy at all. The gospel message would be completely alien to their mindset. In the same way, the Jewish culture expected only that the sinner *must* be punished.

The Jews pressed for punishment. Jesus, knowing He would be taking upon Himself, on the cross, the punishment due to us, preached only salvation (forgiveness, mercy). The gospel is radical. To be merciful calls for us to have the same attitude towards our fellow man as God does. Mercy is unconditional love expressed outwardly. It is the complete reversal of our natural self-centredness and self-protection.

Mercy means love for self will be laid aside in favour of love for both God and mankind *(Matthew 22:36-40)*. This is what Jesus demonstrated throughout His life and ministry as the Son of Man. Such love is very personal and intimate. It is not impersonal, and vaguely general. It means *stopping for the one*, without any hint of discrimination.

We can have a kind of sentimental love for people which is never expressed at a one-to-one level. *Who is my neighbour?* Is he the person in need that I am willing to help if I can? Or is he a nuisance to be avoided? The choice about what to do is always ours. A desire to help, a verbal expression of sympathy, is not *actual* help until it is expressed through *action*. It has been said that *mercy resides in the heart but is revealed in the hand.*

Mercy champions tolerance. Not an easy-going, laissez-faire, turn-a-blind eye kind of tolerance that actually helps no one. No, a tolerance that comes with understanding. The result of making the effort to see things from the other person's perspective.

Mercy leads to forgiveness. Invariably there will be a reason behind someone's negative action. Something will have prompted it, maybe even against their better judgement. A character flaw is often an expression of a deeply buried bitter root that needs to be exposed and healed. Often such roots can be traced back to childhood. Sometimes even beyond that, coming down through the generational line.

It is so much easier to be judgemental if we remain aloof from, or in ignorance of, the many underlying causes of negative behaviour. Anyone who has been involved with inner healing ministries, like Bethel Sozo, will be aware of this. Of how unforgiveness is often the major barrier to both physical and inner (emotional/spiritual) healing.

We have not actually walked in their shoes, endured the same temptations, suffered in similar ways, or been engaged in the same struggles as them. Nevertheless, we should always seek that level of understanding which leads to forgiveness for those who have hurt us. Or others if we are in the position of facilitating ministry.

Mercy promotes help, a help given with consideration. Our help should not cause hurt or humiliation to the one we are aiming to assist. People do not like to receive *charity*, especially if it is *served cold*. But few will turn down the kind of merciful, loving compassion that Jesus always offered. Which He longs to offer now through us.

Thinking of Jesus brings to mind the supreme demonstration of mercy that is the incarnation. As the Son of Man, He identified Himself with all the sins, sorrows, sufferings, and afflictions of mankind. As Emmanuel, He was (and is) *God with us*. He understands. He sympathises. He has compassion.

God is merciful but let us not forget that He is also righteous, holy, and just. He is merciful towards all mankind because He longs for a restored relationship with each one of us. He knows that it is impossible for us to attain His standards of holiness, righteousness, and justice by our own efforts.

God has never set aside His requirements for righteousness and holiness. Our failures must still be dealt with in order for justice to be done. Which is why He sent Jesus as the Son of Man. He has become *for us* wisdom, righteousness, sanctification (holiness) and redemption (*1 Corinthians 1:30*).

Through His sacrificial death and glorious resurrection, He has provided us with forgiveness, healing, and deliverance (the full meaning of the Greek word *sozo*). He has given us a new and abundant life (*John 10:10*) by means of which we can be the people He has called and equipped us to be, the blessed ones!

He has made this provision for the whole of mankind. Christ died for us whilst we were still sinners *(Romans 5:8)*. We know we could never have earned His forgiveness because we were still *lost* when He went to the cross. This is incredible mercy.

This is amazing grace. He took our punishment, at such inestimable cost to Himself, Father God, and Holy Spirit. The requirements of God's justice were met in Him. His righteousness was imputed to us. He was punished for *our* iniquities.

But He was wounded for our transgressions, He was bruised for our iniquities; The chastisement for our peace was upon Him, And by His stripes, we are healed. All we like sheep have gone astray; We have turned, everyone, to his own way; And the Lord has laid on Him the iniquity of us all.

(Isaiah 53:5-6)

This applies equally to those who have hurt us. It does not matter whether or not they have already availed themselves of the blessings of salvation by receiving Jesus as their Saviour. They could make that commitment at any time and immediately their sins would be forgiven by our merciful God. And our loving, compassionate, God wants us to extend such mercy to those who have behaved badly towards us.

If their sins against us are forgivable by Him, who has already forgiven us, then they are forgivable by us. God has been incredibly merciful to us. So, He, can enable us, by His Spirit, as the blessed ones, to be merciful and forgiving also. And, in releasing those who have offended us, we set ourselves free.

Unforgiveness is like someone drinking deadly poison themselves but expecting the person who offended them to die!

For they shall obtain mercy

Love keeps no record of wrongs.

(1 Corinthians 13:5)

I want to begin this second part of the chapter by drawing our attention to a few relevant scriptures. These will help to focus our minds upon the outworking of mercy, of being merciful.

Then Jesus said, "Father, forgive them, for they do not know what they do."

(Luke 23:34a)

And forgive us our sins, for we also forgive everyone who is indebted to us.

(Luke 11:4a)

Then Peter came to Him and said, "Lord, how often shall my brother sin against me, and I forgive him? Up to seven times?"
Jesus said to him, "I do not say to you, up to seven times, but up to 70 times seven."

(Matthew 18:21-22)

Then his master, after he had called him, said to him, 'You wicked servant! I forgave you all that debt because you begged me. Should you not also have had compassion on your fellow servant, just as I had pity on you?'

(Matthew 18:32-33)

Love keeps no record of wrongs.

(1 Corinthians 13:5)

The first four Beatitudes deal primarily with the need of the Christian and with his or her consciousness of that need. As already indicated, we are now beginning to look at a series of consequences of this awareness and realisation. This is essential if, by the grace of God and empowerment of Holy Spirit, we are to live the Christian lifestyle depicted in this portion of scripture.

We all have to deal with those who offend, hurt, reject, or abuse us in some way. The blessed ones are merciful, gracious, and forgiving to such people, without pre-conditions. Being merciful is meant to be a lifestyle, not merely a one-off, gracious response to a specific situation or circumstance.

Receiving undeserved forgiveness (mercy through grace) is an essential part of being born again into God's Kingdom family. Being forgiving (merciful) is an equally essential outward expression of the Christian life we are called and equipped to live thereafter.

Here is my own paraphrase of *2 Corinthians 1:3-4* in which I have substituted *comfort* with *blessing*. *The blessed ones are graced with the ability to be able to bless others with the blessing with which they have been blessed*. In the present context, of course, we are dealing with the blessing of mercy (or forgiveness).

Again, to reverently adapt another scripture *(1 John 4:19)*, not only are we enabled to love Him because He first loved us, but also to forgive others because He first forgave us. There is meant to be a lifelong, experiential aspect to this, not simply a few one-off occurrences.

We will inevitably find ourselves in need of God's forgiveness on 70 times seven (i.e., innumerable) occasions after our initial encounter with Him. In the same way, there will also be countless times when we will have opportunities to forgive others for hurting us, maybe repeatedly. If we have received His gracious, undeserved forgiveness (mercy) towards us, how can we hold back forgiveness from others? Only by being totally selfish and hypocritical. And, if or when we fall into this trap, unless we recognise, acknowledge and repent of our hypocrisy, how can we expect God to forgive us for it?

That is where I believe the apparently pre-conditional aspect of God's mercy and forgiveness towards us must come into consideration (*Luke 11:4a, Matthew 18:35*). It is rather like the chicken and egg conundrum, isn't it? But if we are really walking in the light as He is in the light (*1 John 1:7*), can it really be possible, simultaneously, to be harbouring any unforgiveness (or failing to be merciful)?

God's forgiveness (or mercy) towards us cannot be wholly conditional upon us **first** forgiving (or being merciful to) our brother, as some would contend the scriptures mean. We follow His lead, so that interpretation would completely overturn the crucial blessing of grace. We must be careful to interpret scripture by scripture and not take individual verses in isolation.

If my being forgiven by God is solely dependent upon me having first forgiven, from the heart, everyone who has upset me, I would never be forgiven by Him! There is more to this than meets the unregenerate eye. Grace is the key once again. Remember, it was while we were *still* sinners, that Christ died for us *(Romans 5:8)*.

The point of the parable of the unforgiving servant is that having been forgiven much (comparatively), we should be more than willing to forgive little (comparatively). Having been forgiven by his master, the servant was not willing to forgive his colleague, thus depriving himself of his master's blessing. If I am not willing to be merciful myself, I can never have truly *known* what mercy really is, even if I have benefitted from it. It should be contagious!

But if I am truly repentant and know how blessed I am by the unmerited favour of God's mercy, how could I not want to treat, in the same gracious way, those who offend me? When we are first forgiven by God, I suggest, we have a spirit of forgiveness deposited within us which enables us to be capable of forgiving others (but the choice is still always ours). We learn to differentiate between the sinner and the sin and to remember that Ephesians 6:12 reminds us of who our ultimate enemy is, manipulating gullible people for his own ends.

If we do fail to forgive, to be merciful to anyone, who is it who suffers? Often, only the one who fails to forgive. As mentioned before, practitioners of Christian inner healing ministries (like Bethel Sozo) encounter the barrier of unforgiveness time and time again. If we retain unforgiveness or bitterness it always hurts *us*. I repeat someone has likened unforgiveness to the offended one drinking poison himself but expecting the offender to die!

Please do not lose sight of the fact that it is not uncommon for our offenders to be totally unaware that they have offended us. They may even be mortified if they were to discover that they had somehow managed to do so.

If abuse, particularly in distant childhood, is the problem, it is possible that the perpetrator is no longer alive. But the damage is still there and needs to be dealt with. Forgiving the person is then a matter of choice. It does not absolve them of guilt, it does not *let them off*. Releasing forgiveness to them brings freedom to the survivor. The burden is transferred from the victim to Jesus. He has already dealt with it, on the cross, both the punishment due the perpetrator and the unforgiveness (to date) of the survivor. If the perpetrator never reaches the point of turning to Jesus in repentance in his lifetime, sadly he will not receive God's blessing of forgiveness that was always available to him.

Practising mercy unites us with our merciful Father. Failing to do so separates us from Him. So here we have both a promise and a warning. When we are merciful, we receive His commendation, *Well done, good and faithful servant (Matthew 15:21)*. Our fellowship with Him deepens in intimacy (*1 John 1:7*). He delights in us because we are reflecting His character (*Luke 6:36*). We treat other people as He treats us (*Luke 6:31*). It is right for us to take the initiative rather than to be reactive (*1 John 4:19*).

The Christian life is first about *being*. Our identity is secured in Him and the *doing* aspect follows. When we are Spirit-led and Spirit-empowered, our life is not about striving to match up to a code of ethics. What a Christian *does* is motivated by what a Christian *is*. We are born again (*John 3:3*). We are a new creation (*2 Corinthians 5:17*). We are fully enabled and equipped by Holy Spirit.

When someone hurts us, will we follow our natural response to make them feel guilty or to punish them? Or will we have an overriding, supernatural desire to be gracious to them? By so doing we emulate the response of our gracious God, who is characterised by mercy. Will we concentrate on setting them free? When we show mercy, rather than anger or insist upon obtaining revenge, even by means of justice, we will enjoy the blessing of God.

Blessed are the merciful, for they shall obtain mercy.

7
Blessed Are the Pure in Heart for They Shall See God

Blessed are the pure in heart

> *Create in me a clean (pure) heart, O God,*
> *And renew a steadfast spirit within me.*
>
> (Psalm 51:10)

Some would contend that this is the most demanding of all the Beatitudes. After all, who among us could claim to have been constant in purity of heart? Especially if we were to subject ourselves to a strict and honest examination of our motives in every situation we have been in.

Can we truly say that what would appear to have been the most genuinely selfless of our actions was totally devoid of any hint of pride or self-satisfaction? Even when we were at our most generous were our actions entirely free of a desire for them to have been noted and approved by others?

We may not have been fully conscious of any such taint at the time. But what if we had honestly searched our hearts afterwards? The standard is so high because it has been set to the level of the perfection of Father God and modelled for us by Jesus, His Son!

The first three Beatitudes focus upon both our need and our growing consciousness of that need. This awareness, this humbling, this mourning causes us to hunger and thirst after the Righteous One. In Him, we are satisfied, or filled, as stated in the fourth Beatitude.

Our need is not met through our own effort but by God's gracious provision. It is wholly of grace. A willing cooperation with His prompting and leading is our contribution, as we exercise our freedom to choose. God never overrides our free will.

The following three Beatitudes deal with the result of our being satisfied. We are enabled to be like Jesus: those who are merciful, pure in heart and peacemakers. After that comes persecution for righteousness' sake. That is, if we diligently pursue this new, abundant life made freely available to each of us. Once again, we see the progressive nature of the Beatitudes.

Lloyd-Jones draws our attention to another link between them that is worthy of consideration. We become merciful to others after having realised our own poverty of spirit. When we have mourned over the natural state of our own hearts, we are motivated to seek the remedy of cleansing and purifying them by the grace of God.

As peacemakers, whom we will look at more closely later, we find this task less onerous once we have become personally acquainted with meekness. Therefore, he writes, the three results of our being filled correspond with the three needs that first caused us to hunger and thirst.

The Christian gospel is focussed on the heart. We find this to be so throughout the New Testament record of the teachings and example of Jesus. If we care to look, it is there in the Old Testament too. Jesus rebuked the Pharisees because of their obsession with outward appearances whilst neglecting the necessary inward change of heart.

Their approach to the Law meant they sought to observe every aspect of it They wanted to be seen to comply with the rules through ritualistic practices, right down to the finest detail. In so doing they completely missed the point. The basic requirements of the Law were to be met, first and foremost, in and from the heart.

Conforming on the outside is not at all sufficient if the thoughts of the mind and desires of the heart remain contrary to God's will. Ceremonial purity, the overriding priority of the Jewish leaders, did not involve any change in the inward character of a person. This flaw is at the heart of all *religion*, which focusses on being *seen* to keep the *rules* in order to gain a reward.

An inward change of character (heart) is intended to lead to an outward, often unconscious, observance of the standards set out in the Law. In declaring what the greatest commandments are, Jesus confirmed that a radical inward change of heart leading to outward expression was always the objective. This complete turnaround within the core of our being can only be achieved through re-birth *(John 3:3)* and a new heart *(Ezekiel 36:26)*, both gifts of God's grace

The Christian faith is not simply a matter of what we know in our heads about it. It is not a purely intellectual faith any more than it is only a matter of right conduct or behaviour. Both our understanding and our behaviour are meant to come from the heart.

A heart that has been transformed by a personal encounter with the Living God *(Matthew 12:35)*. A regenerated spirit is the crux of the matter, working outwardly through the soul and body *(1 Thessalonians 5:23)*.

The emphasis of what is called the *social gospel* is on the environment. If we can change a person's habitat or circumstances, then the person themselves will change for the better. That may be so, in some cases, but it is not the work of Holy Spirit.

He brings us into a fundamental change of heart (the core of our being), not mere improvement. That is the true mark of being Christian. I am not saying that rightly motivated social action or reform is either unnecessary or not laudable. But let us not forget that Adam and Eve were in Paradise when they fell!

Blessed are the *pure in heart*? I repeat, which of us would claim such a condition to be naturally our own? Can the heart of any person be completely pure, devoid of any hint of mixed motives? In the light of Jeremiah 17:9, how can we possibly attain such a position, if that is essential for us to be able to see God?

Origen taught what the purity of heart referred to in this verse means. *Not only those who have been rid of fornication, but those who have been rid of all sins, for every sin leaves a stain upon the soul.*

No, we are not considering sexual purity alone in this context. When we look at Matthew 5:27-28, we see a perfect example of the clear distinction that Jesus makes between the external and the internal, the condition of the heart.

We sin if we persistently entertain the *thought* even though we may not translate that impure thought into *action*. There can be no doubt that the required standard is nothing less than perfection *(Matthew 5:48)*. No wonder holiness can be defined as *set apart*!

Are we really expected to be pure, just as Jesus Himself was perfectly pure? Surely that is impossible. But we also read, in the gospels, that what is impossible for man is possible with God. For example:

And they were greatly astonished, saying among themselves, Who then can be saved? But Jesus looked at them and said, With men it is impossible, but not with God; for with God all things are possible.

(Mark 10:26-27)

The writer to the Hebrews states, in relation to a sacrifice acceptable to God, that *If the blood of bulls and goats and the ashes of a heifer, sprinkling the unclean, sanctifies for the purifying of the flesh, how much more shall the blood of Christ, who through the eternal Spirit offered Himself without spot to God, cleanse your conscience from dead works to serve the living God?*

(Hebrews 9:14)

Peter writes similarly, in 1 Peter 1:19, that we were redeemed *with the precious blood of Christ, as of a lamb without blemish and without spot.* He goes on to exhort us, in 2 Peter 3:14, to *be diligent to be found by Him in peace, without spot and blameless.*

John, inspired by Holy Spirit, makes a seemingly incredible statement. *Love has been perfected among us in this: that we may have boldness in the day of judgment; because as He is, so are we in this world* (1 John 4:17).

Let us have a look at what *purity* is. At what being *pure* actually means. The original Greek word is *katharos* or *katharoi*, and it occurs over 150 times in the (Greek) Old Testament.

In the majority of cases, it is used to describe ceremonial purity. Less often, it relates to moral and/or spiritual purity. The former refers to externals and the latter to internals. As I have already pointed out, this highlights the complete contrast between a *religion* of rule-keeping and the holiness of true Christian spirituality.

To provide an example of ceremonial, religious and external purity, we have only to look at the Jewish tradition of ritual washing before a meal. Such washing had little to do with hygiene. It was embraced more for ritualistic, ceremonial reasons. This is referred to in some detail in the gospels, and we find Jesus rebuking the Pharisees for their devotion to externals at the expense of the more important issues of the heart.

Then the Pharisees and some of the scribes came together to Him, having come from Jerusalem. Now when they saw some of His disciples eat bread with defiled, that is, with unwashed hands, they found fault. For the Pharisees and all the Jews do not eat unless they wash their hands in a special way, holding the tradition of the elders.

When they come from the marketplace, they do not eat unless they wash. And there are many other things which they have received and held, like the washing of cups, pitchers, copper vessels, and couches.

Then the Pharisees and scribes asked Him, "Why do Your disciples not walk according to the tradition of the elders, but eat bread with unwashed hands?"

He answered and said to them, "Well did Isaiah's prophesy of you hypocrites, as it is written, These people honour Me with their lips, but their heart is far from Me. And in vain they worship Me, teaching as doctrines the commandments of men."

For laying aside the commandment of God, you hold the tradition of men—the washing of pitchers and cups, and many other such things you do.

(Mark 7:2-8)

Jesus expounds, in the Sermon on the Mount, the true meaning of the Old Testament commandments. *"You have heard that it was said to those of old ...but I say to you ..."* ...cuts right through externals to issues of the heart. It is not enough to hold back from actually doing something known to be wrong.

It is necessary not even to want to do it. This means resisting the temptation before it is translated into action *(James 1:14-15)*. The grace of God enables us to make right decisions and carry them out, but the choice is always ours *(Romans 7:22-25a)*.

We cannot stop negative thoughts or strong temptations from entering our minds. But we can choose whether or not these things are allowed to progress further. That is, in the imagination only—or then to be given outward expression also. Self-control is, after all, a fruit of the Spirit *(Galatians 5:23)* not just a matter of willpower.

Therefore, submit to God. Resist the devil and he will flee from you. Draw near to God and He will draw near to you. Cleanse your hands, you sinners; and purify your hearts, you double-minded.

(James 4:7-8)

Purity of heart means a *united* heart, an *undivided heart (Psalm 86:11, Ezekiel 11:19)*. At its best, the natural human heart, or nature, tends to operate with a degree of mixed motives. This is something Paul expounds in detail in the latter part of Romans 7, as alluded to above.

Purity of the heart also results from being *cleansed (Psalm 51:2)*. Only a heart which has been cleansed will be welcomed into the heavenly Jerusalem *(Revelation 22:14-15)*.

Purity of heart means to be *free from shame or stain*. It contrasts with a divided heart or double-mindedness *(James 1:8)*. It is also a heart *free from bitterness*. Being merciful means that the bitterness caused by unforgiveness, for example, has no place in it.

A pure heart will resist the temptation to unrighteous anger, to lose one's temper. It will resist allowing lustful thoughts to consume us. It will resist the lure of the love of money. Money is not a problem in itself, but the love of money is very much a heart issue *(1 Timothy 6:10)*.

Purity of heart is exemplified by Jesus, the Son of Man *(Hebrews 4:15)*. Jesus kept what He described as the *first and greatest commandment (Matthew 22:36-38)*. Then He goes on, in the following verse, to state the second most important one. In verse 40 He declares, *on these two commandments hang all the Law and the Prophets*. Such *holiness* is absolutely essential if we are to be among the blessed ones who will *see God (Hebrews 12:14)*.

Purity of heart cannot be a matter of attaining sinless perfection. Otherwise, Jesus would not have included a request for God's forgiveness in what we know as 'The Lord's Prayer' *(Matthew 6:12, Luke 11:4)*. The Christian is warned, in 1 John 1:8, not to be deceived by thinking he is *without sin*. The writer goes on to illustrate the remedy for when, not if, we fall short of God's glory.

Quite obviously, there is nothing we can do to make our hearts pure. It can only be accomplished by something God does in us, by grace alone. We have salvation through the death of Jesus and are transformed (enabled) by His resurrection Life, as Romans 5:10 states. *For if when we were enemies we were reconciled to God through the death of His Son, much more, having been reconciled, we shall be saved by His life.*

When the Bible mentions the *heart* it is invariably not referring to the organ which pumps blood around the body. Nor is the definition limited to the *soul*, known as the seat of the mind, will and emotions. The soul, as part of the *flesh*, wars against the spirit *(Galatians 5:17)*.

Those three elements are included, of course, but the heart is more than that. It is the centre of our being, of our personality. It is what uniquely distinguishes each individual, like fingerprints. So, it is the very core of our being that it is the purpose of God to purify. That part of us out of which everything else flows.

Proverbs 4:23 emphasises the importance of the heart by urging us to, *Keep your heart with all diligence, for out of it spring the issues of life.* Our faith is encapsulated by what we believe in our hearts, not just in our minds.

The word is near you, in your mouth and in your heart (that is, the word of faith which we preach): that if you confess with your mouth the Lord Jesus and believe in your heart that God has raised Him from the dead, you will be saved. For with the heart one believes unto righteousness, and with the mouth, confession is made unto salvation.

(Romans 10:8-10)

Believing with the heart is so much more important than mere intellectual assent and head knowledge. Not to put too fine a point on it, what we believe in our hearts is crucial to our salvation.

Believing in our hearts that Jesus died for us and rose again from the dead means not only are we washed and purified by His blood but, simultaneously, our hearts are purified. Not only when we first come to faith but also when the need arises on an ongoing basis (1 John 1:8-9 again, for example).

In exhorting us to *purify our hearts* James and John are making it clear that this is not a passive thing on our part. It involves active participation with the Spirit of God to carry out our resolve experientially.

It began with a sovereign work in our hearts by God when He called us, and we responded. He requires us to co-operate with Him by making right choices thereafter.

Our part in maintaining purity of heart is both to *walk by the spirit* and to keep short accounts with the Lord as and when we fall short. In addition, He wants us to pursue a growing intimacy in our relationship with Him. For, although the heart can contain all that is good and pure, it is also the root of much that is negative in our lives. As Jesus said, again emphasising the distinction between inward motivation and outward show:

Do you not yet understand that whatever enters the mouth goes into the stomach and is eliminated? But those things which proceed out of the mouth come from the heart, and they defile a man. For out of the heart proceed evil thoughts, murders, adulteries, fornications, thefts, false witness, blasphemies. These are the things which defile a man, but to eat with unwashed hands does not defile a man.

(Matthew 15:17-20)

Yes, our heart can hold all that is good, but it can also be the source of what is bad. Both can be given expression in our lives, depending upon whether we are *walking* in the spirit or in the flesh *(Galatians 5:16, 25)*.

For they shall see God

*Beloved, now we are children of God; and it has not yet been revealed
what we shall be, but we know that when He is revealed,
we shall be like Him, for we shall see Him as He is. And
everyone who has this hope in Him purifies himself, just as He is pure.*

(1 John 3:2-3)

Let us begin this section with Barclay's interpretation of this Beatitude. It will provide us with a helpful guide towards what we are seeking to become as the blessed ones. *Blessed are those whose thoughts and motives are absolutely unmixed and, therefore, absolutely pure...the bliss of the heart whose thoughts, motives and desires are completely unmixed, genuine, and sincere.*

This Beatitude is considered by some to be one of the most awe-inspiring statements in the Bible. For any believer, the promise to (all) the blessed ones that they will see Him is incredibly amazing. This is true even if we have a less-than-perfect knowledge and appreciation of who God really is.

In Exodus 33:11, we read that *the Lord spoke to Moses face to face, as a man speaks to his friend.* Yet, when he asked God to show him His glory, Moses received this reply in verse 18. *You cannot see My face; for no man shall see Me, and live.* The revelation of God given to Elijah, in 1 Kings 19, was limited to a *still, small voice.* Awesome, but not a face-to-face encounter.

Matthew 5:8 is not about the initial saving grace received into our hearts by faith. It is about the progression from that point through the process of sanctification that the successive Beatitudes describe. It is that desire, that commitment, to maintain a purity of heart that follows on from the previous Beatitudes.

A hunger for righteousness, that is by faith from first to last *(Romans 1:17),* is essentially heartfelt. Yes, there may still be transgressions in our lives, but we have our Advocate in Heaven who pleads for us *(1 John 2:1).* Thus, due to the grace of ongoing cleansing by the blood of Jesus, we can maintain a pure heart and see Him.

Our human effort is not, and could never be, sufficient. A heart connection with our loving, compassionate, gracious, and merciful God facilitates the perfect remedy *(Romans 7:22-25a).* Yes, with the One who knows all our weaknesses *(Hebrews 4:15-16).* The condition of our hearts determines whether or not we will *see* God.

The blessed ones have been cleansed by the blood of Jesus. They have been drawn closer to God through Holy Spirit. Their motives, thoughts, emotions, and desires are untainted by self. Their reward is a vision of God. A knowledge of Him and an intimacy with Him that is beyond words to describe. Their blessing begins in this life. It will reach completion in the next, as the following verses illustrate.

Therefore, brethren, having boldness to enter the Holiest by the blood of Jesus, by a new and living way which He consecrated for us, through the veil, that is, His flesh, and having a High Priest over the house of God, let us draw near with a true heart in full assurance of faith, having our hearts sprinkled from an evil conscience and our bodies washed with pure water.

(Hebrews 10:19-22)

John tells us, in Revelation 1:7, that one day *every* eye shall see Him. That is *not* a special promise made only to the already blessed ones. Some have maintained that only those who have become pure in heart by attaining a state of sinless perfection will see God.

Their interpretation of Hebrews 12:14 is used to back up this assertion. However, whilst not wishing to minimise our need to cooperate with Him, read 1 Corinthians 1:30. This verse makes it clear that Jesus Himself is *our righteousness, holiness and redemption.*

The promise is that we will see God if we are pure in heart. The purity of heart called for in this Beatitude requires the death of *self* and the Life of Christ in our hearts. This speaks of our participation in Christ's death and resurrection *(Galatians 2:20).*

Without His grace, not one of us could become the blessed ones to whom this amazing promise is given. Only those who become like God, through grace not by personal effort, can see Him and be in His Presence.

This is to be our experience in Heaven, of course. But can we not experience a taste of such privilege in this life, too? For surely, that is what this Beatitude is promising us.

It is a basic tenet of the Christian faith that we will see God when we die and go to meet Him in Heaven. I have no intention of disputing that belief. I share it wholeheartedly. I also believe that there is a *seeing* possible in this life.

In 2 Corinthians 12, Paul testifies to having been taken up into heaven to see indescribable things. He was not certain about whether he saw them with his natural eyesight or, supernaturally, in a vision. Nevertheless, he did **see** them!

You and I have probably come across a number of accounts from people who claim to have *seen* God. Some of those stories are more reliable than others, no doubt. There are certainly stories I have heard or read from people whom I would trust to be sharing a genuine experience. It is not something I have enjoyed myself, to date. However, I am not going to dismiss future possibilities solely because of a lack of past experience in my own life.

Knowledge, experience, and belief will affect our perspective. We might see the same things quite differently from someone else. For example, you will be aware of how the police find that witness statements to exactly the same incident can vary widely from person to person!

My wife, Cathy, views football as nothing more than a bunch of men mindlessly chasing a leather sphere around a field! Having played the game to a reasonable standard in my distant youth, I take a rather different view. This is one of those minor matters it is wise for us both to agree to disagree over!

Seeing God could be described as perceiving some measure of His glory here on Earth. Remember the experience of the priests when the temple was consecrated? It was then that they encountered the Shekinah Glory of the Lord *(2 Chronicles 5:13-14)*. When they saw the cloud, were they not *seeing* a manifestation of the Presence of God?

We read that the Kingdom of Heaven *is at hand (e.g., Matthew 10:7)*. We also read, in John 1:18, that only Jesus has seen the Father face to face. Does it mean that seeing something of the glory of God, like the priests did, or as Moses was permitted to do in Exodus 33:18-23, is all we can expect?

I really appreciate the following statement from R. T. Kendall. *It is nonetheless possible that God can be so real that seeing Him with your naked eye would not make Him any more real to you.*

Maybe, for most of us, seeing God is more about spiritual perception than what is possible for the naked eye? As already pointed out, I am not discounting those who see God in visions. However, such experiences are outside the scope of this book. And what of those awesome occasions when we can encounter His manifest Presence, through many and varied *phenomena* either alone or in a meeting? Can these also be interpreted as *seeing* God?

Moses' heart hungered after experiencing the Presence of God *(Exodus 33:18)*. David, the great worshipper of God, was like-minded about this *(Psalm 17:15; 41:12; 63:2; 140:13)*. What about you and me?

As we go about our daily activities, moment by moment, do we want to be in a position to encounter, to connect with, to see God? Or we are not even aware of this as a possibility? Do we want to draw near to Him or to drift away *(James 4:8)*? Are we increasingly open to connecting with Him or we are shutting ourselves off from the possibility? I would suggest that He actually desires such a connection even more than we (might) do.

I believe that seeing or perceiving God also means entering into a progressive knowledge of Him *(1 Corinthians 13:12)*. Jesus describes Himself as the Truth *(John 14:6)* so this also means knowing or *seeing* the truth. Further, it means entering ever more deeply into a fellowship of agape love with our gracious God, who loves us unconditionally.

So, I would suggest that *seeing* God includes developing a connection with Him through intimacy and Presence. This is the restoration of our relationship with Him that is at the heart of His purpose for each one of us.

There is also the sense in which we *see* God when we personally witness the manifested works of God (healing, miracles, deliverance). Jesus told Nicodemus in John 3 that the Spirit is like the wind. (As you may know, the Greek word *pneuma* can be translated as either *wind, spirit* or *breath*).

We cannot see the wind, but we can certainly see the effects of it. Just think about all the things that can be moved or powered by the unseen wind, from leaves to sailing boats to windmills and more.

There are contemporary records of clouds appearing in church gatherings; also feathers, gems, gold dust, and so on. In my book, 'First Steps into Healing—' I recount a couple of my own experiences of appearances, out of nothing, of such phenomena! I was present during a church meeting when two large gemstones suddenly appeared on the floor in front of the platform during the sermon!

Some people tend to view such sightings as portents of something powerful and highly significant about to happen. Without wishing to belittle in any way such amazing manifestations, I tend to share the belief that they are often simply little signs confirming God's Presence in our midst. Signs to make us wonder, perhaps?

Years before, I remember such manifestations taking the form of tingling hands or fluttering eyelashes. Similarly, there could be tears, laughter, shaking and what is often described as being *slain in the Spirit*. (When someone falls to the ground under the power of God). I have experienced all of these things in some measure, so have I been *seeing* God each time? I think so.

Nevertheless, our focus should always be upon seeking God for Himself, not upon seeking manifestations of His glory, truly wonderful though these are.

Seeing God could involve:

- seeing an angel
- seeing a godly vision
- witnessing a miracle
- an awesome answer to prayer
- divine intervention to transform a situation
- seeing the healing power of God at work

- God *speaking* to us through His Word
- receiving a personal, prophetic word
- being filled with the Spirit
- experiencing His manifest Presence

As we cooperate with Him, may the grace of God continue to maintain our hearts in that purity which will enable us to *see* and experience more of His Presence. May that be increasingly so for us until that glorious Day when we will certainly see Him face to face.

8
Blessed Are the Peacemakers for They Shall Be Called Sons of God

Blessed are the peacemakers

> *Now the fruit of righteousness is sown in peace*
> *by those who make peace.*

> (James 3:18)

In order to become peacemakers, the blessed ones must first know peace and to be at peace themselves. That realisation and experience begins, as Paul informs us, by receiving peace from, and being at peace with, God.

> *Therefore, having been justified by faith, we have peace with God through our Lord Jesus Christ.*

> (Romans 5:1)

Our Lord Jesus Christ is the Prince of Peace *(Isaiah 9:6)* and He *is* our peace *(Ephesians 2:14)*. Only by being equipped with the perfect peace *(Isaiah 26:3)* that is found in Him can we be like Him, as effective peacemakers in this world.

"Peace-making is a God-approved anointing and those who do it are blessed," writes R. T. Kendall.

He also makes a comparison, rightly in my opinion, with anointings to preach or to teach, to bring healing or deliverance, to evangelise. Such anointed people are sons (and daughters) of God, active in the family business of bringing God and people together. Instrumental in reconciling us with one another *(2 Corinthians 5:18-20)* as and when needed.

Peace is central to the New Testament. The Greek word for peace, *eviene*, is found in every book and 88 times altogether. Have you noticed how often it appears in the opening greeting of most of the epistles, certainly in each one of Paul's?

Indeed, it was a normal form of greeting in those days. In John 14:27, Jesus speaks of leaving His peace with us. This 'bequest' has been described as His last will and testament. Of course, He had nothing of material value to leave to His disciples, but this spiritual gift is precious and priceless.

The Hebrew word for peace is well-known *shalom*. In fact, it has a wide range of meanings. Perfect welfare, serenity, prosperity, happiness; and to be in a condition of complete well-being. When it refers to relationships it describes intimacy, fellowship and abiding goodwill, stemming from all that is truly good.

So, peace is more than the absence of conflict, discord, or division. Jesus said there will always be wars and rumours of wars (*Mark 13:7*).

The lack of peace, whether between individuals or nations, stems from the failings of the natural human heart. Remember, *out of the heart comes* (*Matthew 12:34*).

Only when the problem of the sinful human heart is dealt with can there be hope for true and lasting peace (*Jeremiah 17:9*). That is why Father God sent Jesus.

But as many as received Him, to them He gave the right to become children of God, to those who believe in His Name: who were born, not of blood, nor of the will of the flesh, nor of the will of man, but of God.

(John 1:12-13)

It is this change of heart that each one of the Beatitudes illustrates. Without a radical change of heart (both by conversion and the baptism of Holy Spirit) it would be impossible for us to live them out.

Conviction, repentance, regeneration and baptism, all exclusively the work of Holy Spirit, are essential. Therefore, to be a peacemaker requires the same deep cleansing and spiritual empowerment that facilitates all the other qualities highlighted in the Beatitudes.

As we have seen in relation to each of them, the blessed one who is to be a peacemaker cannot be one as a result of his, or her, natural disposition. This description does not apply to the easy-going. Someone who will do anything to avoid trouble.

Someone who is an advocate of peace at any price. Such an attitude may promote a degree of peace. Sadly, this is often at the expense of righteousness or justice.

It is sometimes necessary to make a stand in order to facilitate real peace. If we settle for appeasement, that will rarely do more than postpone the inevitable. Chamberlain's 'Piece of Paper' before WW2, for example. Brushing something under the carpet serves only to create an unsightly mound for someone to trip over in the darkness!

No doubt the vast majority of people in this world could be accurately described as *peace-lovers*. But it takes more than that to be a peace*maker*. Some peace-lovers, faced with problems or difficulties would prefer, *for the sake of peace*, to do nothing to help to rectify such negative situations.

On the other hand, a peacemaker would want to do everything possible to put matters right and be at peace with everyone (*Romans 12:18*). It is not possible for one to be at complete peace in any situation where peace that should be present is obviously lacking. This means the only solution to the problem is to make peace, perhaps at some cost to oneself.

The Jews of Jesus' time on Earth expected their Messiah to come with military power to overthrow the Romans and restore the kingdom of Israel to His chosen people. But Jesus, the Prince of Peace, came as a peacemaker. He came not only to bring peace *to* both Jews and Gentiles but also peace *between* Jews and Gentiles.

And, of course, between Gentiles and Gentiles. Why did the Jews reject the One whom they had been expecting for 100s of years? Because He did not conform to the image that they had created for Him. As a result, they missed the greatest opportunity for peace that could ever have been offered to them.

Peace-making requires our active participation in trying to bring peace into a difficult situation by taking the initiative. Equally, there will be occasions when we need to let peace come by responding positively when the initiative is taken by someone else.

The blessed ones of this Beatitude are those who will do what it takes to increase the well-being and welfare of others, as well as themselves. They will work to make life easier, happier, and more complete by serving the purposes of God.

Sometimes this will not be done consciously but simply because of the peace they *carry* (*Matthew 10:13*). On occasions this may be achieved at a distance, or at least not at an intimate, personal level. Of course, we must consider the realm of closer, and more intimate, relationships as well.

There is the special blessedness of the one who is at peace with himself. One who has Jesus at the centre, as the wellspring of his life. This is living in the blessing of knowing for certain that *the old has gone and the new has come* (*2 Corinthians 5:17, Galatians 2:20*) and living accordingly.

It is being totally secure in our new identity in Christ. To be troubled by internal conflict, or even self-hate, is the very opposite of this blessed state. Paul describes something like this quite graphically in Romans 7. He comes to the inevitable conclusion that the solution is only to be found in Jesus.

Advocating peace and encouraging peace-making is entirely compatible with loving our enemies. Also being willing to forgive anyone who has hurt us. Do we have in us the *meekness* not to stand upon our rights, even if that is justifiable? If so, we have in us the ability to be peacemakers. Not only the ability but also the desire, the inner motivation, to do so.

There are so many potential reasons for division in this world. Paul lists just some of them, from his day, in Galatians 3:28. It does not take very much imagination to come up with an even longer list of contemporary examples. A world in which such divisions are rife can hardly be considered a happy, safe, or peaceful place.

The 12 argued amongst themselves about which of them was to be the greatest (*Mark 9:34*). James and John wanted the best seats in the Kingdom. So, (bravely!) they asked their mother to petition Jesus on their behalf (*Mark 10:35-45*). The same thing even came up during the Last Supper (*Luke 22:24*).

It is Jesus who brings unity and restores relationships. He doesn't ask us to *create* unity. He wants us to *keep* (maintain) the unity that is already ours, in Him, in the bond of peace (*Ephesians 4:3*). This bond accurately reflects that between the Three Persons of the Godhead, the Holy Trinity.

In every family, group, church, community, or country we can always find some who are a disruptive influence. There will be others who are reconcilers. Some who sow strife and others who sow peace (*James 3:18*).

Being reconciled to God is intended to motivate us all to be reconciled with one another, both individually and collectively. The blessed one, who is at peace with God, is the one most disposed to make lasting peace both with and between others.

It is very sad that bitterness and unforgiveness can so easily find a welcome in the human heart. The very presence of such negatives means there is a lack of peace, a barrier between individuals. Peace can reign only when the heart is free of such obstructions. Nothing but our willing cooperation with the grace and healing touch of God can bring the freedom in which such peace thrives.

A significant barrier between parties who need to be reconciled is pride. This barrier can still remain even when a difference of opinion seems to be resolved. Such pride can also come between us and God if we allow it to. Meekness, as we saw earlier in this book, is the primary quality called for in such situations.

Jesus deals with this issue in Matthew 5:23-24. We need to put things right with our friend or neighbour before we are able to *worship in spirit and in truth (John 4:23)*. Or take communion (*1 Corinthians 11:27*).

Writing in reference to this Beatitude, T. H. Robinson declares, *The ideal of God for human society is a spiritual condition in which jealousy, rivalry and hostility have disappeared and a universal harmony prevails. He who is most worthy of congratulation (i.e., is blessed) for his true success in this difficult and complicated world of men and women is he who most perfectly succeeds in producing and upholding this harmony.*

A peacemaker is not one to bury his head in the sand, hoping that a problem ignored is a problem that will disappear of its own accord. Indeed, true peace comes from properly motivated confrontation.

From a desire to do (graciously) whatever it takes to achieve perfect peace in any conflict. A peacemaker is willing to break down the barriers of division. This is the reason why, and how, we have peace with God through our Lord Jesus Christ *(Romans 5:1)*.

Church people are (in)famous for forming committees to look at new ideas from every conceivable angle before they can (if ever!) be put into practice. Sadly, committees tend to take forever to achieve little or nothing.

No doubt you have heard it said that *if Moses was a committee, Israel would still be in Egypt!* Or that, *a camel is a horse designed by a committee!* I am not convinced that a peacemaker would be entirely comfortable sitting on a committee. I think they would rather pray for wisdom and, believing they have received it (*James 1:5-6*), trust God and act as He prompts them to.

Peace-making can never be a matter of theory only. Peace is not made until *action* is taken and *the rubber hits the road*. The proof of the pudding is in the eating, not the recipe book. We may carry the peace of God within us but, to share it, we must do something. Be it by word, action, or sometimes both.

I remember, way back during my teenage years, a group of us were in the southwest of England on a motorcycling holiday. The least financially challenged one of our number purchased a transistor radio for the purpose of entertaining not only himself but the rest of the group (or so we thought).

He brought it back to the tent, where we eagerly gathered around it to listen to some pop music. But he refused to switch it on. His reason, *"because that will waste the batteries!"* His purchase proved to be of no value to anyone because it was not allowed to serve its purpose. What did James say about faith and action?"

Yes, peace-making will usually require *me* to take the initiative to make my enemy a friend. To bring two opponents back together in harmony. It may require *me* to respond positively to the efforts of someone from whom I have been estranged.

To *bury the hatchet* and rekindle our old relationship. Or it could be that someone is appealing to me to be reconciled with a third party with whom I have had a difference of opinion. I need to respond positively to these efforts on our mutual behalf.

In the first example, I am the peacemaker and in the other two examples, it is someone other than me. When I cooperate with their efforts, when I respond positively, it follows that a successful outcome will be achieved. Then I became an active peacemaker too. A peacemaker is one who makes, brokers or embraces peace.

Taking the initiative opens up the possibility of being rejected, of course. But that is not a reason to put off going ahead, whatever the scenario may be. Jesus describes two different sets of circumstances in Matthew 5:23-24 and Matthew 18:15 respectively. Both involve taking the initiative to seek peace.

There will be times when we are the one who needs to forgive and others when we are the one who needs to be forgiven *(Verse 2)*. The onus is upon us to do what is right, regardless of the possible outcome of our actions *(Romans 12:18)*. Willingness on our part is what is called for, at least to the degree that the final outcome depends upon us.

This means that peace-making is not compatible with selfishness. That is especially so when I am the one who needs to make peace with someone who has wronged me. Or perhaps we have embraced only a perception that they did. To step out in this way may actually be a humbling experience for us. Nevertheless, it will be an example of grace in action.

If, by the grace of God at work in us, we have experienced a personal progression through the Beatitudes, then we will also find ourselves equipped by Him to make peace with a friend, colleague, or family member.

Sin, of course, is at the root of all division, dissension, enmity, conflict, etc., both in the world and within the church. This is what God looked upon and it offended His Person and purpose as the God of Peace. So, He did something about it in order to bring peace to the world. He sent His Son, the Prince of Peace (*Isaiah 9:6*). He came willingly and in complete humility (*Philippians 2:5-8*), both to bring peace and to make peace.

In so doing He has also released an anointing to His brethren (*Romans 8:29b*) to become peacemakers. An enabling to follow His perfect example. To be a peacemaker is to be Christlike. It is an expression of godliness. It is a privilege that gives us purpose. In actively pursuing that purpose, we bring glory to our Father.

God is the ultimate peacemaker. He has made it possible for us to be at peace with Him by reconciling the world to Himself through Jesus. Now, He has committed to us the message of reconciliation (*2 Corinthians 5:19*).

In order to make perfect peace with one another, and to make it a priority, we must first be at peace with God ourselves. This would be impossible if He had not taken the initiative because of His unconditional love for us and His great desire for a relationship with us. So, what is a peacemaker?

A peacemaker is free from self-interest, self-concern, self-protection, and self-seeking. He or she is not self-centred, looking at every situation from the perspective of how it affects them. Allowing selfishness to determine both their attitude and their actions.

You will no doubt recall that we have already discovered that these are the characteristics which mark the meek. These blessed ones don't take sides. They are concerned, first and foremost, about others and bringing peace to both parties in a dispute. They work equally hard for the people on both sides of a difference of opinion.

A peacemaker seeks to bring people together, to remain friends whatever the problem may be. Being seen to be right is considered less important than being at peace. Even if it means amicably agreeing to disagree about something, the goal is to restore the relationship.

Good friends don't have to share identical opinions about everything to remain good friends. The blessed ones seek reconciliation. They prioritise their friendships. They want to maintain peace.

A peacemaker is neither quarrelsome nor a troublemaker. He is not someone who seeks to impose peace through a wrong motivation. He is truly a peacemaker from the heart. The kind of pure heart that we considered in the previous chapter.

Yet another example of the progressive nature of these Beatitudes. The goal is to bring peace into the hearts of others. Not simply to cover over every outward, visible aspect of hostility or dissension.

A peacemaker will not support racial discrimination or any other harmful barriers between people and people groups. He will do whatever he can to dismantle any such *walls* that have been erected. Whether they arise from a specific conflict situation, or an unhelpful cultural trait being manifested.

I am given to understand (rightly or wrongly) that Irving Berlin composed all his music using only the black keys on his piano. If so, even as a non-musician, I am certain that it would sound even better transposed into a different key. Then both black and white keys would played together in harmony.

A peacemaker will seek to repair divisions (barriers) within the church. Any such divisions are the antithesis of the message of this Beatitude. They should never be tolerated anywhere in the church universally, in the first place. Sadly, it is the reality we are often faced with. And such a reality falls short of the ideal!

As mentioned earlier, the ultimate concern of the peacemaker is the glory of God. That is what motivated Jesus as the Son of Man. When the Presence of God is brought into a situation it changes.

Jesus did only what He *saw* the Father doing and spoke the words the Father gave Him. He calls and equips us to do the same, made possible only by the Presence of Holy Spirit within us.

The Son of Man was equally, and will always be, the Son of God. When we emulate Him, empowered by the Spirit, we are also sons (and daughters) of God. We are *carriers* of His Presence, actively doing the works He has prepared in advance for us to do (*Ephesians 2:10*). The blessed ones are prepared even to endure suffering (e.g., rejection) in order to bring peace into a situation. All this for and to the glory of God.

For they shall be called sons of God

*For as many as are led by the Spirit of God, these are **sons** of God.*

(Romans 8:14)

The promise to the blessed ones who are peacemakers is that they shall be called *sons of God*. There can be no higher accolade than that we should be given that title by God Himself. How awesome to be known in Heaven as a peacemaker on Earth. And, if we are doing God's bidding in this respect, there will be no ignorance of our endeavours in hell either (*Acts 19:15*)!

A peacemaker is a child of God and, as such, carries the family likeness of the Father. The *God of Peace* is an expression found more than once in the New Testament. Peace is more than a characteristic of God, it *is* Him. In the same way that He is more than simply the Healer but *is* healing itself (*Jehovah Rapha—Exodus 15:26*).

We have a new status, as adopted sons and daughters of the King. It is our privilege, and our destiny, to inherit the family traits, just as Jesus displayed them (*Colossians 1:19 and John 14: 9-10*). We are junior partners in the family business of reconciliation and restoration of relationships. Whether between God and man or between individuals and groups within mankind.

What better and more blessed task can there be than to carry out God-like works? To help to build and grow the Kingdom of God on Earth (as it is in Heaven)? For the expression, *sons of God* equates with *godliness*. This has prompted Barclay to interpret this Beatitude as, *Blessed are those who produce right relationships in every sphere of life, for they are doing a God-like work.*

God Himself is the foremost establisher of right relationships. And our own relationship with Him is the most important of all. It is the source of every good thing that enriches our lives (*James 1:17*).

The Father gave His own Son to establish the right relationship between God and mankind (*John 3:16, Romans 5:1*). Our precious calling is therefore to seek to do likewise. Whether that is to do the work of an evangelist (*2 Timothy 4:5*) or to meet the needs of those in want (e.g., *Acts 6:1-6*).

The Christian church has been prominent in many essential reforming and charitable works down the centuries. I am sure you don't need me to provide you with examples of those.

Barclay pointed out that the Hebrew language is deficient in adjectives. It compensates for that by using the words *son of...*, coupled with a virtue or quality. In *(Acts 4:36)*, for example, we find Barnabas described as S*on of Encouragement*. Reading further on, we find just how much he encouraged Saul of Tarsus.

After his conversion, Saul was doubted by many in the church because he had been persecuting them for their faith. No doubt, this welcome encouragement was instrumental in setting Saul/Paul on his way into the most fruitful of ministries as the Apostle Paul.

God has adopted us into His Family as sons (and daughters). Yet it has been my experience to find that too many Christians go through their lives seeing themselves more as either sinners or servants. We *were* sinners but now we *are* sons. We are not just servants, but we are sons who serve.

Too often we live in denial of our true identity and purpose in Christ. All that He has achieved on our behalf, at such cost to Himself, that we might be and live as sons (and daughters) of God. That is really a whole different subject that it is not my purpose to consider in further detail in this chapter.

We have encountered the Father, in and through Jesus. Let us embrace the status of the sonship that He offers us. Then our attitudes will change. We will find ourselves seeking Him rather than trying to avoid Him or to flee from His Presence (*Genesis 3:8, Jonah 1:3*).

In fact, we will find ourselves both at home and at peace in His Presence (*Psalm 23*). When we are at peace with Him, we are ready to become a peacemaker. We perform this anointed task in His image and to His glory.

It seems fitting for me to give Jude, the last words in this chapter: *Mercy, peace, and love be multiplied to you.*

9
Blessed Are Those Who Are Persecuted for Righteousness' Sake for Theirs Is the Kingdom of Heaven

Blessed are those who are persecuted for righteousness sake

A servant is not greater than his master.
If they persecuted Me, they will also persecute you.

(John 15:20)

I am sure you will be fully aware of the many promises of God to us, as voiced by Jesus. But have you noticed that not all of them are the sort of promises that we would prefer to receive? In the last chapter, we considered the blessing we have in terms of peace with God. However, there may be a caveat to that.

These things I have spoken to you, that in Me you may have peace. In the world you will have tribulation; but be of good cheer, I have overcome the world.

(John 16:33)

The Beatitude we are now contemplating is unlike those which have preceded it. It is not so much a positive description of a Christian characteristic but a depiction of the inevitable worldly reaction to the kind of life to be lived by the blessed ones. A life which will not be deflected off course when opposition comes its way. Opposition is clearly described as an inevitable consequence.

Barclay has observed that, by the end of the first century AD, the Greek word *martus*, meaning *witness*, had already taken on the joint meaning *martyr*. This is hardly surprising in an era when martyrdom had become a common experience for many of those who faithfully confessed and lived out their Christian faith.

Tertullian wrote, *If the Tiber floods the city, or if the Nile refuses to rise, or if the sky withholds its rain; if there is an earthquake, a famine, or a pestilence, at once the cry is raised: The Christians to the lions!* There is also a phrase of Augustine's which became a proverb in North Africa, *If there is no rain, blame the Christians!*

Of course, the mention of persecution will immediately bring martyrdom to mind. This has been, is and will be an actual experience for some. It is all too common in various parts of the world as I write this sentence. But, for most of us, to date, persecution is, for the most part, likely to take more subtle forms.

For instance, having rushed home to share your conversion experience with family and friends, who were not believers, were you greeted with apparent indifference or misunderstanding? *That's nice, dear. Now come and eat your supper. You have to be up early for work in the morning.*

Or what about coming into a genuine, new experience of the Spirit in your life? Did you get a similar sort of negative reaction from fellow church members when you shared with them what had happened to you? *Oh, how lovely. Now about the jumble sale on Saturday.*

Have you known the healing touch of God in your body or emotions only to have your joyful testimony of this life-changing experience pooh-poohed by some, or all, of the people you recounted it to? *Just a coincidence, son. We've already told you all that became unnecessary after the original disciples died.*

Have you been blessed by God in being used to release His healing grace into someone's life? When talking about this with a relative or friend with a similar condition, and offering to minister to them, was your offer refused? *Thank you, dear, I know you mean well. But that sort of thing is not for me.*

These are examples of persecution in the form of rejection. As you may have deduced, they are not a million miles from my own experiences. If you know my history or have read my earlier book '*First Steps...*', you will know that I have a passion for the recovery of the healing ministry in the church universally.

As someone who has been freed by God's grace from the affliction of rejection, I find it particularly difficult to handle the apparent willingness of some to remain trapped in an infirmity from which I am convinced God would desire to heal or set them free!

Throughout the New Testament Epistles, great emphasis is placed on the joy of sharing in the sufferings of Jesus. This can range from self-denial in comparatively minor matters, through rejection, to actual martyrdom. The underlying principle is the same whatever form our suffering may take.

We recognise that Jesus gave everything for us and so is worthy of us giving everything to and for Him, the Righteous One *(Philippians 1:29)*. Christ identified with us, as Paul so movingly describes in Philippians 2. We can also identify with Him, in His sufferings and death, in order that we might also share in His (resurrection) life *(Romans 8:17)*.

I am sure that the Apostle Peter not only had this Beatitude in mind but also the circumstances in which he lived when he wrote the following verses. These emphasise the blessing that is the due reward of those who suffer for the sake of righteousness, or the Righteous One.

But even if you should suffer for righteousness' sake, you are blessed.

(1 Peter 3:14)

If you are reproached for the name of Christ, blessed are you, for the Spirit of glory and of God rests upon you. On their part, He is blasphemed, but on your part, He is glorified.

(1 Peter 4:14)

I am told that the Greek word translated as *persecuted* derives from *dikoo*, which means *to follow*. Persecutions, of one sort or another, will follow the blessed ones because of who they are in Christ. The potential they carry, and are perhaps already giving expression to, to widen the influence of God's kingdom realm.

The Pharisees and Teachers of the Law pursued Jesus relentlessly. The Apostle Paul was continually stalked by Judaizers and others who opposed his preaching of the gospel of grace. Even though the message was confirmed by demonstrations of God's healing power, or signs and wonders *(2 Corinthians 12:12)*.

Persecution, although never intended to be such by the perpetrator, is a real compliment to the blessed ones on the receiving end of it. It amounts to proof of the genuineness and sincerity of an anointed lifestyle of faith that it can provoke such a negative reaction from the worldly.

Someone whose version of the Christian life amounts to little more than an outward conformity to religious observance, lacking an inward change of heart, is not going to be persecuted. For one thing, such a lifestyle presents no threat to our ultimate enemy. No, to be persecuted is to be recognised and complimented as a genuine Christian, one who really does *walk the walk*.

Jesus was never less than honest when He spoke about what it could, or would, mean to follow Him *(Matthew 10:16-22 and 16:24, Mark 13:9, Luke 21:17)*. His words in John 16:2 refer to someone like Saul of Tarsus prior to his dramatic encounter with Jesus on the Damascus Road.

Human nature, or *the flesh*, apart from God, is fundamentally opposed to one who has been transformed by God, from the inside out and is living by the Spirit. It means that, if we are genuinely following Jesus, opposition is to be expected from the *world*. And the world has been defined as *human nature organising itself without God*.

Our Lord could not have expressed it more simply and effectively than He does in John 16:33, could He? Yes, this verse provides a promise from God we would prefer to remain unfulfilled in our lives. But it is merely confirming the inevitable—if we are truly serious in our commitment to Him.

Paul knew, from the beginning *(Acts 9:16)*, that this was something he would have to embrace. And embrace it he certainly did. This he makes clear both in Philippians 3:10 and in the list of troubles he sets out in 2 Corinthians 11:23-29.

The apostles collectively, and new believers generally, were never given free rein, by the *world* and the *powers of darkness*, in their mission to *turn the world upside down*. They had to face the possibility of severe opposition and persecution from the *world*. But, by the grace and power of God, they achieved their aims to do the will of God.

Peter and John were persecuted when God used them to bring healing to the crippled man at the Beautiful Gate of the Temple in Jerusalem *(Acts 3 & 4)*. When they reported back to their fellow believers there was a wonderful Spirit-inspired response to the threats that had been made against them all.

God caused the venue for their meeting to be shaken and Holy Spirit to be poured out in a fresh anointing. Clearly, we must expect opposition to every

Kingdom manifestation. We counter that with Spirit-led strategies to demonstrate the unconditional love and compassion of God for those in our communities who do not yet know Him.

Jesus ascended to Heaven after declaring the words that have come to be known as the Great Commission *(Matthew 28:18-20)*. See also the parallel passage in Mark's Gospel *(Mark 16:15-20)*. He commissioned the disciples (and us) to change the world by cooperating with His Spirit in bringing Heaven's culture to Earth, an apostolic calling. We are to be fully involved in the advancement of His Kingdom realm into our communities. This will inevitably stir up opposition. It certainly does where I live!

Our own church was involved with a major spiritual breakthrough. A real cause for Kingdom celebration. But within a short time, all of us on the leadership team suffered health issues of one kind or another. We know what the primary enemy strongholds are in our area. We are aware of how opposed they are to us. So, we did not put this *backlash* down to coincidence. We simply trusted God to see us through the difficulties—and He did!

We cannot rule out the possibility, even in our own lifetime, that this will involve severe persecution. Perhaps even martyrdom, for this is a common reaction against the church in parts of the world today. It can, and maybe will, happen if we do not compromise our calling and actively believe that the Kingdom of Heaven is *ours*.

Christians are intended to be markedly different from the *worldly*. Not only did the early church family turn the world upside down. They also did the same to worldly thinking and attitudes.

People who are *different* tend to be regarded with suspicion at the very least. Children who are *different* from their peers are invariably bullied by them. So, it begins at a young age!

Emperor worship brought a form of unification into the widely stretched Roman Empire. It embraced great numbers of people with many different customs and beliefs. Interestingly, the Romans made this worship compulsory for all their subjects but the Jews!

However, it was rarely more than nominally supported by the other races, and then primarily only to ensure their personal safety. Worship prompted by fear is hardly being offered in spirit and in truth *(John 4:23)*.

Trouble ensued when Christians came into conflict with a pagan, emperor-worshipping, savage, conquering power. Or when they encountered a religious elite, like the Pharisees and Sadducees, who had made an idol out of the 'Old Testament Law'.

They were following a Saviour who had taken the letter of the Law a whole stage further. He applied it to the heart (see the remainder of the Sermon on the Mount), so there was a negative reaction to His followers. This was at the root of the mockery of the trial and execution that Jesus Himself underwent.

Persecution, whatever form it takes, presents us with a difficult challenge. This challenge will touch different aspects of our lives, according to its form and our basic character. But it will always challenge our faith.

We have a righteousness that is by faith alone and is from God and not from ourselves *(Philippians 3:9)*. It is because of this righteousness that we will be blessed when we are persecuted. If persecution comes our way for any other reason, we must question just how much we have embraced Kingdom life and values. It is only the blessed ones who are persecuted because of this imputed righteousness. Those believers who are recognised as sons and daughters in the Kingdom of Heaven *(Matthew 7:21-23)*.

Of course, we will always face temptation to *avoid* persecution or any sort of opposition to the free expression of our faith. Our enemy will make a point of seeing to that. However, evading such problems rather than facing them will almost certainly lead to shame and regret. Thomas Cranmer signed six recantations of his faith in order to preserve his life.

But, in the end, he stood bravely for the truth. When he was burned at the stake, he made a point of extending the hand that had held his pen into the flames first. For him, the joy of martyrdom finally outweighed the perceived benefits of hypocritical escape. He went to be with his Lord at peace both with himself and God.

We must never lose sight of the fact that Jesus is *not* saying we are blessed if we are persecuted *per se*. Only if we are persecuted for righteousness' sake. It is for being like Him, the Righteous One. Living the right way, doing the right thing *(John 15:18-20),* and walking by the Spirit *(2 Timothy 3:12)*.

To be persecuted for the sake of righteousness does not, on the face of it, appear to create expectation of any kind of blessing. Jesus is teaching that we can be blessed and persecuted simultaneously, an incongruous mix. In fact, persecution confirms that there is an anointing upon us for Kingdom business.

That we have Heaven's approval. Luke's gospel turns this Beatitude on its head. It views it from another perspective to show that being treated well, for the wrong reasons, is nothing to be thankful for in the end.

Woe to you when all men speak well of you, for so did their fathers to the false prophets.

(Luke 6:26)

Let's look at some negatives for a moment. We are not blessed if we bring persecution or suffering upon ourselves due to our own foolishness. A *holier-than-thou* attitude is not popular with anyone. It certainly does not please Father God. Being objectionable, difficult, self-righteous, or judgemental; or lacking in wisdom is not going to win us any friends.

Unless they are like-minded, I suppose! There is no blessing in being rejected (persecuted) on account of such attitudes. Let's be honest, all Christians are not immune from all such faults all of the time *(1 Peter 4:15)*.

We are not even considered among the blessed ones if we are persecuted for doing something *good*. Good works may be laudable but that does not make them righteous. A good deed is most unlikely to attract persecution to us in the way that a righteous attitude or act could do. There can be a subtle difference between goodness and righteousness *(Romans 5:7)*.

We can be sure our enemy will recognise it, even if we cannot. It will prompt the appropriate (in his terms) response, usually through people who serve his evil purposes, either knowingly or otherwise.

Jesus has always attracted many secular admirers. They admire Him for His goodness. For the things they perceive He stands for and teaches. But they don't *know* Him. They don't properly recognise the Righteous One. If they did, they would either bow their knee—or persecute Him (or His followers).

Just as Jesus said it would happen *(Matthew 10:34-37)*, adoption of the Christian faith can lead to divisions within families. We come across examples of this in other cultures, particularly when someone from an established religion accepts Christ.

They are, at best, ostracised by their family. This serves only to underline what Jesus said about His requirement for us to love Him above all others being the cause of such family issues *(Matthew 10:37)*.

Sadly, we must also be aware that rejection/persecution can be found even within the church. We find earlier examples in the lives of the Old Testament prophets. Then with the apostles and early church members, right down through church history to our own day. Of course, we see it in great measure in the life and ministry of the Son of Man.

It arises most often when genuine Christian spirituality encounters both religion and religious traditions. This is especially so where the latter have become strongholds in different elements of the church right across the denominations.

The truth is that every active follower of Jesus will experience persecution to some degree whenever they encounter someone entrenched in this world, or in bitterness or unforgiveness. Even from someone in the church who cannot recognise and accept it when God is *doing a new thing (Isaiah 43:19)*.

I am a firm advocate of 'Treasure Hunting[1], as you will know if you have read my earlier book 'First Steps…'. But walking up to a complete stranger in the street does not come naturally to me. Indeed, I would find it difficult to do that in a meeting at a church I was visiting, although it would be much less of a problem for me to get up on the platform and speak to the congregation! But enough of my foibles. You probably have your own!

It is breaking the ice with the initial approach to open a conversation that is so difficult for me. I am much happier if there are two of us Treasure Hunting together (as there would normally be) and my partner is bold enough to make the first move. Nevertheless, it is something that I believe the Lord has called me out of my comfort zone to get actively involved in—and I have been obedient (most of the time!).

Going out on the streets involves a degree of risk. People may mock us, reject us, or even abuse us. Just the thought of such possibilities puts off a lot of Christians from even trying to share their faith. That is a fear of persecution by any other name.

So, the *fear* of persecution can be just as potent as the real thing. But it is not being persecuted for righteousness because *God* does not give us a spirit of fear *(2 Timothy 1:7)*. Even so, fear (e.g., of persecution) is a very successful tool of our enemy to keep us from stepping out to extend God's Kingdom further into our communities.

Incidentally, I have been on many Treasure Hunts, and I have rarely been brushed off by anyone. When I have, it has usually been with no more than a brusque, *No thanks*. No doubt prompted by their own fears in many cases. Most people are polite and much more receptive than you might think if you have never done something like that before.

How the blessed ones positively express their (new creation) life, is a threat to our enemy. Therefore, we can expect him to respond. If we want a quiet life, then don't *do* anything.

Don't go anywhere carrying the Presence of God and His Kingdom influence. Then neither the enemy nor his various minions will bother us. Mind you, then we will most likely become both bored and boring!

Furthermore, we will probably struggle with the difficulties that everyday life brings. That contrasts us with those who believe that nothing can separate us from the love of God *(Romans 8:38-39)*. What happened to Paul and Silas in the jail at Philippi is a prime example of persecution and endurance. They were rewarded by the joy of seeing the Lord bring good out of extreme difficulty.

If we have followed and been part of the progression of these Beatitudes, we have been immersed into in His righteousness. Being persecuted, as Jesus was, and the prophets before Him, is a confirmation of Holy Spirit's *seal* upon us.

We know that we are truly His when we are called upon to experience something of what He did. If we are to share in His glory then, as already stated, we must be prepared to share in His sufferings. One is an inevitable consequence of the other. It's an example of cause and effect. By this, *we* will know that we are His disciples.

For theirs is the Kingdom of Heaven.

> *But watch out for yourselves, for they will deliver you up to councils,*
> *and you will be beaten in the synagogues. You will be brought*
> *before rulers and kings for My sake, for a testimony to them.*
> *And the gospel must first be preached to all the nations.*
> *But when they arrest you and deliver you up, do not*
> *worry beforehand or premeditate what you will speak.*
> *But whatever is given you in that hour, speak that;that.*
> *for it is not you who speak, but the Holy Spirit.*
> *Now brother will betray brother to death, and a father his child;child.*
> *and children will rise up against their parents and cause them to be put to*
> *death.*

And you will be hated by all for My name's sake.
But he who endures to the end shall be saved.

(Mark 13:9-13)

There is a debate over whether there are eight or nine Beatitudes but, as I stated earlier, I am opting for eight in this writing. Although the word *blessed* is included in both verses 11 and 12, these verses could be interpreted as an expansion, or extension, of verse 10.

For theirs is the Kingdom of Heaven is the only promise to the blessed ones that is repeated within the Beatitudes. It is contained in both the first and the last of them, both at the beginning and at the end. This indicates, to me at least, that eight is most likely the right number.

This repetition must, at the very least, underline the enormous significance of this particular promise. And, of course, our need to take a firm hold of it, whatever the prevailing circumstances of our life might be.

Verse 12 elaborates on the promise of verses 3 and 10 by declaring, *Great is your reward in heaven*. It seems fair to say that the Kingdom of Heaven and its accompanying rewards are virtually synonymous. And let us not forget that *the Kingdom of Heaven is at hand*, so we are looking at both a present and a future blessing. The Kingdom of Heaven is with us already if we have been adopted into God's Kingdom Family.

The promise to the blessed ones who are persecuted is a reminder that our primary reward is citizenship of the Kingdom of Heaven. This same reward is at least implicit in the promises contained in the previous Beatitudes. His Kingdom is not of this world, but it has invaded this world.

The blessed ones are called to be part of that peaceful but radical invasion for the full extent of their remaining natural lifespan on Earth. So, it is here and now that we can encounter persecution, not after we are welcomed into Heaven. There will be no persecution there!

Jesus exemplified that, in the event of persecution, retaliation is not an option *(Isaiah 53:7, Matthew 5:39)*. He even offered forgiveness to those who were crucifying Him. In so doing, He provides those who are persecuted now with an example to follow.

> *My kingdom is not of this world. If my kingdom were of this world, my servants would fight*
>
> (John 18:36)

Retaliation is not what His Kingdom is about *(Matthew 5:44)*. Jesus healed the man whose ear was sliced by Peter's sword in Gethsemane. Bless those who persecute you and *you* will be blessed is His message. As always, Jesus turns normal human expectations and responses upside down.

He is very different. He is radical. He calls us to be like Him. He equips us to share His Kingdom blessings with those we encounter on a daily basis. His purposes are grounded in grace, not in what people may or may not deserve.

If we are destined for persecution, even to the shedding of our blood, our hope in our future life can sustain us. This hope will help us to endure what we must in the meantime. I hope so anyway for, unless or until such times come upon us, how can we be sure how any of us will react?

We know, at least in theory, that God in us can enable us to do the seemingly impossible. It is up to us to put our trust in Him if and when severe persecution comes upon us. When the rubber hits the road.

It is part of the normal Christian life to experience God doing the impossible, both in us and through us. In every circumstance when we step out in faith as He leads us. As we cooperate with Him, we see evidence of the Kingdom of Heaven at work.

Through prophecy, healing, and other gifts of the Spirit. This evidence creates a firm foundation on which to build our faith to contend with the worst of what may befall us in the years ahead.

It is also true that the Spirit of God (the Kingdom) seems to be more active during times of severe persecution. We know that the church invariably grows more rapidly in those countries where the Christian faithful are most under threat.

There are innumerable stories of people being healed, raised from the dead and experiencing many other kinds of miracles whilst undergoing extreme persecution. God never abandons His suffering people, especially when they pursue righteousness, regardless of what they may be subjected to as a response to their faith. Such Christians demonstrate a righteousness that is by faith from first to last *(Romans 1:17)*. Nothing can separate them from the love of God *(Romans 8:39)*.

The threat of persecution for righteousness' sake provides an opportunity to demonstrate loyalty to our Saviour and Lord. A chance to declare with Paul that we are *not ashamed of the gospel (Romans 1:16)*.

We are offered the privilege of following the many who have gone that way before us *(Matthew 5:12, Hebrews 11 & 12)*. Are you familiar with the old saying, *the blood of the martyrs is the seed of the church*?

A martyr endures by the grace of God. His, or her, mind is focussed upon what is of ultimate, fundamental importance to them and keeps them immune from compromise.

Persecution can come when we respond to the prompting, and trust in the enabling, of the Spirit of God *(1 Peter 4:14)*. It becomes a kind of mark of authenticity. Of ownership of us and our actions, on His part *(1 Peter 2:19)*.

We are carriers of the Presence of God. We are citizens of His Kingdom. We can be demonstrators of His power—ambassadors for Christ *(2 Corinthians 5:20)*. This is the very pinnacle of the Christian experience. To have Holy Spirit indwelling us is the ultimate joy and privilege. It is a special taste of Heaven before we reach our destination at the end of our time on Earth. There is nothing to surpass it.

What Jesus describes in the Beatitudes as the characteristics of the blessed ones is what the normal Christian life expresses. There is a before and after. Death must precede resurrection. The old man must be replaced by the new creation. Humility comes before exaltation in His Kingdom. If we want to be His blessed ones, we must be prepared for anything to happen to us.

We must always remember that the world is opposed to the Kingdom of God, as the flesh is to the spirit. They are inevitably at enmity with one another. So, as representatives of Heaven on Earth, we cannot expect to be welcomed by the world with open arms.

Except by those upon whom the Spirit of God is already working and drawing to Himself. Jesus, the Son of Man, carried the Spirit without limit *(John 4:34)*. He was rejected by both Jews, God's chosen people, and Gentiles. He promises us the same reaction from them *(John 15:8)*. Something which Paul also emphasised *(2 Timothy 3:12)*.

Now, I am not suggesting for one moment that we should ask for, or even look forward to persecution. Especially at levels beyond which we may have experienced it to date Only that we should be prepared, ready and not taken by surprise, whenever it may come. The kingdoms of this world may be against us.

But, if we are being persecuted for righteousness, the Kingdom of Heaven is simultaneously confirmed as being ours.

God's presence, comfort and blessing will be available to all those who are persecuted for the sake of the Righteous One. Let us remember that in the day of our trouble. Count it all joy *(James 1:2)*, knowing that the joy of the Lord is our strength *(Nehemiah 8:10)*.

Have you been inspired to share a special prophetic word with someone that who has really blessed them? Have you been used by God to bring physical healing to someone? Have you had the privilege of being led by Him to bring a person out of the emotional pain of deep trauma?

Have you cooperated with Him in releasing someone from the grip of demonic oppression? Above all, have you had the joy of leading someone to Christ and His Kingdom?

If so, you already know something of what it is to see the Kingdom of Heaven manifested in the here and now. You know already that, to some degree, the Kingdom of Heaven is yours. You have tasted and seen that the Lord is good *(Psalm 34:8)*. And yet, all of this is a pale imitation of what is still to come.

We have been blessed. We are blessed. We will be blessed. But let us not be surprised when we encounter opposition because of it!

1. *'The Ultimate Treasure Hunt'*, Kevin Dedmon, Destiny Image Publishers Inc.

Enabled to Be
Postscript 1

Most assuredly, I say to you, unless one is born of water and the Spirit,
he cannot enter the Kingdom of God. That which is born of the flesh
is flesh, and that which is born of the Spirit is spirit.

(John 3:5-6)

Therefore, if anyone is in Christ, he is a new creation;
old things have passed away; behold, all things have become new.

(2 Corinthians 5:17)

The answer to Shakespeare's question, as posed in the Introduction, is most definitely *to be*, and not *not to be*. By the grace of God, as Christians, we have been enabled to *be*. In order to embrace our truly awesome position in Christ we have had to *be born again*. Nothing less would suffice to make us be both who we are and what we are—in Him.

This is clearly not something we could accomplish by our own natural effort, strength, and abilities. No matter how morally good and upright we may have been. No matter how admired and respected we might be by all those who know us. That we can become such amazing, incredible people on this planet is entirely God's doing. Our only contribution to this transformation is our cooperation with Him in embracing His initiative *(John 15:16)*.

For by grace, you have been saved through faith, and that not of yourselves;
it is the gift of God, not of works, lest anyone should boast.

(Ephesians 2:8-9)

By the grace of God, the blessed ones have followed a heavenly-prescribed path of progression, both individually and corporately.

(From those who—)

- are poor in spirit
- mourn
- are meek
- hunger and thirst after righteousness

(To become—)

- merciful
- pure in heart
- peacemakers

(To those who—)

- are persecuted for righteousness' sake.

In these Beatitudes, we find the essence of the Christian being. A description of who a Christian is or, if you prefer, *what* a Christian is. These are the essential *be-attitudes* of a Christian. All of them are unique to the Christian. All of them are made possible only by the indwelling Holy Spirit.

He is not only the author of the life by which we were born again but also the source of the new life that sustains us. That makes it possible for us to *be* all that we are meant to *be* if we appropriate the truths of the Beatitudes. Therefore:

- We have humbled ourselves and come to terms with the limitations of what our natural selves can achieve, despite our best intentions.
- We have mourned over the natural inadequacies of the *old man*.
- In meekness, we have ceased to be self-reliant and left behind the need to defend ourselves from criticism and the like.
- Having now realised our great need, we have hungered and thirsted after righteousness, after the Righteous One. Only in Him can we be accepted, forgiven, fulfilled, and satisfied.

- Appreciating His love, grace, compassion, and mercy towards us has led us to become more merciful and forgiving towards others.
- Mourning over the natural state of our own hearts has motivated us to seek the purifying of our hearts by the supernatural grace of God.
- Through embracing meekness, we find that we are now drawn towards making peace, both with and between others.
- We have experienced the supernatural power of the grace of God to transform our character from inadequate, natural inclinations into godly expressions. We can now expect opposition, having become a threat to the enemy of our souls.

Knowing we have been empowered to *be*, albeit experientially as a *work in progress* this side of Heaven, we will find ourselves equipped to *do* that which pleases Him. That which He has even prepared in advance for us to do!

Christian *doing* is the subject of Part 2 of this book. I would love it if you would accept my invitation to join me there.

I'm not what I ought to be, I'm not what I'd like to be, I'm not what I hope to be, but I'm not what I was, and by the grace of God, I am what I am.

(John Newton)

A Christian is something before he does anything, and we have to be Christian before we can act as Christians.

(D. Martyn Lloyd-Jones)

Part Two
Blessed—Empowered to Do

Introduction (2)

Blessed be the God and Father of our Lord Jesus Christ, who has BLESSED us with EVERY spiritual blessing in the heavenly places in Christ.

(Ephesians 1:3)

I don't have to be a genius to conclude that, if I have been blessed with *every* spiritual blessing, there can be *no* spiritual blessing that is unavailable to me, by active faith in His promise.

Most Christians must have come across this verse many times. The question is, how many different conclusions about its meaning have been reached by those who have read or heard it?

Reference is made to *heavenly places*, so does that mean that every blessing is ours only when we arrive in heaven after we have died? From the day we were born again until the day of our death, are we supposed to sit patiently in *Heaven's waiting room*, just thanking God that our sins have been forgiven? (Of course, that alone *is* a major reason for gratitude!).

But God, who is rich in mercy, because of His great love with which He loved us, even when we were dead in trespasses, made us alive together with Christ (by grace you have been saved), and raised us up together, and made us sit together in the heavenly places in Christ Jesus.

(Ephesians 2:4-6)

Here, Paul, inspired by Holy Spirit, has written that we *are* sitting *together in the heavenly places in Christ Jesus*. This was so from the moment we were born again. It is as though we have been granted the amazing privilege of being in two places at once! Which was equally true of Jesus, according to the words quoted below from His conversation with Nicodemus.

If I have told you earthly things and you do not believe, how will you believe if I tell you heavenly things? No one has ascended to heaven but He who came down from heaven, that is, the Son of Man who is in heaven.

(John 3:12-13)

According to Jesus, *the Son of Man who is in Heaven* is simultaneously standing on Earth having a conversation with a Jewish leader! Notice that He does not refer to Himself as the Son of God in this statement.

Could the *whole* of the Son of God, the second Person of the Trinity, be contained within the human body of the Son of Man? (An interesting question to ponder another time, perhaps).

Therefore, from now on, we regard no one according to the flesh. Even though we have known Christ according to the flesh, yet now we know Him thus no longer. Therefore, if anyone is in Christ, he is a new creation; old things have passed away; behold, all things have become new.

(2 Corinthians 5:16-17)

If we focus solely on our bodies, it is impossible to understand how we can be here on Earth whilst being simultaneously seated in heavenly places *in Christ Jesus*.

But, if we view these things from a spiritual perspective, considering that we are now *a new creation* and the *old things have passed away*, surely anything is possible. Especially if *He* says it is so.

Love has been perfected among us in this: that we may have boldness in the day of judgment; because as He is, so are we in this world.

(1 John 4:17)

Do I fully understand that statement? No, I don't! Can I easily explain what it means? No, I can't! Can I believe it, nonetheless? Yes, of course I can! If I am willing to embrace by faith the often-unfathomable mysteries of God.

And without faith, it is impossible to please Him (God)

(Hebrews 11:6a)

Jesus Christ is the risen, ascended, glorified Lamb of God who took away the sins of the world. He is now seated in heavenly places, on the throne, at the right hand of the Father. That is where He *is* right now. Look again at what the above verse tells us. As He is (now), so are we (now) in this world!

Once again, we have a Holy Spirit-inspired statement that seems impossible for us to get our heads around. Do we have faith to believe the seemingly impossible? If so, we can also have faith to believe all that His Word tells us. Even if we do not (yet) have a full understanding to go with it.

The spiritual realities of the Kingdom of Heaven are far superior to the physical realities of this world. Try as we might, there are some things which we simply cannot fully comprehend without first receiving divine revelation.

The secret things belong to the Lord our God, but those things which are revealed belong to us and to our children forever, that we may do all the words of this law.

(Deuteronomy 29:29)

When we remember that we have been adopted into the royal family of heaven, the following verse takes on special meaning in this context, too.

It is the glory of God to conceal a matter, but the glory of kings is to search out a matter.

(Proverbs 25:2)

We begin with faith, then trust that we will grow in our level of understanding, with some ability to teach or explain. But only when, and indeed if, He deems it necessary. Without revelation, this can be a difficult *pill* for the specialist Bible teachers among us to swallow.

Therefore, faith, not (in)sight is the one essential requirement for each of us. There is a need for us to view things from our new spiritual position, seated in heavenly places in Christ, whilst we are physically located here on Earth.

For My thoughts are not your thoughts, nor are your ways My ways, says the Lord, for as the heavens are higher than the Earth, so are My ways higher than your ways, and My thoughts than your thoughts.

(Isaiah 55:8-10)

There are a number of descriptions of Heaven as a *place* in the Bible *(e.g., Revelation 4)*. We tend to expect that place to be somewhere up yonder, way out of natural reach. Yet the Bible also speaks of the (Kingdom of) Heaven being much nearer. Maybe it is more of a *dimension* than an actual place?

For instance, in Matthew 3:2, 4:17 and 10:7, we read that *the Kingdom of Heaven is at hand*. So, do we have to go literally to another place in order to be *seated in heavenly places in Christ Jesus*?

If Jesus could be in two places at once and *in Him, we live and move and have our being (Acts 17:27b-28a)* why should that not be true for us right here and now on Earth? Surely, even if Jesus says something that I cannot get my head around, I can still believe it by exercising (the gift of) faith. His Word should be sufficient for us.

But you are a chosen generation, a royal priesthood, a holy nation, His own special people, that you may proclaim the praises of Him who called you out of darkness into His marvellous light; who once were not a people but are now the people of God, who had not obtained mercy but now have obtained mercy.

(1 Peter 2:9-10)

Yes, in God's eyes, we are a chosen, precious, and special people, who are all loved unconditionally. We are not only enabled but also *equipped* to share His love and power with those around us. This is true whether we are inside or outside of the four walls of our church buildings. He has enabled us to *be* in order to equip us to *do*.

For we are His workmanship, created in Christ Jesus for good works, which God prepared beforehand that we should walk in them.

(Ephesians 2:10)

We means all of us. No exceptions. And what is it that we are meant to do? I think the following will be plenty to excite us—if we believe it—don't you?

Most assuredly, I say to you, he who believes in Me, the works that I do he will do also; and greater works than these he will do, because I go to My Father.

(John 14:12)

God did not choose us to *be* a special people with nothing to *do* before we are welcomed into Heaven at the end of our earthly lives. He has even prepared in advance the things He has called and equipped us to *do*. The sort of works that Jesus did.

The only limiter tends to be the *"leetle grey cells"* located between our ears. I repeat, if we can learn to think and live from a heavenly perspective, rather than out of the doubt and unbelief of a natural, earthly view, why should anything He says of us be an impossibility for us?

Do you not believe that I am in the Father, and the Father in Me? The words that I speak to you I do not speak on My own authority, but the Father who dwells in Me does the works. Believe Me that I am in the Father and the Father in Me, or else believe Me for the sake of the works themselves.

(John 14:10-11)

The only *rule* for a doer to follow is, *always to listen to Holy Spirit and obey His prompting and direction,* trusting that He has fully equipped us for every good work *(2 Timothy 3:17)*. The works that have been already prepared in advance for us to do *(Ephesians 2:10)*.

As You (Father) *sent Me into the world, I also have sent them into the world.*

(John 17:18)

So, Jesus said to them again, "Peace to you! As the Father has sent Me, I also send you."

And when He had said this, He breathed on them, and said to them, "Receive the Holy Spirit."

(John 20:21-22)

Jesus was sent into the world to *do*, and we have been given the same mission as Him—except for the (actual) cross. Having said that, taking up *our* cross to follow Jesus is the essence of self-denial and Jesus requires that of us as His followers called to represent Him on Earth.

If anyone desires to come after Me, let him deny himself, and take up his cross, and follow Me. For whoever desires to save his life will lose it, but whoever loses his life for My sake will find it.

(Matthew 16:24-25)

When we go out to *do* what Jesus has called each one of us to *do*, we can be confident that we go with His commissioning and with His authority delegated to us. We are being sent out to be His ambassadors. We are His envoys, representing Heaven on Earth, tasked to bring Heaven's culture to Earth.

This is the essence of an apostolic calling. Before Jesus applied the term to His first followers, an apostle was a government envoy sent out to impose the conquering nation's culture upon the occupied nation.

And Jesus came and spoke to them, saying, "All authority has been given to Me in heaven and on Earth. Go therefore and make disciples of all the nations, baptising them in the name of the Father and of the Son and of the Holy Spirit, teaching them to observe all things that I have commanded you; and lo, I am with you always, even to the end of the age."

(Matthew 28:18-20)

The operative word is *Go*! This must include venturing outside the four walls of our church buildings with the full gospel. We cannot rest content with just *being*. It is essential that we get into *doing*, as He leads, prompts, and equips us. One is intended to follow the other as surely as night follows day.

We are each called to play our unique part in bringing into being that which Jesus taught us to pray in 'The Lord's Prayer'.

Your kingdom come; your will be done on Earth as it is in heaven.

(Matthew 6:10)

His intention is that we should be active participators, not spectators. That is our cooperative contribution to bringing into being the answer to this prayer. That is both His expectation of and His requirement from His children.

And they went out and preached everywhere, the Lord working with them and confirming the word through the accompanying signs.

(Mark 16:20)

Let us obey Him and *Go!* out to *do* the impossible both in and with the One who *has blessed us with every spiritual blessing in the heavenly places in Christ*.

A definition of Grace that I like very much is, *the power of God to do the will of God.*

(Robby Dawkins, 'Do What Jesus Did', Chosen Books, 2013)

1
Blessed by His Perfect Example

Jesus was poor in spirit, and He is the King of Heaven.
Jesus mourned over the sins of the world, and He brought comfort.
Jesus was meek and He has inherited the Earth.
Jesus was Righteousness and He has fully satisfied the Law.
Jesus was merciful and He personifies Mercy.
Jesus was pure in heart, and He always sees (Father) God.
Jesus was a peacemaker, and He is the only begotten Son of God.
Jesus was persecuted for righteousness' sake and vindicated as the King of kings and Lord of lords.

The blessed ones have been blessed to become increasingly more like Jesus. The character of Jesus, the Son of Man, shines through in the supernatural characteristics of the Christian (born-again human) *being* that we looked at in Part One. Jesus is our model, our template, our perfect example, not only in how to *be* but also in how, and what, to *do*.

The Son is the radiance of God's glory and the exact representation of his being,

(Hebrews 3:3a, NIV)

Jesus was a perfect representation of the Father. We are called and equipped to *progress*, by the process of sanctification and by grace, towards becoming (as near as it may be attainable) perfect representations of Him. That profound statement, made by the writer to the Hebrews, echoes what Jesus said to Philip when the latter asked Him to show them the Father.

Jesus said to him, "Have I been with you so long, and yet you have not known Me, Philip? He who has seen Me has seen the Father; so how can you say, 'Show us the Father?' Do you not believe that I am in the Father, and the Father in Me? The words that I speak to you I do not speak on My own authority, but the Father who dwells in Me does the works."

(John 14:9-10)

Jesus had earlier confirmed that He represented the Father by *doing* His works as the Son of Man.

Most assuredly, I say to you, the Son can do nothing of Himself, but what He sees the Father do; for whatever He does, the Son also does in like manner.

(John 5:19)

Jesus came to show both Jews and Gentiles what the Father is like. Loving, gracious, merciful, slow to anger and full of compassion *(Psalm 145:8)*. He has commissioned us to become like Him. To demonstrate the reality of this grace gift through our actions. Each of them is to be carried out in the authority of His Name, with His Power and at His direction.

Most assuredly, I say to you, he who believes in Me, the works that I do he will do also; and greater works than these he will do, because I go to My Father.

(John 14:12)

Anyone who knows me knows that this is one of my favourite inspirational verses. It both encourages me and gives me something to aspire to. I know I can't do it on my own. But I know that I can do it because He has promised it. He has made it possible for me.

Even if it's a struggle to imagine what it could involve in practice. I have had various experiences over the years that have provided much encouragement through the knowledge that the goal of this promise is totally real, believable and, therefore, achievable (in Him).

Yes, of course, I still let Him down, as well as myself, all too often. But He forgives me and provides me with another chance. Confession and genuine repentance on my part, and forgiveness on His part, combine to make possible further opportunities.

He is infinitely more concerned about maintaining the relationship with me He initiated than I could ever be, no matter how pure my motivation. I am standing permanently on a rock, not on quicksand. This, despite what my feelings might sometimes tell me to the contrary, most especially when I am emotionally at my lowest ebb.

All Scripture is given by inspiration of God, and is profitable for doctrine, for reproof, for correction, for instruction in righteousness, that the man of God may be complete, thoroughly equipped for every good work.

(2 Timothy 3:16-17)

It is through feeding upon the scriptures, as we read them or hear them expounded through preaching, that we are enabled to digest, to absorb them into our beings. Then to turn theory into glorious practice in our lives as we seek the opportunities God provides to bless others through us.

As Paul writes to Timothy, this ensures not only that we are equipped but also that we are *thoroughly* equipped for every good work. Clearly, God's purpose for us is to become *doers* of the Word.

But be doers of the word, and not hearers only, deceiving yourselves.

(James 1:22)

James goes on, in a humorous way, to point out what being only a hearer of the Word is like. But he is being completely serious in his message. It is not enough to have a faith that is based upon what we have heard or read.

We should not be limited to what we know, only expressing it verbally. *Action* is called for. Not merely regurgitating what we have learned in our subsequent conversations, discussions, or even teaching.

For as the body without the spirit is dead, so faith without works is dead also.

(James 2:26)

We know that James is in perfect agreement with Paul, whose teaching is always emphasising that we are saved through faith and not by works. James is simply advocating that, having been saved by faith alone, the faith that we have is to be expressed through works, by deeds, by our actions.

A friend has illustrated this point by saying that no one goes into a restaurant only to read through and then eat the menu (document) rather than the food it describes. Or, by the same token, what is the point of having lots of glossy cookery books on a shelf in your kitchen if you never turn the recipes into appetising meals to serve at your table?

For by grace, you have been saved through faith, and that not of yourselves; it is the gift of God, not of works, lest anyone should boast. For we are His workmanship, created in Christ Jesus for good works, which God prepared beforehand that we should walk in them.

(Ephesians 2:8-10)

The wonderful thing is that God knows in advance what He wants us to do, what opportunities He will bring our way. For not only has He set up these situations but also the faith to believe He has equipped us with everything we need to tackle them.

Our part is to recognise His hand at work and boldly step out of our comfort zone to do what He wants us to do, in cooperation with Him. That might mean sharing an encouraging prophetic word, ministering healing, providing some practical, compassionate help, etc.

Now Peter and John went up together to the temple at the hour of prayer, the ninth hour. And a certain man lame from his mother's womb was carried, whom they laid daily at the gate of the temple, which is called Beautiful, to ask alms from those who entered the temple.

(Acts 3:1-2)

For the man was over 40 years old on whom this miracle of healing had been performed.

(Acts 4:22)

We need to recognise a *God moment* when it comes our way. Listen to Him, then boldly and obediently step out to do whatever it is that He wants us to do at that time. Just as Jesus did. Holy Spirit prepares the scenario in advance. So, it is all about His *timing*, as the above verses admirably illustrate.

The crippled man was lame since birth, we are told. He was taken to the same place at the temple every day. He was over 40 years old when he encountered Peter and John. During the three years or so of Jesus' public ministry, He visited Jerusalem and the temple on a number of occasions. No doubt many more times than are actually recorded in the gospels.

Some, if not most, of those visits would have involved Him, and the disciples, passing through or near the Beautiful Gate. He would have seen this crippled man on each occasion, but He didn't heal Him.

None of those occasions could have been the Father's time for this miracle to be performed. It was prepared in advance for Peter and John. When they knew it in their hearts, they stepped out in faith and God healed the man.

Do you not believe that I am in the Father, and the Father in Me? The words that I speak to you I do not speak on My own authority; but the Father who dwells in Me does the works. Believe Me that I am in the Father and the Father in Me, or else believe Me for the sake of the works themselves.

(John 14:10-11)

For the works which the Father has given Me to finish—the very works that I do—bear witness of Me, that the Father has sent Me.

(John 5:36)

Jesus spoke the words the Father gave Him to speak. He did the works the Father directed Him to do. The words would be spoken, and the works would be done, both in accordance with the Father's plan and His timing. I conclude from this that there is a perfect *time* for everything that God has prepared in advance for us to say or *do.*

Therefore, on at least some of the occasions when things don't work out as we might have hoped, I think it can only be because the timing is not His. However, I believe that does not mean He would not be pleased with us for stepping out, though. We learn best from our *mistakes.*

I struggled with *M.E.* for some 10-11 years. During that time, I was prayed for on several occasions. Invariably I experienced the Presence of God as people prayed, but I was not healed. Then, on that awesome night in May 2008—whilst watching God TV—*that* was my time! Why then? I have no idea! Jesus Himself was aware that the power of God was more obviously present to heal on some occasions than on others.

Now it happened on a certain day, as He was teaching, that there were Pharisees and Teachers of the Law sitting by, who had come out of every town of Galilee, Judea, and Jerusalem. And the power of the Lord was present to heal them.

(Luke 5:17)

Five years after my precious experience, I was a ministry team leader at an annual conference in Kent. A young lady came forward after the speaker had made an appeal at the end of the message. She fell down in the Spirit a few feet from the platform.

My wife spotted her and went over to see what assistance might be required. The young lady told Cathy that she had not come forward in response to what the appeal was about. It was because this was the only evening on which she could attend the week-long conference and she was desperate for God to heal her.

She then informed Cathy that she was suffering with *M.E.* So, I was sent for (as one who had already been healed from this affliction). It is important to bear in mind that what God has done before is something that He can and will do again.

If we have experienced a healing from a particular affliction and, later, God brings across our path someone who is suffering with the same problem, it is likely to be a God-incidence rather than a coincidence!

To cut a longer story short, she was wonderfully set free and healed by a loving and compassionate God that evening. We left her on her knees worshipping Him, lost in wonder, love, and praise. She had suffered for about 20 years and, for reasons known only to God, that was *her* time!

Why then? Again, I have no idea! He is Sovereign. We need to trust Him to know what is best for each one of us. He does not *have* to explain Himself!

For the testimony of Jesus is the spirit of prophecy.

(Revelation 19:10b)

In the root of the word translated into English as *testimony* is the sense of *repeat* or *do again*. Something God has done before He can willingly do again—simply in response to a testimony about what He has done before. This is a verse that Bill Johnson uses to illustrate that principle.

Some teachers, whilst agreeing with the reasoning behind the teaching, do not feel this verse is specifically relevant to that principle. I am not sufficiently qualified as a theologian to enter that debate. But I certainly know the value of the testimony, from personal experience, to see God repeat what He has done before to bless even more lives.

Cathy and I have been members of ministry teams who have made it a practice to come together before a meeting gets underway to pray together. We would share testimonies of the known healings God has been ministering recently.

These could be either in our own experiences or through what we have heard from people whose stories we trust. This is an extremely effective faith-builder before a time of ministry begins. We also recommend a debrief for a team after a meeting. A major part of this should involve sharing testimonies of what God had done during the ministry time just ended.

In 1 Corinthians 12:8-10, we find a list of spiritual gifts: *word of wisdom, word of knowledge, faith, healings, working of miracles, prophecy, discerning of spirits, different kinds of tongues and interpretation of tongues.* Looking through these, we can be reminded of different times during Jesus' time on Earth, when these gifts were manifested in His ministry.

I cannot find a record in the gospels of Jesus speaking in tongues or interpreting a tongue. Even so, that cannot completely rule out the possibility that He did so, however unlikely it may seem to us. What of the others?

The queen of the South will rise up in judgment with this generation and condemn it, for she came from the ends of the Earth to hear the wisdom of Solomon; and indeed, a greater than Solomon is here.

(Matthew 12:42)

In John 4:17-18, we have an example of Jesus expressing a *word of knowledge*. *The woman answered and said, 'I have no husband.' Jesus said to her, 'You have well said, I have no husband, for you have had five husbands, and the one whom you now have is not your husband; in that you spoke truly.'*

In my opinion, Jesus was expressing tremendous *faith* in the Father for His resurrection from the dead when He submitted to crucifixion on our behalf: *who for the joy that was set before Him endured the cross (Hebrews 4:2).*

Then His fame went throughout all Syria; and they brought to Him all sick people who were afflicted with various diseases and torments, and those who were demon-possessed, epileptics, and paralytics; and He healed them.

(Matthew 4:24)

Mark 6:42-44 provides just one example of the many *miracles* that Jesus performed during His ministry. *So, they all ate and were filled. And they took up 12 baskets full of fragments and of the fish. Now those who had eaten the loaves were about five thousand men.*

In Matthew 24:2, we find one of the times when He was exercising the gift of *prophecy*. *And Jesus said to them, "Do you not see all these things? Assuredly, I say to you, not one stone shall be left here upon another, that shall not be thrown down."*

The gospel records inform us, on several occasions, that Jesus not only *discerned* what people were thinking but also what the motivation (the spirit) behind their thinking was.

But Jesus did not commit Himself to them, because He knew all men, and had no need that anyone should testify of man, for He knew what was in man.

(John 2:24-25)

There are various other spiritual gifts available to the blessed ones as the need arises. For just about every single one, we can find examples of them being employed by Jesus during His earthly ministry as the Son of Man. This is especially so when we consider the gifts/offices Paul describes as gifts *to* the church.

And He Himself gave some to be apostles, some prophets, some evangelists, and some pastors and (some) *teachers.*

(Ephesians 4:11)

Jesus came as an ambassador from Heaven to introduce Earth to the culture of Heaven (*apostle*). He always spoke the words of Father God authoritatively (*prophet*). He welcomed disciples into His Kingdom realm (*evangelist*). He was the Good Shepherd to His little flock of followers (*pastor*), and He was the greatest *teacher* there has ever been.

In conclusion, then, when we have recognised what God has called us and equipped us to *be*, we can legitimately aspire to all that He is calling us to *do*. Always whilst looking to Jesus for inspiration as our perfect example. And trusting Holy Spirit to equip us for the task ahead.

Now, as we move on with Part Two, we will be looking at more specific ways in which this truth may be actively applied in our lives as the blessed ones.

2
Blessed by Spiritual Gifts

There are diversities of gifts, but the same Spirit.
There are differences of ministries, but the same Lord.
And there are diversities of activities,
but it is the same God who works all in all.
But the manifestation of the Spirit is given to each one for the profit of all: for
to one is given the word of wisdom through the Spirit,
to another the word of knowledge through the same Spirit,
to another faith by the same Spirit,
to another gifts of healings by the same Spirit,
to another the working of miracles,
to another prophecy,
to another discerning of spirits,
to another different kinds of tongues,
to another the interpretation of tongues.
But one and the same Spirit works all these things,
distributing to each one individually as He wills.

(1 Corinthians 12:4-11)

As part of my preparation for the writing of this chapter, I decided to do a little online research about the gifts of the spirit. I consulted different websites that referred to themselves as one sort of Bible study resource or another.

In most cases, I found these to offer explanations, or definitions, of at least some of the gifts. Sadly, for me, most of them were quite at odds with the understanding and experience I have accrued over the years and which I wanted to convey in these pages.

Many of my readers may have consulted the same sources in their search for teaching on this subject. Therefore, I must make it clear that what follows is a personal view. It is an interpretation which I stand by, at least until such time as Holy Spirit may show me otherwise. You don't have to agree with me!

So, I propose to go *back to basics* to an extent that I was not anticipating when I began this project. I must apologise to any reader who feels that I am *teaching my granny to suck eggs*.

I am simply attempting to convey an understanding that I believe is more practical and relevant than much of what I found online. This is primarily for the benefit of those who have either received no teaching, or a *different* teaching. I ask such people to pray for our gracious God to reveal to them the interpretation which is closest to the truth.

Now concerning spiritual gifts, brethren, I do not want you to be ignorant is how 1 Corinthians 12 opens. And 1 Corinthians 14 begins with these words, *Pursue love, and desire spiritual gifts*. When you read the New King James Version you discover that, in both verses, the word *gifts* is printed in italics.

This is because, in the original Greek, there is no word for *gifts* found in either verse. Translators have put it there. Commentators have commented on it. Preachers have taught about it. Each as though it was there, presumably because *gifts* is the *substance* of the following verses of both chapters.

Am I splitting hairs or is this important? If Paul was not intending to refer specifically to gifts at that initial stage, what was he dealing with? The original Greek text implies, at the very least, that he was referring to the spiritual.

Or to spiritualities or spiritual life. Or to a supernatural *lifestyle*. Whichever of these possibilities you choose to embrace, the gifts themselves are an important, but not exclusive, expression of it.

The Corinthians seemed to be making a bigger deal of spiritual gifts than Paul was comfortable with. Or, at least, they were making too much of what might be considered the least important gift. They were *showing off*, competing with one another perhaps. Maybe trying to demonstrate who was the greatest.

When the first disciples behaved like that Luke 9:46, 22:24, Jesus was not pleased. Neither He nor Paul considered this sort of behaviour to be acceptable in Kingdom culture. In each instance, they both brought correction to their disciples.

In Part One of this book, we looked at what it is to *be* Christian. At what sort of characteristics would be the marks of a blessed one. We noted that none of these things come from the natural man, only from one who has been born again of the Spirit of God and been transformed into a new creation.

A person enabled to live out a supernatural lifestyle from a spiritual life source rather than from a carnal one. And living, or giving expression to, a supernatural lifestyle unquestionably involves being equipped to *do*. Hence the gifts.

In beginning the Corinthian chapters as he did (there were no chapters and verses in the original letters, of course), Paul is following a similar path. Those who trust Holy Spirit to live in and work through them are those able to manifest the gifts of the Spirit.

And this is not to draw attention to themselves or to boost their egos but for the blessing of others. People either within the church family or out in the wider community in which they lived.

Back in the early days of my Christian experience, elements of the charismatic lifestyle were beginning to impact upon the traditional evangelical culture that I was originally introduced to. At that time there was a teaching about spiritual gifts which I absorbed but would not accept now.

This was that in each one of us, God has deposited a *specific* spiritual gift. *Our* job is to identify and use it. It is possible that the repetition of *to one* or *to another* and the words, *to each one individually* are what prompted this point of view.

I believe it was John Wimber (Vineyard) who was particularly instrumental in questioning that teaching. He believed that any one of us could be used to operate in any one of the spiritual gifts at any time that God called upon us to meet an arising need. There was never to be a sense of exclusivity at all. Simply a requirement for openness, expectancy, and willingness to cooperate as required.

I found this teaching not only to make much more sense but also to remove the pressure of the self-imposed responsibility to discover *my* gift. Over the ensuing years, experience has shown me time and again that it is not about what we have already *got*.

It's about what we are open to be *given* at the point of another's need. Alternatively, it is what Holy Spirit chooses to select, for the issue immediately before us, from the complete range of potentials placed within us.

Given to each one for the profit of all

The *(NIV)* translation renders the latter part of this phrase as *for the common good*. The blessing is primarily intended for the one on the receiving end, not the one through whom it is given. Of course, being used by God in these ways is a blessing to the man, woman or child concerned. But that is not the main objective.

If we *eagerly desire* to be used by God to manifest the gifts of the Spirit, it should always be focussed on their benefit to another. When we read about the ministry of Jesus in the gospels, we notice that this is always His motivation. The Son of Man was motivated always by unconditional love and compassion. We are meant to follow His example.

The word of wisdom

For it is written, I will destroy the wisdom of the wise and bring to nothing the understanding of the prudent. Where is the wise? Where is the scribe? Where is the disputer of this age? Has not God made foolish the wisdom of this world? For since, in the wisdom of God, the world through wisdom did not know God, it pleased God through the foolishness of the message preached to save those who believe.

For Jews request a sign, and Greeks seek after wisdom, but we preach Christ crucified, to the Jews a stumbling block and to the Greeks foolishness, but to those who are called, both Jews and Greeks, Christ the power of God and the wisdom of God. Because the foolishness of God is wiser than men, and the weakness of God is stronger than men.

(1 Corinthians 1:19-25)

Even the natural wisdom of the wisest person on Earth pales to insignificance by comparison with the wisdom of God. His wisdom is personified in the books of both Proverbs and Ecclesiastes.

Even more significantly, in and through the incarnation of the Son of God. Therefore, God is the source of this word of wisdom spoken through the lips of a man or woman of God.

There are those who teach that such wisdom is a superior level of intellect that God gives to certain chosen people. They advocate that the first apostles required such wisdom for the founding and establishing of the infant church. Such thinking is indicative of a Cessationist stance, suggesting that only the limited timeframe of *their* ministries was necessary for this purpose.

My argument would be that we are dealing with heavenly revelation here. We are definitely not considering an enhancement of human intellect, even if it is sovereignly provided by God. Whilst I would *never say never* where the sovereignty of God is concerned, my assertion remains that this is a revelatory gift. It is given at specific times for specific situations, not necessarily for life. I believe that this is what James is referring to.

If any of you lacks wisdom, let him ask of God, who gives to all liberally and without reproach, and it will be given to him.

(James 1:5)

Under the old covenant, we find that Solomon asked for and received wisdom from God to sustain him throughout his reign as king of Israel. But it was a wise and discerning heart that he was given *(1 Kings 3:12)*. Of course, the heart referred to here is not the organ that pumps blood around our bodies, but the soul and/or spirit.

Under the old covenant, certain people were given a measure of Holy Spirit for certain tasks for a certain time, like Solomon. But we live in an age where the Spirit *has been poured out on all flesh*, beginning at the Day of Pentecost in Jerusalem *(Joel 2:28, Acts 2)*. Now, *one size fits all*, if it is not irreverent to put it like that!

I believe that we receive a *word of wisdom* by revelation when we find ourselves in a situation that calls for wisdom. This could be either for us or (more likely) for another person.

Its purpose would be in order to resolve some sort of dilemma confronting either us or them. Something beyond our natural ability. A product of the supernatural; a *download* of heavenly wisdom from God through the operation of Holy Spirit.

The word of knowledge

Once again, we should beware of equating the knowledge referred to here with something produced by human intellect, even a Divinely enhanced human intellect. The latter is a view I found in my research, put forward by some within the church.

But we are dealing with a gift of the Spirit, a spiritual gift. So, it must be supernatural, not natural. We are being provided with knowledge supernaturally which we could not have acquired by natural means.

I devote a whole chapter to Words of Knowledge in *First Steps* because this gift has proved to be invaluable. Not only for me but for anyone involved in the healing ministry to any degree. I will not go into such detail here but, instead, provide a brief overview. However, please note that I am not suggesting that a word of knowledge is exclusively a tool for those ministering healing.

Sometimes a church ministry team gathers for preparatory prayer before a service or meeting. Holy Spirit then gives them information about ailments or problems that people who will be present in that meeting will have.

He does this because He wants to heal or set free those persons through ministry. This could be either during or after the main meeting time, however He leads. These supernaturally revealed 'words' are also a faith-builder for the team.

Dr Randy Clark teaches seven different ways by which Holy Spirit imparts words of knowledge. Five of them were taught to him by a Vineyard minister before Randy's first-ever healing service. Two were added by him that were gained through his own subsequent experience. If you are familiar with his international healing ministry, you will know that words of knowledge still have a prominent place in all his meetings.

Feel it; Read it; See it; Say it; Think or *Know it; Dream it* and *Experience it*, are the seven. I have been blessed with revelations in each of the first five categories on various occasions. The most common one for me is to *Read it*. For Cathy, it is *Think* or *Know it*. I will explain each one very briefly here and provide just a couple of examples by way of illustration.

Feel it is when you experience a pain or sensation in your body, usually very briefly. Unless you are aware that Holy Spirit works this way, you could miss it (as having come from Him). This would be a pain that you know is not your own. It is a revelation of what is happening in or to the body of someone else.

An Eastgate Healing Centre colleague and I were asked to pray a blessing on a lady attending a Christian conference for the medical profession. Whilst doing so, I experienced a short, sharp pain in my back between the shoulder blades. I asked her if she had such a pain. Surprised that I could have known, she confirmed that she had and gave us permission to minister healing.

As we were doing this, I felt the same pain again. This time it was worse, and then it disappeared immediately. Afterwards, when we asked her what had been happening, she replied that she was now pain-free. So, I enquired if, just before the pain left, it had got worse. She confirmed that indeed it had. Two words of knowledge *felt* for the same person!

Read it is when you see, in your mind's eye, certain words that you can read. Just like you would out of a book, a newspaper, or on a computer screen.

See it is very similar but, this time, you see a picture or image in your mind's eye. This could be either static or moving. In the latter instance, some might prefer to describe it as a vision.

Say it is when you find yourself saying a word or phrase that you had not processed through your mind before the utterance came out. I was once in a ministry situation on the streets where a colleague and I were talking to a young lady. Thanks to a prior revelation, we discovered she had back pain caused by a trapped nerve.

During our conversation I suddenly found myself saying to her, "You're not an accident, you know!" Both my friend and I were wondering where that had come from.

Then, to our astonishment, the lady said, "But I always thought I was!"

She told us her very sad back-story and we were able to pray into her situation and share with her about a Father who loved her and would never desert her.

Think it or *Know it* is when a thought comes into your mind, that you are pretty sure is not your own thought. Or it's as if you just *know* something that you couldn't possibly have known if Holy Spirit had not just revealed it to you.

This is something that Cathy has experienced on many occasions, usually *during* ministry times. She often receives such revelation when preparing herself ahead of a Bethel Sozo ministry session. This invariably facilitates a breakthrough in a situation which, otherwise, might not have been resolved so quickly.

Dream it, is simply something that you have dreamed at some point in the past. Then, in a subsequent ministry situation, God brings it back to your mind as a *word of knowledge.* This proved to be just what was required at that moment in order to progress the ministry.

Experience it, is very similar, except that what Holy Spirit brings to mind is the memory of a past experience of yours. It provides the key to dealing with the matter at hand.

These things do not always make obvious sense to us, being seemingly quite random. However, when we have the courage to share them, invariably we find that they meet the presenting need exactly.

Bearing in mind that we are all quite capable of *getting it wrong* sometimes, one should never exhibit overconfidence in delivering a word of knowledge. Prefacing it by saying something like, "I believe the Lord may be saying—" is recommended.

This is also preferable when speaking out a prophetic word, rather than a, "Thus says the Lord—" emphatic kind of Old Testament opening phrase.

Faith

The gift of faith that we are considering here should not be confused with what we might call *basic* faith. The faith that we have to believe, receive, or live out in everyday matters. It is not the faith (even though that was itself a gift) that brought us into the Kingdom in the first place *(Ephesians 2:8).* It is not even that *basic* faith on a sliding scale, say from a mustard seed to coconut size! It is something more, something quite separate.

When Paul referred to his ministry in 1 Corinthians 12:12, he wrote that *the signs of an apostle were accomplished among you with all perseverance, in signs and wonders and mighty deeds* and he was including miracles here. Let me use *miracles* here to illustrate what seems to me to be the difference between faith and the *gift* of faith.

In Acts 19:11 we are told that *God worked unusual miracles by the hands of Paul,* (the NIV says, extraordinary miracles). How on Earth, or even in Heaven, do you calibrate miracles? Aren't they all unusual or extraordinary, from a human perspective at least? Does our all-powerful God ever have to evaluate conditions in terms of degrees of difficulty (as medical science might)?

Luke goes on to elaborate by writing, *so that even handkerchiefs or aprons were brought from his body to the sick, and the diseases left them, and the evil spirits went out of them.* So, it would appear that those are extraordinary miracles, and all the other ones were ordinary!

Randy Clark's teaching is helpful when considering how faith and the gift of faith could be different. He refers to the *gift* of faith being manifested when, in human terms, something unusually difficult presents itself to someone ministering. Some *extraordinary* faith is required to deal with it.

This faith, he contends, is what you have when *you know that you know that you know* that God is going to come through even against seemingly impossible odds.

Although I certainly did not analyse it this way at the time, possibly I needed the gift of faith on the first occasion I saw God grow out a shortened (and/or misaligned) leg. But, when my confidence in Him in this aspect of healing grew, perhaps the more normal level of faith was sufficient.

Actually, the first time I prayed for someone with this condition nothing happened. So, maybe the gift of faith was provided subsequently when wonderful healings of this nature did occur.

Gifts of healings

That brings us on to the subject of healing and the first thing to notice is that both the words *gift* and *healing* are stated in the plural form. I must be honest and say that I don't know why this is so, I can only speculate for now.

It could be that there is such a variety of conditions, and different sorts of healing gifts can be employed, according to the need presented, to bring about healing by the power of God. As a simple example, we have both physical healing and inner healing, and it could be argued that different gifting is required to minister to people with those very different kinds of infirmities.

Cathy is involved in Bethel Sozo ministry. As I take the role of her *second* on occasion, I know that God has really gifted her in this form of inner healing ministry. I also know that I could not do what she does. I do not feel called to do any more than to assist her, happily, whenever required to do so.

Then again, if we are in a situation where some deliverance ministry is required, she prefers to leave that to me. She has done it herself, of course, but she usually asks me to take the lead when we are ministering together in this way.

The working of miracles

How do you differentiate between a miracle and a healing miracle? Obviously, there are miracles that do not involve healing. Turning water into wine, stilling a storm, and multiplying food, for example. But what is the difference between a miracle and a miracle of healing? If indeed there is one.

The most helpful explanation I have come across to date is to apply the term *healing* to a condition, like a pain in the back between the shoulder blades. Healing occurs when the pain, and the cause of the pain, disappear.

A healing could be described as a *miracle* when, for example, God creates a foot at the end of a leg where there was none immediately before His intervention. I have no experience of this myself (yet). But I know of people, whom I trust to share honestly, who have testified to such, and similar, occurrences. Something like a replacement body part appearing out of *nowhere* is often described as a *creative miracle*. That is the best answer I can propose—at the moment.

As to the non-healing kinds of miracles, I have no personal experience to date to share with you. However, the gospels are full of them. There are plenty of testimonies around, from a wide variety of ministries, to be encouraged by. Remember, our God is the God of the impossible.

Jesus says that anyone who believes in Him can do the things He did—and even greater things *(John 14:12)*. So, let us never limit Him by succumbing to temptations to doubt, or retreat into unbelief, when He wants to work through us in amazing ways!

Prophecy

We have to be aware that there is a difference between *anyone* being enabled to prophesy on occasion (i.e., being prophetic in the local church environment) and being designated as a prophet. By the latter, I mean a recognised ministry wholly dependent upon the gift of prophecy being developed, sometimes with a national, or international, influence.

I want to go into this subject in some detail. Not here but in chapter 9 when we look at the office, or ministry, of a prophet as one of the five-fold ministries described in Ephesians 4:11. Suffice it to say, for now, that most of us will fall into the category of being prophetic. Our gifting will fall under the current heading. Only a few will be called more specifically to minister as prophets.

Discerning of spirits

We have probably all had the experience at one time or another of feeling inexplicably uncomfortable in certain surroundings or in the company of certain people. Conversely, of feeling very much at peace in either of those scenarios.

This *picking up the atmosphere* in a place or around a person can be described as discernment. When this is more than just a natural ability but is something that Holy Spirit has enabled us to do, we are talking about the spiritual gift of *discerning of (or between) spirits*.

It is not exactly unknown for witches or other occultists to infiltrate church meetings for negative purposes. People with this gift can usually detect their presence and even identify them. There is a wonderful story from Smith Wigglesworth's early ministry when just such a little group came to the Bowland Street Mission in Bradford where he was ministering.

He knew in his spirit that something was wrong. Holy Spirit enabled him to identify the source of the problem. He overturned the bench, on which these witches were sitting and *praying* against him, before ejecting them all from the building!

Another spiritual gift, related to our present subject matter, is known by some as *reading the room*. A person with this gift is able to become aware in their spirit of either something negative (as above) or something positive.

They pick up on what God is doing or wants to do. If such a person is leading the meeting, they can change the direction it is taking. Or whatever it may be that Holy Spirit is prompting them to do.

Buildings and places have spiritual *atmospheres*, positive or negative. The spiritually discerning can *read* these, too. Dawna de Silva has written an excellent book, 'Shifting Atmospheres'[1], which covers this subject very well. She explains how Christians can *read* and *change* the atmosphere they are encountering, if negative. Alternatively, to *press into* a positive atmosphere.

When I went out on the streets of Gravesend, with my fellow students from ESSL[2], we were usually divided into three groups. One group would be going out on to *treasure hunt*. Another would be offering *free hugs* and *prophetic readings* from a gazebo. The third group would be *shifting atmospheres*.

The latter entailed going around the streets praying and making positive declarations, as the Lord led the participants. Sometimes, the leaders would point out in advance that Holy Spirit had revealed to them that a certain area of town needed particular attention. So, the *troops* would be sent there first.

Prayer Walking can have the same objective if a certain spiritual issue has been discerned in a particular area. Holy Spirit will prompt either someone or a group to go out to pray and make declarations against it.

We have been involved in something very like this in the town where we live now. The prayer walking was prompted by a *prophetic picture* given by Holy Spirit to one of our church leadership team members. The initiative should always be His.

Different kinds of tongues

One day 120 people came running out of a building in Jerusalem shouting the praises of God in multiple languages that they had never learned. This phenomenon was linked once and forever with the Christian church *(Acts 2)*. As we follow the development of the early church, we see that there were occasions when apostles came across a group of new believers. The first thing they seemed to do was introduce them to the *baptism of the Holy Spirit*. This was invariably confirmed by these believers speaking in tongues.

It was the gift that the Corinthians seemed to fixate upon, to the detriment of the other (more important?) gifts. So, in his first letter to them, Paul seeks to correct this imbalance.

He shows us that there is both a private and a public aspect to speaking in *tongues*. The private aspect means that individually, and sometimes in silence, we can praise or pray to God, employing our spirit rather than our mind. This is invaluable when we have a burden to pray but struggle to find the right words to express ourselves *(Romans 8:26-27)*. It is also powerfully effective in some ministry situations and certainly in 'spiritual warfare'.

Sadly, there are still parts of the church generally where this gift is not accepted and is even attributed to the devil. It seems to me to be very clear that this is a spiritual gift of God to His church. Paul goes to great lengths, in 1 Corinthians 14, both to promote it and to explain how it is best used. Particularly in a public context. Those who view this gift negatively are often Cessationists, who would not endorse the use of *any* of the gifts today.

The interpretation of tongues

In 1 Corinthians 14:13, Paul writes, *let him who speaks in a tongue pray that he may interpret*. If there is no *interpretation* of a message spoken out publicly in tongues, then it is obviously of no value because no one will have understood it. This gift is given in a public meeting in conjunction with the previous one.

Then a message from God can be given to the people in a language they will understand. So, it carries the same value as a prophecy in their native tongue. Perhaps delivering the message in this dual form may command more attention than a traditional prophetic utterance would.

Outside of the Pentecostal denominations, I am not sure how widespread the employment of these two gifts is in churches today. I was a regular worshipper in an Anglican church when they became a more common part of my experience.

Although I must admit, I was not one who was privileged to speak out like this in a meeting. This usually happened during a monthly informal service in the church hall rather than in the main services. The latter usually followed liturgical formats (with some freedom of expression). The former was more relaxed and *free*.

However, I was leading one of the regular morning meetings one Sunday when somebody stood up and gave a public message in tongues. The vicar was away, and I must confess to imitating a *swan* with my reaction. I was calm on the surface but paddling madly below the waterline!

I managed to ask if there was anyone who could give an interpretation. Much to my relief, the worship group's keyboard player stood up and shared the message in English.

When he had finished, I quickly announced the next worship hymn/song and then slipped down to speak to one of the churchwardens. He was to be the preacher later on. I asked him what he thought about this situation. Not only did he reassure me that I had responded correctly but also said that the interpretation was fully compatible with the sermon he was about to preach!

Much encouraged, I carried on with leading the rest of the meeting. At the close, the preacher and I stood at the main doors shaking the hands of folk as they left. A retired vicar, who was part of our regular congregation, tore me off a strip on his way out.

"Why did you not *rebuke* him?" he demanded.

I explained how I came to the decision I took but to no avail. So, I rang the vicar later to put him in the picture. He also kindly reassured me that I had adopted the right procedure and promised to deal with any negative feedback.

By the way, I am still baffled about the person who spoke out. He was not recognised by anyone I questioned about him. He didn't leave the building through the doors where we were standing to say goodbye to folk as they left! An angel?

But one and the same Spirit works all these things, distributing to each one individually as He wills.

The above are not the only spiritual gifts, of course. They are a selection that Paul, inspired by Holy Spirit, provides in this letter to illustrate his point. There are more later in chapter 12 of 1 Corinthians and in Romans 12, for example.

Now you are the Body of Christ, and members individually. And God has appointed these in the church: first apostles, second prophets, third teachers, after that, miracles, then gifts of healings healing, helps, administrations, varieties of tongues. Are all apostles? Are all prophets? Are all teachers? Are all workers of miracles? Do all have gifts of healings? Do all speak with tongues? Do all interpret? But earnestly desire the best gifts.

(1 Corinthians 12:27-31)

Some of the gifts from earlier in 1 Corinthians 12 are repeated here. But Paul also adds *"helps"* and *"administrations"* as well as mentioning *apostles* and others for the first time. The latter are referred to here as *appointments* (or *placements* in the NIV) rather than *gifts*. Some clarity can be found in Ephesians 4:11, followed by a few words to explain their purpose. We will look at those aspects of ministry in more detail in (chapter 9).

Helps

This is essentially another way of describing *serving* and we will consider that in a moment when we get to the list of gifts in Romans 12.

Administrations

There are not many gifted church *leaders* who are also proficient in the art of administration. Many would have great difficulty organising the proverbial *booze-up in a brewery*! They probably attract a lot of criticism because of that deficiency.

Especially if church funds don't stretch to cover an efficient PA! Administration should not be expected to be part of every leader's role. If there are no funds to pay someone capable of handling such tasks, surely gifted volunteers could be found to put in a few hours of service here and there?

A good administrator is worth his or her weight in gold. The larger and busier a church may be, the more vital the role becomes. It may not attract the same kudos as the pastor, teacher, or evangelist positions, but those guys would be lost without someone efficient to organise them and pick up the pieces!

Having then gifts differing according to the grace that is given to us, let us use them: if prophecy, let us prophesy in proportion to our faith; or ministry (serving), *let us use it in our ministering; he who teaches, in teaching; he who exhorts, in exhortation; he who gives, with liberality; he who leads, with diligence; he who shows mercy, with cheerfulness.*

(Romans 12:6-8)

Ministering

Let us not confuse this term with *full-time* or *part-time* paid Christian ministry. What is being referred to here, as the NIV renders more helpfully, is *serving*. This relates to those who operate out of a servant's heart in a variety of roles within the church environment.

More often than not this means the less glamorous, but nonetheless essential, jobs. Things like serving refreshments or cleaning the facilities. This is a reminder to us that every job has value. If we are doing what He calls us to do, our role has equal value with any other.

I am reminded of the *widow's mite* being nothing, in strict monetary terms, compared with the size of the gifts that rich people were putting onto the plate. However, Jesus pointed out that, in Kingdom terms, her tiny donation had significantly more value than theirs *(Mark 12:41-44)*. To change the wording slightly to emphasise my point, *she put everything she had into it*—she did her very best with the very *little* she possessed.

Exhortation

A certain man called Joseph was nicknamed *Barnabas*, meaning *Son of Encouragement*. We read this in Acts 4:36-37. Encouragement in the church is seriously undervalued. Most of us are much quicker to complain than to encourage, particularly if someone has not done something quite as well as we might have wanted.

But, if they tried hard and did their best, they should be encouraged. That way, they are more likely to do better in future. Whereas to be the subject of complaints is not only totally off-putting but also the epitome of *discouragement*. Maybe all they need is a little help (or training)?

We can put off saying, "Well done!", to a person whose contribution we have appreciated because of the possibility that praise might go to their heads.

Well, it might—but take the risk anyway! What they do with your compliment is not your responsibility. It is between them and God. Others appear ever so humble and anxious to deflect away from themselves every compliment.

"It wasn't me; it was the Lord," they respond, looking down at their boots.

Yes, it *was* you, in cooperation with Him, just as it should be. Take the compliment for your contribution and give Him the glory when you are alone with Him.

Liberality

Churches are famous, some would say infamous, for asking for money. There is no smoke without fire, but I think that is an exaggeration. At least it is in my experience. But then, I don't give in to every TV exhortation to *sow a seed* (money) to receive a blessing. I don't worship a God who apparently needs to be *bribed* to act favourably towards me. I worship a God who is exceedingly generous and would like me to be just the same.

> *Now Araunah said to David, "Let my lord the king take and offer up whatever seems good to him. Look, here are oxen for burnt sacrifice, and threshing implements and the yokes of the oxen for wood. All these, O king, Araunah has given to the king."*
>
> *And Araunah said to the king, "May the Lord your God accept you."*
>
> *Then the king said to Araunah, "No, but I will surely buy it from you for a price; nor will I offer burnt offerings to the Lord my God with that which costs me nothing."*
>
> *So, David bought the threshing floor and the oxen for fifty shekels of silver.*
>
> (2 Samuel 24:22-24)

Giving can be quite a controversial issue in some circles. It can be riddled with misunderstandings and misinterpretation of motives, all manner of negative things. Paul is simply suggesting that, if you are giving, be as generous as you can. Not only in church but also in a hotel or restaurant. Indeed, any secular establishment in which you have been served well—even if *it is their job*!

Giving is not just about money either, is it? If we don't have money but we do have time, why not give that? Go and visit a lonely person at home. Talk to that nervous-looking individual who doesn't seem to know whether to go or stay when it is time for coffee after a church meeting.

Talk to someone when you are out on the street if God prompts you to. Who knows what that may lead to? You and I certainly won't find out if we never respond to His leading. However, let's remember to approach them with love and compassion, trusting Him for the right words to say. Don't spout some carefully rehearsed patter.

Eagerly desire to be spiritual (supernatural) and remember that there are a whole lot of *tools* (gifts) for Holy Spirit to select from to meet every need. He can equip us for each and every task He prompts us to undertake for Him.

Any gift we receive comes to us solely by God's grace, not through our own merit. If we are obedient and cooperative so that much good results, then all the glory goes to Him. These gifts are spiritual and supernatural, and He stewards the Kingdom toolbox they are all stored in.

As I have already indicated, we will consider prophecy and teaching (along with leadership) later in chapter 9. We already looked at the subject of mercy quite extensively in Part 1, so I will not elaborate further here.

1. *'Shifting Atmospheres',* Dawna de Silva, Destiny Image Publishers Inc
2. *Eastgate School of Supernatural Life,* visit eastgate.org.uk (ESSL tab)

3
Blessed by Spiritual Fruit

But the fruit of the Spirit is
love, joy, peace, longsuffering, kindness,
goodness, faithfulness, gentleness, self-control.
Against such, there is no law.

(Galatians 5:22-23)

In the previous chapter, we looked at spiritual *gifts*. These *gifts* are the *tools* with which the blessed ones are enabled to accomplish the *works*. And God, who knows the end from the beginning, has prepared them in advance for us to do Ephesians 2:10.

They have both *natural* equivalents and anti-Christian counterfeits. We have already discovered that, no matter how worthy natural gifts may be, they do not possess supernatural value in God's Kingdom. Of course, that is even more obviously true in respect of the counterfeits!

We come now to spiritual *fruit*. Again, although there are laudable, natural equivalents, neither do these have special value or significance in God's kingdom realm. To borrow a catchphrase from an old TV quiz show, *It's good, but it's not* (quite) *right*.

The other thing we discover is that, whilst *gifts* appear in the plural form, *fruit* is in the singular. This is even though nine examples are listed! I want to suggest, therefore, that the one (singular) fruit derives from the Spirit of God.

That fruit is given expression in multiple different ways through His connection with our human spirit. And I don't believe those examples listed in *(Galatians 5)* are the only varieties. Any way in which the life of the Spirit is made more evident through us is an example of abundant life expressed through either *a gift* or *good fruit*.

Jesus said, *"For a good tree does not bear bad fruit, nor does a bad tree bear good fruit. For every tree is known by its own fruit. For men do not gather figs from thorns, nor do they gather grapes from a bramble bush. A good man out of the good treasure of his heart brings forth good; and, and an evil man out of the evil treasure of his heart brings forth evil. For out of the abundance of the heart his mouth speaks."*

(Luke 6:43-45)

Both these verses and the varieties of fruit listed describe good expressions emanating from a good heart. They relate primarily to the spirit-prompted, emotional responses or reactions made possible by the changes Holy Spirit inspires in us from our conversion onwards.

Jesus makes it clear that the words we say, and the way in which we say them, are major indicators of the condition of our heart. This is the *heart* which is the core of our being, not the blood-pumping organ. There may be physical expressions also, but perhaps not to the extent that is clearly obvious when many of the *gifts* are manifested.

It is my contention that the fruit of the spirit comes under the heading of doing, more than being. It is only because we are already enabled to *be* that it is now possible to *do*. And this doing is expressed in the form of verbal, emotional or physical fruit. Holy Spirit is the ultimate source of all spiritual fruit, and the expression of it comes through our submission to, and cooperation with, Him.

I am the vine; you are the branches. He who abides in Me, and I in him, bears much fruit; for without Me you can do nothing.

(John 15:5)

Bill Johnson contends that *faith is not effort but surrender.* I believe the same principle applies to bearing spiritual fruit. We don't have to strive to *work up spiritual* love, joy, peace, etc. What we need for any given moment is either there to be drawn upon, or it isn't. Holy Spirit determines the possibilities.

Sometimes, to surrender to the promptings of the Spirit, it may be necessary to suppress a wrongly motivated reaction or response. One that is initiated by *the flesh*. But that is the only real effort that comes into it.

When the Spirit is given free rein, the outworking of His Presence within us and His influence upon us comes through without the need to strive and strain to produce it.

I was born and brought up in Kent, known as the Garden of England, where orchards proliferate (or used to!). I have never walked through one of those in summer and heard the trees groaning with effort to produce the fruit appearing on their branches. It happens naturally. Works always require a degree of effort. Fruit is a naturally supernatural product of our willing submission to God.

Love

Agape is the Greek word for unconditional love, such as a parent has for a child. This is the love that God has for His people (Romans 8:35) and it is the greatest of the gifts of the Holy Spirit (1 Corinthians 12:31; 13:13). Jesus calls his people to agape their enemies (Luke 6:27). When Jesus quotes Deuteronomy 6:4 in Matthew 22:37, *the gospel writers (again) use the Greek word agape.*

(theopedia.com)

It is hardly a surprise to find that love heads the list of spiritual fruit because love is the essence of God's character. God does not simply love, He *is* Love.

God is love, and he who abides in love abides in God, and God in him.

(1 John 4:16b)

Love is also the foundation of the changed character that He wishes to see both formed *in* us and expressed *through* us as His blessed ones. We are equipped to love, as He does when we know He first loved us.

(1 John 4:19

A new commandment I give to you, that you love one another; as I have loved you, that you also love one another. By this, all will know that you are My disciples, if you have love for one another.

(John 13:34-35)

We may be blessed abundantly with gifts, both natural and supernatural but, without expressing them through love, we will not please God. This was one of the shortcomings in the Corinthian church that prompted the writing of Paul's first letter to them.

The problem wasn't a lack of spiritual gifts but the way in which they gave expression to them. They were abusing the privilege they had been granted and we should beware of ever doing the same.

Though I speak with the tongues of men and of angels but have not love, I have become sounding brass or a clanging cymbal. And though I have the gift of prophecy, and understand all mysteries and all knowledge, and though I have all faith, so that I could remove mountains, but have not love, I am nothing. And though I bestow all my goods to feed the poor, and though I give my body to be burned, but have not love, it profits me nothing.

(1 Corinthians 13:1-3)

These are just the opening verses of Paul's inspired treatise on Love (agape). It is a passage of scripture ranked among the finest examples of literature ever produced. What is more important, of course, is that it is inspired by Holy Spirit. It is therefore the embodiment of truth.

This highlights the difference between the best of our natural selves (good) and the heavenly supernatural (Godly). Love is a fundamental necessity of the Christian life from which everything else flows. We see this exemplified in the life and ministry of Jesus, our prime example of a Kingdom lifestyle.

God demonstrates His own love toward us, in that while we were still sinners, Christ died for us.

(Romans 5:8)

God's love for us is so powerful because it is unconditional. If Christ died for us whilst we were *still* sinners, then it is abundantly clear that we could have done nothing to earn His love, compassion, and grace. Without Holy Spirit's empowering it is difficult, if not humanly impossible, for us to love totally unconditionally.

We are prone to give our love as a reward to someone who has pleased us. And to withdraw it, at least temporarily, from someone who has offended us. Even our very best can be diluted by a certain fickleness.

This is a characteristic we can easily display to our children when we are bringing them up. We would never stop loving them because they are naughty sometimes. However, we should be wary of prompting such an inaccurate perception in their hearts when showing our displeasure with their behaviour.

We should ensure that they do not adopt the view that they must always do well to earn our love. That is something which can so easily carry over into adulthood, even if unconsciously. It is not uncommon within church circles, especially where *keeping the rules* is an unwritten condition of acceptance and belonging.

The late prophet, Bob Jones, died and, on entering Heaven, was asked, "Bob, did you learn to love?"

He felt unable to answer honestly in the affirmative, especially in the context of unconditional love. So, he was given a second chance and sent back to Earth to try again! He was graciously given another stab at life and made a point of sharing this important lesson. He aimed both to inspire and encourage others—as well as himself.

Our motivation to share love cannot be a desire to keep the rules or to earn acceptance, even within a church setting. That is not unconditional love. A love that puts the other person first. It is actually selfish. It can easily become a springboard to pride. If we want to see love in action, then we only have to look at Jesus. If we want to find a perfect description of love, there is no need to look further than 1 Corinthians 13.

Joy

Joy is a state of mind and an orientation of the heart. It is a settled state of contentment, confidence, and hope...something or someone that provides a source of happiness. It appears 88 times in the Old Testament (in 22 books); 57 times in the New Testament (in 18 books).

(theopedia.com)

The Lord your God in your midst, the Mighty One, will save; He will rejoice over you with gladness, He will quiet you with His love, He will rejoice over you with singing.

(Zephaniah 3:17)

To be a fruit of the Spirit, joy must first have been integral to the character of God. We find many examples of expressions of joy in the Old Testament. This verse in Zephaniah is especially lovely because it expresses the great joy of the Lord over His people.

Considering how often and how much they (and we) let Him down, it can only spring from His unconditional love. We find Jesus expressing Himself in much the same joyful way when the 70 reported back to Him after they had been sent out on their apostolic mission.

Then the 70 returned with joy, saying, "Lord, even the demons are subject to us in Your name."

And He said to them, "I saw Satan fall like lightning from heaven…In that hour Jesus rejoiced in the Spirit."

(Luke 10:17-18, 21a)

The NKJV translation betrays a little of our British understatement here. Jesus' reaction was apparently much more boisterous than the words at the beginning of verse 21 convey. The Passion Translation rendering is rather more in tune with the original text. *Then Jesus, overflowing with the Holy Spirit's anointing of joy.* It seems very likely that He literally danced for joy!

*So, the ransomed of the Lord shall return, and come to Zion with singing, with everlasting joy on their heads. They shall obtain **joy** and gladness; sorrow and sighing shall flee away.*

(Isaiah 51:11)

The well-known verse in Nehemiah (8:10) tells us that the **joy** of the Lord is our strength. His joy in us actually strengthens us. The nearest human nature would come to this is probably *mind over matter*. That is, perhaps, a denial of reality. The joy of the Lord doesn't deny the reality of a difficult time or situation in our lives. It actually strengthens us both to endure it and to come through it.

This joy is not always a bubbly overflow of happiness and delight. It can sometimes be a simple, quiet confidence in Him. A peaceful assurance that He has the matter in hand. We know we can trust Him to be with us throughout, just as He has promised. It will prevent us from descending into the negativity of depression and inadvertently opening ourselves up to the subtle wiles of the enemy. God's joy and our joy are inextricably linked in our spirits.

These things I have spoken to you, that My joy may remain in you, and that your joy may be full.

(John 15:11)

Acts 13:52 describes one of the many occasions when the disciples were filled with *joy* and with Holy Spirit. This particular time was when, once again, the Jews rejected Paul's preaching of the gospel in their synagogue.

Both he and his companions were forced to continue their teaching elsewhere for the blessing of both Jews and the Gentiles who responded to their message. Such joy will always be ours when we react wisely to the negative reactions or threats of those who reject us.

For the Kingdom of God is not eating and drinking, but righteousness and peace and joy in the Holy Spirit.

(Romans 14:17)

What a wonderful definition of the Kingdom of God this is! We each receive righteousness, peace, and joy as grace gifts and anointings from God. Joy is a quality that is intended to be an ever-present mark of our citizenship of His Kingdom, in all circumstances. This seems to have been a particular characteristic of the Macedonian Christians.

Moreover, brethren, we make known to you the grace of God bestowed on the churches of Macedonia: that in a great trial of affliction, the abundance of their joy and their deep poverty abounded in the riches of their liberality.

(2 Corinthians 8:1-2)

In the midst of trials, and notwithstanding their financial poverty, these people became gracious givers for the blessing of their brethren in Jerusalem. They did not give grudgingly or unwillingly but with great joy, counting it a privilege to be able to contribute.

That can only have been Spirit-inspired, a true fruit of His Presence in and with them. Paul also writes about giving cheerfully, the original language actually meaning giving *hilariously*, a mark of true joy.

So, let each one give as he purposes in his heart, not grudgingly or of necessity; for God loves a cheerful giver.

(2 Corinthians 9:7)

Finally, John expresses the heart of God, I believe, when he writes about joy in his third epistle. Holy Spirit is the Spirit of Truth. As we walk (live) in Him, sensitive to His promptings and guidance, He is the One who leads us into all truth. This is not just in respect of what we *know* but also through what we do. How we express ourselves in many different ways, with integrity—always with an underlying joy in any and every circumstance.

I have no greater joy than to hear that my children walk in truth.

(3 John 1:4)

Peace

Peace has been defined as, *freedom from disturbance, tranquillity; a state or period in which there is no war, or a war has ended;* as well as *mental or emotional calm*. These definitions manage to provide a reasonable understanding of what peace is. We could easily elaborate on these few words. But the point I am making is that, in Kingdom terms, peace is so much more than what the secular dictionaries usually tell us.

The peace of the church is the unity of the Body of Christ, which is made by the destruction of mutual hostility by the cross of Christ, into which the nations are invited through the Gospel of repentance and faith in Him, and it is the norm of the fellowship of Christians according to the grace of God.

(theopeadia.com)

Be anxious for nothing, but in everything by prayer and supplication, with thanksgiving, let your requests be made known to God; and the peace of God, which surpasses all understanding, will guard your hearts and minds through Christ Jesus.

(Philippians 4:6-7)

The peace that God gives is so powerful that it is beyond our understanding. It is too much for us, for the natural man, to comprehend. To me, this means that we can experience peace in God even in situations in which it would defy simple, human logic for us to know, or even expect, peace of mind and heart.

These things I have spoken to you, that in Me you may have peace. In the world you will have tribulation; but be of good cheer, I have overcome the world.

(John 16:33)

The peace that is available to us from God is different to any kind of peace the world can offer. Jesus carried that peace throughout His life and ministry. Now, He has bequeathed it to us, His church. Initially to His disciples on the night that He knew He was about to be betrayed, tortured, and executed.

Peace, I leave with you. My peace I give to you; not as the world gives do I give to you. Let not your heart be troubled, neither let it be afraid.

(John 14:27)

The peace of God is something precious we can carry—and pass on too. This was the case with the disciples when they were first sent out to minister two by two, pre-Pentecost. It's a foretaste of the Great Commission that is given to each one of us.

And when you go into a household, greet it. If the household is worthy, let your peace come upon it. But if it is not worthy, let your peace return to you.

(Matthew 10:12-130)

When we seek to share the Kingdom with others, and they receive it, we also share His peace with them. Indeed, people tend to be more receptive to our ministry when they feel comfortable and at peace, with us.

If they are not so receptive, even hostile, we will resist any temptation to lose our cool. Instead, we will retain our peace and move on graciously, seeking more opportunities to share God's love elsewhere. *Shaking dust off the feet* is perhaps as negative as we should be!

Then (Jesus) *arose and rebuked the wind, and said to the sea, "Peace, be still!"*
And the wind ceased and there was a great calm.

(Mark 4:39)

Jesus was asleep in the boat when the storm struck and caused the disciples to panic. This was despite some of them being experienced fishermen. He was at peace Himself. On being wakened, He rose in peace and released His peace to the wind and the waves with a word of command.

Bill Johnson teaches that *we have authority over any storm we can sleep through.* In other words, we cannot release a peace that we *do* not already have. This is especially true when a peace that *surpasses understanding* is called for.

I remember witnessing a friend ministering to a lady who was manifesting demonically in the middle of a meeting.

She quietly whispered, "Peace, be still," to her until she calmed down, ready for the next stage of ministry.

So, Jesus said to them again, "Peace to you! As the Father has sent Me, I also send you."

And when He had said this, He breathed on them, and said to them, "Receive the Holy Spirit."

(John 20:21-22)

John doesn't give us as much information as the other gospel writers about this first encounter of the resurrected Jesus with His disciples. We know, from the other accounts, that they were understandably shocked, fearful even. He had just walked through the wall into a room that was securely locked!

At once He met their immediate need by releasing calm, His peace, to them. When He commissioned them, He released peace again—and Holy Spirit. He would become the source of their ongoing peace within all the rigours of their calling.

It is notable that, almost every time an angel appears to someone in a Bible passage, their greeting begins with, "Fear not."

Another way of releasing peace to someone who is alarmed—to say the least!

For to be carnally minded is death, but to be spiritually minded is life and peace.

(Romans 8:6)

It is important for peace to be maintained within the church. Not only within individual local expressions of the body but also nationally and internationally. We can learn to agree to disagree, especially about non-essentials, without falling out with one another.

I, therefore, the prisoner of the Lord, beseech you to walk worthy of the calling with which you were called, with all lowliness and gentleness, with longsuffering, bearing with one another in love, endeavouring to keep the unity of the Spirit in the bond of peace.

(Ephesians 4:1-3)

We have made this difficult for ourselves down through the years, with all our denominations and other kinds of divisions. From time to time, there are different efforts made to bring about unity (peace) between different parties that have become divided. But we are not called to do that. Our call is to maintain the unity that already exists in the Spirit through the bond of peace.

The Holy Trinity is the epitome of unity. Peace has always existed in God. We share it through Holy Spirit's connection with our human spirit. Sadly, we can so easily step outside of this peace because of our fleshly differences.

And let the peace of God rule in your hearts, to which also you were called in one body; (and be thankful.)

(Colossians 3:15)

The process of sanctification is necessary for the development of Christian maturity. It applies from the time we are born again until we leave this life. We submit to this process through the ministrations of the God of Peace.

Now may the God of Peace Himself sanctify you completely; and may your whole spirit, soul, and body be preserved blameless at the coming of our Lord Jesus Christ.

(1 Thessalonians 5:23)

Peace is a fundamental ingredient of our new life and nature. It is equally an essential outward expression of it. He imparts His peace to us so that we can share it with and impart it to others.

Pursue peace with all people, and holiness, without which no one will see the Lord.

(Hebrews 12:14)

And peace is even a weapon! For it is the God of Peace, not of war, who will crush Satan under our feet *(Romans 16:19b-20a)*.

Can you think of anything more infuriating and frustrating than this for our enemy? Having thrown everything in his armoury at us, we continue to give expression to the peace that surpasses understanding. Our God of Peace has planted it within us for us to draw upon in such times of need.

Finally, let us remember that peace is invariably part of the greeting from the writers of the New Testament epistles to their readers. Amen, let it be so.

Longsuffering

"Someone who patiently puts up with a lot of trouble or unhappiness, especially when it is caused by someone else" (synonyms: *uncomplaining, patient, resigned, forgiving*).

(Collins Dictionary)

Longsuffering means *suffering long*, although that might be a little too simplistic for some of us. The word translated from the Greek in our Bibles is made up of two words which mean *long* and *temper*. This results in *long-tempered*. That contrasts with a more familiar expression, short-tempered.

It actually means *to exhibit self-restraint when stirred to anger* (hopefully, righteous anger!). The NIV says *forbearance*, the NLT favours *patience* and the Passion Translation reads *patience that endures*, which is probably the most helpful rendering for the modern ear.

God has been patiently enduring the vagaries of mankind ever since the fall. He constantly gives us opportunities to come to repentance. To enter into His Kingdom by means of the salvation offered through Jesus. We know that He is the only Way to the Father and the only means of reconciliation with God. One of my favourite Bible verses confirms this.

Or do you despise the riches of His goodness, forbearance, and longsuffering, not knowing that the goodness (or kindness) *of God leads you to repentance?*

(Romans 2:4)

In the same way, He has patiently endured the Jewish nation's rejection of their Messiah. His arms of love are ever open in order to welcome their return to Him. He confirmed this by submitting to nails to hold them open on a cross!

What if God, wanting to show His wrath and to make His power known, endured with much longsuffering the vessels of wrath prepared for destruction, and that He might make known the riches of His glory on the vessels of mercy, which He had prepared beforehand for glory,

(Romans 9:22-23)

Those of us who are part of the Christian church soon make an unwelcome discovery. Despite everything God has graciously done for us, provided for us and equipped us with, we let Him down. We fall out with each other as well.

When such differences occur, He wants us to treat one another as He treats each of us. Paul emphasised this when he was writing to both the Ephesians and the Colossians.

I, therefore, the prisoner of the Lord, beseech you to walk worthy of the calling with which you were called, with all lowliness and gentleness, with longsuffering, bearing with one another in love, endeavouring to keep the unity of the Spirit in the bond of peace.

(Ephesians 4:1-3)

Some have joked, perhaps with serious undertones, that *the church could be perfect if it wasn't for the people in it!*

Therefore, as the elect of God, holy and beloved, put on tender mercies, kindness, humility, meekness, longsuffering; bearing with one another, and forgiving one another, if anyone has a complaint against another; even as Christ forgave you, so you also must do. But above all these things put on love, which is the bond of perfection.

(Colossians 3:12-14)

We do tend to fall out with one another when we permit our *flesh* to pop up above the parapet. It keeps trying to override our spirit. It's a sad fact of life that not even the best human relationships achieve perfection on a consistent 24/7 basis. But that is the target.

That is the standard set before us. When we fall short of the glory of God, we need to put things right with one another (and with Him) as soon as conviction overtakes us. This is intended to be our default action to *maintain* unity in the bond of peace.

Christ Jesus came into the world to save sinners, of whom I am chief. However, for this reason, I obtained mercy, that in me, first, Jesus Christ might show all longsuffering, as a pattern to those who are going to believe on Him for everlasting life.

(1Timothy 1:15b-16)

When we hit a bump in the road in our relationships, we need to remember something simple. When we point our forefinger at someone else, there are three other fingers pointing back at us. Let our focus be on our part in the problem, not that of the other person. Let us seek to put things right from that perspective. We cannot be responsible for the other person's response, only for our own *(Romans 12:18)*.

The Lord is not slack concerning His promise, as some count slackness, but is longsuffering toward us, not willing that any should perish but that all should come to repentance.

(2 Peter 3:9)

Sometimes, when we are preaching, teaching, or evangelising our listeners don't seem to *get it*. When that happens, let us learn to be patient with them. Don't give up. Don't walk away. Don't look for greener pastures. Listen for the voice of God and respond obediently to Him.

His timing is always perfect. He alone knows when a person is *ready* to enter His Kingdom. We can be carried away by our own enthusiasm and our desire to obtain a *scalp*.

Peter makes the point that God Himself is longsuffering with His stubborn and stiff-necked people. His love and compassion for them overrides any thought of writing them off. As if He would have such thoughts! But *we* can, and we do, so we need to follow His example and graciously persist.

Preach the word! Be ready in season and out of season. Convince, rebuke, exhort, with all longsuffering and teaching.

(2 Timothy 4:2)

At those times when we need to be longsuffering with one another, it is important that we *keep our love on*, as Danny Silk would put it. Avoid falling out with one another, especially over trivial matters. We may be convinced that we are right, and the other person is wrong.

Nevertheless, we need to be careful about pursuing our argument if, at that time, it is unlikely that they are ready to change their minds. For clarity, I am not advocating compromise. Instead to lay aside our strongly held opinions until a more opportune time for an amicable discussion.

We really need to listen to Holy Spirit so that we press on, gently, only when He prompts us to. It is selfish to prioritise winning an argument over keeping a friend. Trusting in God's timing makes far more sense. He is more than capable of choosing the right moment and the right way to bring correction.

Kindness

Goodwill, understanding, charity, grace, humanity, affection, patience, tolerance, goodness, compassion, hospitality, generosity, indulgence, decency, tenderness, clemency, gentleness, philanthropy, benevolence, magnanimity, fellow-feeling, amiability, beneficence.

(thefreedictionary.com)

We aim to learn to love others as God loves us. To let His compassion flow through us unhindered towards them. One way to do this is through *random acts of kindness*. Kindness is not meant to be an abstract quality. On the contrary, it's something demonstrated through actions: *doings*.

Paul includes kindness right in the middle of the following passage. I have included the whole thing because it seems good to me to see it in the full context of what Paul is conveying through these verses. In the midst of all manner of negative experiences, the positives shine through.

Clearly, Paul *paid a price* in realising a fruitful and effective ministry. We must come to terms with the prospect of encountering such things if we choose to follow a similar path in responding to God's call upon our lives. We are ambassadors of a heavenly Kingdom that is invading a hostile planet, thanks to the *prince of this world (Ephesians 2:2)*.

We give no offense in anything, that our ministry may not be blamed. But in all things we commend ourselves as ministers of God: in much patience, in tribulations, in needs, in distresses, in stripes, in imprisonments, in tumults, in labours, in sleeplessness, in fasting; by purity, by knowledge, by longsuffering, by kindness, by the Holy Spirit, by sincere love, by the word of truth, by the power of God, by the armour of righteousness on the right hand and on the left, by honour and dishonour, by evil report and good report; as deceivers, and yet true; as unknown, and yet well known; as dying, and behold we live; as chastened, and yet not killed; as sorrowful, yet always rejoicing; as poor, yet making many rich; as having nothing, and yet possessing all things.

(2 Corinthians 6:3-10)

Having already responded to the gospel, however it was preached or made known to them, the blessed ones have experienced the kindness of God. It is good, and humbling, to consider from time to time all the things we have been rescued from and brought through. All courtesy of the unlimited kindness of God. And, of course, when the time comes, we go to a much better place that He has already prepared for us.

But God, who is rich in mercy, because of His great love with which He loved us, even when we were dead in trespasses, made us alive together with Christ (by grace you have been saved), and raised us up together, and made us sit together in the heavenly places in Christ Jesus, that in the ages to come He might show the exceeding riches of His grace in His kindness toward us in Christ Jesus.

(Ephesians 2:4-7)

In recalling, contemplating, and meditating upon the kindnesses of God towards us, it becomes ever more beholden upon us to treat those around us in the same way. Thankfully, God has made it possible for us to do that, because of His Spirit within us.

It has been said, "We become like the one we worship."

My prayer is that we will hear, "Well done, my good and faithful servant," because we have wisely invested all the kindness and other qualities He has entrusted us with.

Therefore, as the elect of God, holy and beloved, put on tender mercies, kindness, humility, meekness, longsuffering; bearing with one another, and forgiving one another, if anyone has a complaint against another; even as Christ forgave you, so you also must do. But above all these things put on love, which is the bond of perfection. And let the peace of God rule in your hearts

(Colossians 3:12-15a)

It is, or should be, much easier for us to be gracious and compassionate towards the people who cross our paths from time to time, by not forgetting what we were like before we were saved by grace.

For we ourselves were also once foolish, disobedient, deceived, serving various lusts and pleasures, living in malice and envy, hateful and hating one another. But when the kindness and the love of God our Saviour toward man appeared, not by works of righteousness which we have done, but according to His mercy He saved us, through the washing of regeneration and renewing of the Holy Spirit,

(Titus 3:3-5)

It seems to go against the grain of what I have been writing so far in this book when we find what Peter writes in the following verses. Other translations exhort us to *make every effort to add*. Yet we have already concluded that we cannot either achieve or add to our salvation by our own efforts.

But also, for this very reason, giving all diligence, add to your faith virtue, to virtue knowledge, to knowledge self-control, to self-control perseverance, to perseverance godliness, to godliness brotherly kindness, and to brotherly kindness love.

(2 Peter 1:5-7)

To be consistent with other Holy Spirit-inspired scriptures, it cannot be that Peter is calling us back. Of course, he isn't. Despite what many unbelievers would contend, the Bible is not full of contradictions. A careful reading, after asking Holy Spirit to guide and teach us, will lead us to the truth of what is being said to us.

My contention is that Peter is focussing on our cooperation with Holy Spirit in the process of sanctification. I have been emphasising that, at every turn of the road of life, we are faced with choices. We can either go God's way (of the spirit) or the *old man's* way of the *flesh*.

Peter, in my opinion, is encouraging us to make every effort to reject the *flesh* and choose the way of the Spirit. Doing so with confidence that enabling grace is released in us as that right choice is made. Kindness is not the only fruit of the spirit in Peter's list. We have already established that it is the grace and power of God in us that enables us to be spiritually fruitful.

Christian maturity is marked by the progression of the changes in our character that will produce *fruit that will last* (John 15:8).

Goodness

The state or quality of being ***good****; moral excellence; virtue; kindly feeling; kindness; generosity; a euphemism for God: (Thank goodness).*

(dictionary.com)

One of my favourite contemporary Christian worship songs, at the time of writing, is *Goodness of God*, from Bethel Music. If you are not familiar with it, then let me encourage you to track it down on YouTube. Just let the words flow over you and refresh your spirit. Goodness is the essence of God. *God is good* is one of the fundamental truths undergirding the culture of Bethel Church, Redding; and something for us all to absorb.

And he (Moses) *said, "Please, show me Your glory."*
Then He (God) said, "I will make all My goodness pass before you, and I will proclaim the name of the Lord before you."

(Exodus 33:18-19a)

Moses had found much favour with the Lord and so he boldly, but humbly, asked to see God's glory. What God revealed to Him, in answer to that request, was His goodness. God and goodness are inseparably one. He *is* goodness.

So, whenever we say, "Thank goodness," I believe we are simply saying, "Thank God,"—even if we don't realise it.

Or do you despise the riches of His goodness, forbearance, and longsuffering, not knowing that the Goodness of God leads you to repentance?

(Romans 2:4)

The original Greek word is usually translated as either *goodness* or *kindness* in our English versions of the Bible. Either conveys essentially the same truth. A compassionate, gracious God seeks to draw us to Himself by stretching out His loving arms towards us. He doesn't threaten us with His wrath so that we come to Him out of fear instead of (voluntarily) loving Him through recognising that He has first loved us *(1 John 4:19)*.

Therefore, consider the goodness and severity of God: on those who fell, severity; but toward you, goodness, if you continue in His goodness.

(Romans 11:22a)

Nevertheless, as Paul spells out to the Christians in Rome, He is a God of Justice. First towards the Jews and then the Gentiles. He makes Himself available to us all (I do not claim to understand exactly how this works, but I trust Him) and gives us free will to make our own choices.

If we receive Jesus, then the wrath and justice we deserve have been put on Him, at Calvary, on our behalf. If we reject Jesus, then He cannot stand before the judgement seat in our place, and we must take the consequences.

Now I myself am confident concerning you, my brethren, that you also are full of goodness, filled with all knowledge, able also to admonish one another.

(Romans 15:14)

The blessed ones have been born again by the Spirit of God. They are new creations, being transformed into His likeness. Aspects of His character will begin to be seen in us. Therefore, something of *His* goodness, for example, will become evident in the way we conduct ourselves.

For you were once darkness, but now you are light in the Lord. Walk as children of light (for the fruit of the Spirit is in all goodness, righteousness, and truth), finding out what is acceptable to the Lord.

(Ephesians 5:8-10)

When we have, by the grace of God, been transferred out of the kingdom of darkness into the Kingdom of Light, we are gifted with the ability to live our lives in harmony with His Kingdom. We can bear spiritual fruit to the glory of God.

Therefore, we also pray always for you that our God would count you worthy of this calling and fulfil all the good pleasure of His goodness and the work of faith with power, that the name of our Lord Jesus Christ may be glorified in you, and you in Him, according to the grace of our God and the Lord Jesus Christ.

(2 Thessalonians 1:11-12)

As representatives of Jesus on this planet, we are graced with the ability, at least in potential, to do the things that He did. By grace, we can live our lives as He lived His. Just as Jesus perfectly represented the Father on Earth *(Hebrews 1:3)*, so we are called and enabled to represent Him too. This scripture makes it clear that something of His goodness can be seen in us as we exercise faith and release His power in our communities. Ministering always in the name, power, and authority of Jesus to the glory of God.

Faithfulness

Faithfulness is the concept of unfailingly remaining loyal to someone or something and putting that loyalty into consistent practice regardless of extenuating circumstances. It can also mean keeping one's promises no matter the prevailing circumstances, such as God's covenant to love his people. Literally, it is the state of being full of faith in the sense of steady devotion to a person, thing, or concept.

(en.wikipedia.org)

Our understanding of faithfulness comes from seeing and experiencing the faithfulness of God towards His people. His character is consistent under both the old and new covenants. The people of Israel were often unfaithful in former times. We ourselves are not incapable of letting Him down. Yet He remains true to His character. He remains faithful always.

Through the Lord's mercies, we are not consumed, because His compassions fail not. They are new every morning; great is Your faithfulness.

(Lamentations 3:22-23)

Through the prophet Hosea and, I believe, to help us to understand better His intentions, God demonstrates what this faithfulness means. He illustrates it for us within the context of engagement (betrothal) before marriage.

I will betroth you to Me forever; Yes, I will betroth you to Me in righteousness and justice, in lovingkindness and mercy; I will betroth you to Me in faithfulness, and you shall know the Lord.

(Hosea 2:19-20)

God is faithful because, in effect, He *is* faithfulness. That is a very important aspect of His divine character. Just as He *is* Love, Joy, Peace, etc. If He were to be unfaithful, for even a moment, it would be a denial of Himself, of who He is. That's something which *is* impossible for God, who will always be true to Himself.

This is a faithful saying: 'For if we died with Him, we shall also live with Him. If we endure, we shall also reign with Him. If we deny Him, He also will deny us. If we are faithless, He remains faithful; He cannot deny Himself.'

(2 Timothy 2:11-13)

There is an inevitability about our stumbling and falling occasionally. Especially when our faith is tested by trials or temptations. Even so, His faithfulness will sustain us. We can return to Him, under conviction of sin, confessing our failing with true repentance. We will find Him standing by to help us through.

No temptation has overtaken you except such as is common to man; but God is faithful, who will not allow you to be tempted beyond what you are able, but with the temptation will also make the way of escape, that you may be able to bear it.

(1 Corinthians 10:13)

It is very important to have faithfulness established in our own lives. Especially if we are asking God to trust us in increasing measure with His various giftings to be expressed through us for the common good. Just as sanctification is a process over time, faithfulness develops in us as we mature in Him. The more we mature in Him the more He can trust us with powerful ministry in His Name. His faithfulness will respond to our growing maturity.

He who is faithful in what is least is faithful also in much; and, and he who is unjust in what is least is unjust also in much. Therefore, if you have not been faithful in the unrighteous mammon [i.e., money], *who will commit to your trust the true riches?*

(Luke 16:10-11)

His faithfulness towards us is such that we can be sustained through both times of blessing and times of difficulty. When we put our trust in Him in every single circumstance of our lives, we, too, are being faithful. By His grace, we can emulate His faithfulness in our relationships with our brothers and sisters in Christ. Even when they may say or do things that cause us pain for a season.

Gentleness

A common misconception is that gentleness is weakness or passivity. True gentleness, however, is just the opposite. It requires great strength and self-control. Gentleness comes from a state of humility. Someone who lacks gentleness is often prideful and easily angered or feels the need for revenge.

(gcu.edu)

Those of us of a certain age will probably recall singing as children about *Gentle Jesus, meek and mild.* Jesus was all of those things, but He could never be described as *weak*. Surely nobody who has ever lived can have demonstrated greater strength of character than Him.

He laid aside His Majesty and deity and came from Heaven to Earth to seek and save the lost. To restore the broken relationship between God and mankind. We know only too well all the things He endured in order to complete His mission. Yet He was always gentle. Except with the demonic realm and the religious hypocrites of the day, that is.

Come to Me, all you who labour and are heavy heavily laden, and I will give you rest. Take My yoke upon you and learn from Me, for I am gentle and lowly in heart, and you will find rest for your souls. For My yoke is easy and My burden is light.

(Matthew 11:28-30)

It is vitally important that church leaders are gentle, but firm, with members of their church families. Especially in situations where a degree of discipline is to be exercised.

Brethren, if a man is overtaken in any trespass, you who are spiritual restore such a one in a spirit of gentleness, considering yourself lest you also be tempted.

(Galatians 6:1)

We are inclined to deem punishment to be the essential remedy, placing that ahead of restoration. If someone is caught in a misdemeanour and is genuinely prepared to confess and repent, why do we still so often prioritise punishment over restoration? We strip them of their position within the church, at least temporarily. Then we send them off to meditate upon their failure until such time as *we* consider they are ready to be restored.

Now I, Paul, myself am pleading with you by the meekness and gentleness of Christ.

(2 Corinthians 10:1a)

It is different, of course, if the person is *not* prepared to acknowledge their error, even when it is established by two or three witnesses (*Matthew 18:16*). It is important that we establish a Culture of Honour [1] within our churches, not least when it comes to providing discipline. Gentleness but firmness, backed by spiritual authority, should be employed. And always with the primary aim of restoration.

Gentleness, of course, is not solely an important requisite of the disciplinary process, but of our lives as a whole. How can we be loving and not gentle with people, both inside and outside of the church? Gentleness is implicit in God's kindness/goodness that leads to repentance *(Romans 2:4)*.

It applies whether we are dealing with church family members or pre-Christians whom we have encountered on the streets. It is a characteristic of Jesus that it is vital for us to walk in (by His Spirit), but without compromise.

I, therefore, the prisoner of the Lord, beseech you to walk worthy of the calling with which you were called, with all lowliness and gentleness, with longsuffering, bearing with one another in love, endeavouring to keep the unity of the Spirit in the bond of peace.

(Ephesians 4:1-3)

Notice again that the bond of peace is something we keep, not create. Jesus is the ultimate peacemaker and the unity of peace (and love) that is found in the Godhead is something in which every believer is called to participate *(2 Peter 1:4).* If the Gentle One is present with us and in us, how can we be less than gentle with one another?

Let your gentleness be known to all men. The Lord is at hand.

(Philippians 4:5)

Paul writes to Timothy about negatives like the love of money and encourages him not to be taken up by such things but to pursue positives, including gentleness. And that is a Holy Spirit-inspired word for each of us, not just for him.

But you, O man of God, flee these things and pursue righteousness, godliness, faith, love, patience, gentleness.

(1 Timothy 6:11)

"Gently does it."

Self-control

Restraint is exercised over one's own impulses, emotions, or desires.

(merriam-webster.com)

We are often inclined to react very negatively towards those who offend us in some way. Whatever guises we may dress up our anger and indignation in, it is invariably little more than a desire for revenge, for retribution. That is not the way Jesus responded or wants us to respond to provocation.

Jesus rebuked James and John saying, *Don't you realise what spews from your hearts when you say that? (Luke 9:55, TPT)*

He was concerned at the lack of self-control prompting their request for punishment to be inflicted on the people they felt were doing things which only Jesus and His disciples were authorised to do.

In both the following verses from the NKJV, the NIV translates the references to ruling over one's spirit as self-control. In the first instance, one who is self-controlled is equated with someone who is slow to anger, someone who can control their temper. In the second example, a person lacking self-control is considered to be defenceless, and wide open to being taken advantage of by our enemy.

He who is slow to anger is better than the mighty, and he who rules his spirit than he who takes a city.

(Proverbs 16:32)

Whoever has no rule over his own spirit is like a city broken down, without walls.

(Proverbs 25:28)

Saul of Tarsus was a fiery zealot for the traditional Jewish religious lifestyle. He showed no restraint when he oversaw and approved the stoning of Stephen. This continued when, as authorised by the Jewish leaders, he travelled about to hunt down Christians to have them imprisoned or even executed. Following his conversion, and as he matured as a Christian, he changed dramatically. He provided an excellent example for new believers.

Now as he (Paul) *reasoned about righteousness, self-control, and the judgment to come, Felix was afraid and answered, "Go away for now; when I have a convenient time, I will call for you."*

(Acts 24:25)

Never was this more striking than when he suffered at the hands of the Jewish authorities himself. Particularly true in Jerusalem and when he had to be taken under guard to Caesarea for his own protection. It is interesting that he was talking about self-control when he appeared before Felix.

Clearly this caused the latter to suffer a crisis of conscience when he seemingly came under conviction. Even to the extent that he struggled to handle that situation wisely. Fear triumphed over a potential change of heart (and life).

But know this, that in the last days, perilous times will come: for men will be lovers of themselves, lovers of money, boasters, proud, blasphemers, disobedient to parents, unthankful, unholy, unloving, unforgiving, slanderers, without self-control, brutal, despisers of good, traitors, headstrong, haughty, lovers of pleasure rather than lovers of God, having a form of godliness but denying its power. And from such people turn away!

(2 Timothy 3:1-5)

Not only when he spoke but also in his letters Paul clearly placed great emphasis upon the need for self-control to be exercised. He said it would be sadly lacking in the lives of so many who did not repent and turn to Jesus. Peter takes up a similar theme. In his second epistle, he presents it in a more positive scenario. He exhorts us to lead lives that are marked by both this and other expressions of the fruit of the spirit.

But also, for this very reason, giving all diligence, add to your faith virtue, to virtue knowledge, to knowledge self-control, to self-control perseverance, to perseverance godliness, to godliness brotherly kindness, and to brotherly kindness love. For if these things are yours and abound, you will be neither barren nor unfruitful in the knowledge of our Lord Jesus Christ.

(2 Peter 1:5-8)

Again, I am sure it is obvious that the *knowledge* Peter refers to here is not an intellectual grasp of facts and information. It's not simply a knowing *about* Jesus, but a growing, intimate, *relational* knowledge *of* Him.

Against such, there is no law.

The fruit of the spirit may be expressed in and through us in a wide variety of ways. However, if it happens, it will always be a product of the amazing grace of God. He abides in us, and we abide in Him. His grace makes it possible for us to bear much fruit. Although such fruitfulness will not be confined exclusively to the nine examples provided in Galatians.

I am the vine; you are the branches. He who abides in Me, and I in him, bears much fruit; for without Me, you can do nothing.

(John 15:5)

When we live out this fruitful life, it derives solely from the Spirit of God at work in us. It is expressed through the righteous things we think, say, and do. In doing thus, it is impossible for us to be transgressors of the law. We are living in Christ, and He is the fulfilment of the law *(Matthew 5:17)*. Keeping the law, without striving to do so, is an inevitable fruit of a naturally supernatural lifestyle.

For the law was given through Moses, but grace and truth came through Jesus Christ.

(John 1:17)

When our lives are marked by *love, joy, peace, longsuffering, kindness, goodness, faithfulness, gentleness* (or) *self-control,* we are living as Jesus lived. This is the fulfilment of His perfect will and purpose for us. It was what His death, resurrection and ascension were intended to bring about. The fact that He was prepared to go to the cross to make this possible for each one of us, is a perfect illustration of the unlimited love of God for mankind.

1. For more on this subject, I thoroughly recommend *'Culture of Honour'* by Danny Silk, Copyright © 2019, Destiny Image Publishers Inc.

4
Blessed by Abundant Life

A.

The thief does not come except to steal, and to kill, and to destroy.
I have come that they may have life,
and that they may have it more abundantly.

(John 10:10)

No doubt there are many and varied opinions about what constitutes a life which can be accurately described as *abundant*. I am offering my personal opinion here, based on my understanding of scripture and a little experience.

An abundant life is a Holy Spirit-empowered life that, to some degree, reflects the perfect example set for us by Jesus Christ as the Son of Man. It is the free and fulfilled spiritual life that only He can provide. It is enabled exclusively by grace, through faith. This life expresses good spiritual fruit and facilitates the exercise of spiritual gifts for the common good. In fact, it is the antithesis of religious systems based on duty and performance instead of on love and grace.

This abundant lifestyle does not meet with universal approval because of an enemy who is totally opposed to it. He is against anyone who seeks to live it out to the glory of God. Our enemy seeks only to steal, to kill and to destroy.

He does this either in an effort to keep people from entering the Kingdom in the first place or, if that strategy fails, to prevent, or limit, their fruitfulness as citizens of the Kingdom.

When Jesus came to Earth, He brought His Kingdom with Him. He made it possible for us to enter that Kingdom so that we may be blessed with *every spiritual blessing in the heavenly places in Christ (Ephesians 1:3)*. To be in that precious position, of course, we have first to be gifted with **abundant** life through being born again of the Spirit of God *(John 3:3)*.

In Him was life, and the life was the light of men.

(John 1:4)

Abundant life was revealed to us in the life of Jesus of Nazareth (who never ceased to be the eternal Son of God) during the three or so years of His ministry on Earth. I believe He was also modelling that life, as the Son of Man, for us to aspire to and to emulate—insofar as that is possible for us (in Him).

The extent of that possibility goes beyond anything I was taught both at the beginning of my Christian Walk and for (too) many years afterwards. My hope and my prayer is that, you do not find yourself in a similar situation.

Or, if you do, those days will come to an end very soon. We live an abundant life by faith, which reminds me of something I read recently, *Faith thinks and sees outside the box*. Let's remember that truth, especially if the *box* is religiosity.

For if, by the trespass of the one man, death reigned through that one man, how much more will those who receive God's abundant provision of grace and of the gift of righteousness reign in **life** *through the one man, Jesus Christ!*

(Romans 5:17)

We believers know that, in coming to Christ, we receive forgiveness of our sins. And we will meet Him face to face when we die physically and go to be with Him in Heaven. For many of us, the abundance of that life seemed to consist of acquiring ever-increasing knowledge about Him and His Word. That was certainly where I was at one time.

There is nothing wrong with either of these things, of course. However, they do not necessarily constitute spiritual abundance. At least not the abundance that I believe we are promised when we embark on the life of the Spirit. Knowledge is only part of living out our relationship with God, not the goal of it!

An abundant provision of grace enables an abundant life. A life which means that we can reign with Him in life *now*—not just in life after physical death! When we are born again, we become new creations. The old has gone—the new has come.

The *old man* is not just patched up and sent on his way to make the best of it this side of Heaven. He/she becomes a new person, blessed with a new (spiritual) source of life. This blessing is meant to be shared with others in order to bless them. The gospels show clearly how Jesus modelled this **abundant** life for us. *Christian* means *little Christ*. We are created in His image to do good works, even greater works than He did. My Bible says so!

Enter by the narrow gate; for wide is the gate and broad is the way that leads to destruction, and there are many who go in by it. Because narrow is the gate and difficult is the way which leads to life, and there are few who find it.

(Matthew 7:13-14)

We have come through that narrow gate, from darkness into light. We have left behind the rule and reign of the prince of this world. True, whether or not we realised that we were under it. We have become subjects of the King of kings and Lord of lords. He has called us, and He will equip us for everything He wants us to do to extend His Kingdom here on Earth.

Jesus answered and said to her, "Whoever drinks of this water will thirst again, but whoever drinks of the water that I shall give him will never thirst. But the water that I shall give him will become in him a fountain of water springing up into everlasting life."

(John 4:13-14)

The *water* that Jesus gives us is, of course, Holy Spirit. It is Holy Spirit who has brought us into this new, abundant life. He has, in a sense, invaded our space. He has revealed Jesus to us, convicted us of our need for Him and given us new birth.

He does not stop there although, sadly, that is where some Christians do stop. There are still those who do not accept what is called the *baptism of the Holy Spirit*, even though it is a totally biblical concept. We cannot possibly emulate the life of Jesus of Nazareth unless we are baptised in Holy Spirit to equip us for life and ministry, as He was.

Jesus was baptised by John in the Jordan. Not because he needed a baptism of repentance (as we do) but to model that experience for us. As He came up out of the water, Holy Spirit descended from Heaven like a dove. He alighted upon the Son of Man and remained. In this way, Jesus also modelled for us the *second baptism*, as some describe it.

You search the Scriptures, for in them you think you have eternal life; and these are they which testify of Me. But you are not willing to come to Me that you may have life.

(John 5:39-40)

I am at a loss to understand how so many can read all this in the scriptures and yet not recognise that we are all invited to share both immersion experiences. We find in the gospels that the Pharisees and other learned Jews saw and heard all that Jesus was doing and saying.

Still, they failed to understand that He was the embodiment of the Messiah as revealed in so many places in the Old Testament. The very scriptures that they studied to the *nth* degree! The blind man (see John 9) had no such trouble when he experienced what Jesus did for Him!

And Jesus said to them, "I am the bread of life. He who comes to Me shall never hunger, and he who believes in Me shall never thirst."

(John 6:35)

Abundant life requires us to be fed a diet rich in spiritual nutrients. In Part One, we looked at how those who hunger and thirst after righteousness, or the Righteous One, will be filled, will be satisfied. In the Spirit of Jesus, we find everything we need to sustain our abundant lives here on Earth for all the (remaining) days of our lives. He is the Bread of Life who provides the water of life just as He is the Vine who supports and sustains the branches (us).

It is the Spirit who gives life; the flesh profits nothing. The words that I speak to you are spirit, and they are life.

(John 6:63)

Abundant life is the supernatural life of the Spirit, released by the Spirit of God into the spirits of mankind. We have left behind the life of the flesh, the unregenerate body and soul. It no longer has dominion over us. Insofar as we do not come into agreement with it, that is.

And with our enemy who tempts us through it. That which we think, say, or do in the spirit produces fruit and works with a Kingdom value. Nothing produced by the flesh, even at its best, can ever come close.

*Jesus said to her, "I am the resurrection and the **life**. He who believes in Me, though he may die, he shall live. And whoever lives and believes in Me shall never die. Do you believe this?"*

(John 11:25-26)

In raising Lazarus from the dead, Jesus demonstrated the power that He stewarded. He carried an abundance of life that could even conquer death. That life is now in us. That life enables us to be overcomers and to do the things that Jesus did. We need only submit ourselves to Him. Just as He modelled for us, we can say what we *hear* the Spirit *saying* to us. We can do what we *see* Him *doing*.

I put those words in italics simply because Holy Spirit does not only communicate with us through an audible voice or a vision. I have already provided several alternative examples when looking at the various ways *words* of knowledge can be received from Him.

Jesus said to him, "I am the way, the truth, and the life. No one comes to the Father, except through Me."

(John 14:6)

Jesus is the only One through whom we can receive the abundant Life of which He speaks. We believe also that He is the only Way to the Father. The only one who can restore that relationship with God which was broken at in the Fall. In addition, we believe that He is the embodiment of Truth.

And this is eternal life, that they may know You, the only true God, and Jesus Christ whom You have sent.

(John 17:3)

Eternal life and abundant life are, I believe, synonymous. They speak of a restored relationship with the Godhead. That restored relationship was the reason for the incarnation as well as the death, resurrection and ascension of Jesus Christ, the Son of Man, the Son of God.

Knowing Him, not simply *about* Him, is the supreme purpose of our lives on Earth. And the joy is that this intimacy of relationship will continue even after we breathe our last breath. He has given us everlasting life to enjoy with Him for ever.

For the letter kills, but the Spirit gives life.

(2 Corinthians 3:6b)

Religiosity brings us rules and regulations and invariably overlooks grace. A total dependency upon works in a vain attempt to obtain salvation and/or sanctification. Religion is death to us, but the Spirit is, and brings, Life. The sad thing is the extent to which the church so easily absorbs *rules-based* or *works* versions of life. Even what we might call the *liveliest* of churches are not necessarily totally immune from this error.

Wherever and whenever we find grace and rehabilitation set aside in favour of some form of discipline, in the form of punishment, for the genuinely repentant, religion has circumvented life in the Spirit. Finding ourselves sticking rigidly to the letter, rather than the spirit, of the law, is the most obvious warning indicator.

And this is the testimony: that God has given us eternal life, and this life is in His Son. He who has the Son has life; he who does not have the Son of God does not have life.

(1 John 5:11-12)

"*I have come that they may have life,*" Jesus said.

John expands upon this phrase in order to make its meaning perfectly clear to us. If we want Life, we need Jesus and Jesus alone. Without Him, we cannot have His Life in us. We are lost and hopeless, adrift in a world under the (temporary) control and influence of the enemy of our souls. Just as Moses set a choice before the Israelites in the desert *(Deuteronomy 30:19-20)*, so we have a choice set before us. Jesus and abundant life—or neither of those.

Let me close this half of the chapter by quoting these glorious words of life from the end of the last book of the Bible:

And he showed me a pure river of water of life, clear as crystal, proceeding from the throne of God and of the Lamb. In the middle of its street, and on either side of the river, was the tree of life, which bore 12 fruits, each tree yielding its fruit every month. The leaves of the tree were for the healing of the nations. And there shall be no more curse, but the throne of God and of the Lamb shall be in it, and His servants shall serve Him. They shall see His face, and His name shall be on their foreheads. There shall be no night there. They need no lamp nor light of the sun, for the Lord God gives them light. And they shall reign forever and ever.

(Revelation 22:1-5)

B.

I have been crucified with Christ;
it is no longer I who live, but Christ lives in me;
*and the **life** which I now live in the flesh I live by faith in* (of)
the Son of God, who loved me and gave Himself for me.

(Galatians 2:20)

In the first part of this chapter, I have sought to refresh our memories with regard to the abundant life that God, in His amazing grace, has richly provided for us. Now I would like to explore a little more of the practicalities of the day-to-day living out of this life. I have chosen the above verse from Galatians as a lead into what my thoughts are on this subject.

I would also recommend a thorough study of Romans 6-8. There, a Holy Spirit-inspired Paul sets out in detail the transition from death to life that each of us goes through. It begins as a once-and-forever change at conversion. It also works out on a day-to-day basis experientially until we are called *home*.

And so it is written, The first man Adam became a living being (soul). *The last Adam became a life-giving spirit* (pneuma).

(1 Corinthians 15:45)

For each one of us, our natural, physical life derives from our one common ancestor, Adam. Jesus Christ is the last Adam. As we know already, our supernatural, spiritual life derives from Him. We are born again spiritually whilst we are still alive physically. When we die physically, we remain alive spiritually with Him forever (and with a glorious, new body).

For the wages of sin is death, but the gift of God is eternal life in Christ Jesus our Lord.

(Romans 6:23)

When Adam sinned, the entire human race was affected throughout the history of this world. We inherited a sinful nature from him. Consequently, each one of us has sinned, thereby falling short of the glory of God, which is perfection. His absolutely perfect purity and holiness.

For the law of the Spirit of life in Christ Jesus has made me free from the law of sin and death.

(Romans 8:2)

There are spiritual laws just as there are physical laws. I am not referring to *rules* that have to be kept but *laws* that can be observed. An obvious example is the *law* of gravity. If I drop an object, a handkerchief perhaps, it will always fall straight to the ground.

Nothing can prevent that unless I catch it before it lands. That means something stronger has to intervene to prevent the inevitable consequence of the original action.

Death is the inevitable consequence of sin, which Paul describes as the *law of sin and death*. But Jesus is stronger. Through our faith in His death and resurrection on our behalf, we are saved from the consequences of our sins by *the law of the Spirit of Life* in Him.

But if the Spirit of Him who raised Jesus from the dead dwells in you, He who raised Christ from the dead will also give life to your mortal bodies through His Spirit who dwells in you.

(Romans 8:11)

When we receive Jesus as our Lord and Saviour, we are born again through the work of Holy Spirit, who comes to dwell in us. Our mortal bodies now receive a new *source* of life. An uncreated Life which is the essence of the Godhead. When we undergo baptism in water, this is what that act of faith is representing, both to us and those who witness it happening.

Baptism in water is an illustration of the spiritual reality of the death and resurrection of Jesus being shared by us. This is something Paul expects us to know, according to the New King James translation.

The Passion Translation emphasises that by asking instead, "Have you forgotten?"

Do you not know that as many of us as were baptised into Christ Jesus were baptised into His death? Therefore, we were buried with Him through baptism into death, that just as Christ was raised from the dead by the glory of the Father, even so, we also should walk in the newness of life.

(Roman 6:3-4)

Baptism illustrates that we are co-buried with Him so that we can share in His triumph over sin and death. Not by our own worthiness but through faith in His alone. This is not something I was taught until I had been a Christian for several years.

I am concerned that this may be true of too many other believers down the years. It is a fundamental spiritual truth we should all be familiar with from the beginning of our new life in Him. There is more, of course.

For if we have been united together in the likeness of His death, certainly we also shall be in the likeness of His resurrection, knowing this, that our old man was crucified with Him, that the body of sin might be done away with, that we should no longer be slaves of sin. For he who has died has been freed from sin. Now, if we died with Christ, we believe that we shall also live with Him, knowing that Christ, having been raised from the dead, dies no more.

Death no longer has dominion over Him. For the death that He died, He died to sin once and for all; but the life that He lives, He lives to God. Likewise, you also, reckon yourselves to be dead indeed to sin, but alive to God in Christ Jesus our Lord.

(Romans 6:5-11)

Death could not hold the sinless Son of Man. He conquered it and was raised to life. He had a new resurrection body that could even pass through a wall or a locked door *(John 20:19, 26)*. Being co-resurrected with Him, we are enabled to step into a new (source of) life for the remainder of our days on Earth (by reckoning ourselves dead to sin) and ever after.

It is surely an indisputable fact that dead people cannot sin. We have shared in the death and resurrection of Jesus. Therefore, in our new life, we are also dead to sin. So, it must be that old 'flesh' life of ours that remains susceptible to temptations.

[18] For I know that in me (that is, in my flesh) nothing good dwells; for to will is present with me, but how to perform what is good I do not find. [19] For the good that I will to do, I do not do; but the evil I will not to do, that I practice. [20] Now if I do what I will not to do, it is no longer I who do it, but sin that dwells in me.

(Romans 7:18-20)

When we are tempted, we can stand firm in our faith in the efficacy of what Jesus has done for us. We can employ the spiritual power of this new life to say *No* to every temptation of our flesh. Our flesh will not die until our bodies finally do. In the meantime, we can rely upon that new spiritual source of life to empower our mortal bodies *(Romans 8:11)*. We just have to *reckon* it to be so. The word translated as *reckon* is a pure mathematical term. Remember, mathematics is an exact science, so this reckoning is not wishful thinking!

I have been crucified with Christ; it is no longer I who live, but Christ lives in me; and the life which I now live in the flesh I live by faith in (of) *the Son of God, who loved me and gave Himself for me.*

(Galatians 2:20)

Most English translations of the Bible refer to faith *in* the Son of God in this verse. I understand a more accurate translation would use the word *of* instead of *in* (as The Passion does). I live my new supernatural life by the faith *of* the Son of God. He went to the cross for you and me in certain *faith* that His Father would reward Him with *the joy set before Him* (Hebrews 12:2). The joy that motivated His supreme sacrifice was made so that *we* would be saved!

We *know* that we have been co-crucified with Christ, and co-resurrected with Him. Therefore, we should *know* that the old mortal body-life no longer has the power to control us. This new life that we now live in the flesh is more powerful. It is the hand that can stop gravity from taking my falling handkerchief right down to the ground.

In addition, we should know that God will always provide a way out when we are tempted *(1 Corinthians 10:13)*. But we still have a *choice* to make. Do we follow the flesh and give into temptation? Or do we go with our empowered spirit and whatever way out God provides?

Our free will is never violated by God. But our new life source is powerful enough to resist every temptation that comes our way. The more we choose to follow the Spirit, the more we will upset our enemy. That means we can expect to be targeted by him.

And he who does not take his cross and follow after Me is not worthy of Me. He who finds his (soul) *life will lose it, and he who loses his* (soul) *life for My sake will find it.*

(Matthew 10:38-39)

We can deny the old ways of life by resisting temptation. Such denial of the flesh is what I believe taking up our cross to follow Jesus means. I understand the original Greek of the above verse to refer to a soul-based life. Sadly, our English translations often do not convey that depth of meaning.

The soul is the seat of our mind, will and emotions. Before we were born again and entered the life of the Spirit the (soul) life would have dominated us. Now our spirits have been quickened with new life. Now our spirit is enabled to reign over both the soul and the body. In harmony with Holy Spirit that will always be the case. Except when we exercise our free will and make wrong choices.

For he who sows to his flesh will of the flesh reap corruption, but he who sows to the Spirit will of the Spirit reap everlasting life.

(Galatians 6:8)

When we exercise our free will to make choices, we are either *sowing* to the flesh or to the Spirit. The spirit is always willing, but the flesh is often weak. The irony of that is that such weakness of the flesh can sometimes be strong enough to influence our choices wrongly.

The spirit will always be stronger than the flesh. But not to the extent that it will be permitted to override our free will. We are not robots or puppets; we must always choose where we *sow*.

Grace and peace be multiplied to you in the knowledge of God and of Jesus our Lord, as His divine power has given to us all things that pertain to life and godliness, through the knowledge of Him who called us by glory and virtue, by which have been given to us exceedingly great and precious promises, that through these you may be partakers of the divine nature, having escaped the corruption that is in the world through lust.

(2 Peter 1:2-4)

What a powerful verse with which to end this chapter! Our new birth, our co-resurrection with Jesus, has even enabled us to become *partakers of the divine nature*. God's nature now works within us, through Holy Spirit. The divine power of His grace has gifted us with *everything* we need for a life of godliness.

But, because of free will, we can either choose to let Him use the freedom He has paid the price for to work within us, or to go the way of the flesh. Do you or I not *know*? Have we already *forgotten*? Or will we choose to embrace His gracious gifts and live this new life by His power and to His glory?

5
Blessed by Freedom

Therefore, if the Son makes you free, you shall be free indeed.

(John 8:36)

Stand fast therefore in the liberty by which Christ has made us free, and do not be entangled again with a yoke of bondage.

(Galatians 5:1)

An alternative rendering of Galatians 5:1 reminds us that *it is for freedom that Christ has set us free.* At first glance that might seem like a statement of the blatantly obvious. But how many of us Christians, and to what extent, do we truly live in the freedom won for us?

Holy Spirit is emphasising for us here the two-fold aspect of our freedom in Christ. First, we are set free *from* something (e.g., our sin). At the same time, we are freed *to,* or into, something (the power and ability to live out our new life in Him).

It is one thing to be granted complete freedom. It is quite another to exercise it well. What we do with our freedom, in line with the plan and purpose of God for our lives, is what illustrates and confirms that we are free indeed. For we are set free to be conformed to His likeness. We can become like Him, *because as He is, so are we in this world (1 John 4:17).* And He is free!

When Jesus sets us free, we are indeed free. But that does not mean we are incapable of sacrificing (some or all of) that freedom. Either by deliberately or inadvertently returning into captivity, or bondage.

Doing nothing with our freedom, when we are freed for a purpose (as we are) is as unacceptable as abusing it. For total passivity is the equivalent of burying our 'talent' in the ground until the master returns. We know that the unprofitable servant was not exactly commended for his action. Or, rather, for his inaction, for his passivity. He was rebuked because he did nothing positive with what he was given for a purpose.

Suppose someone gives me a gift, perhaps some sort of tool or implement. They are not going to be pleased with me if I never take it out of the box and do something useful with it. Something it was specifically designed for. Or something the giver specifically wanted me to do with it. Because the gift was given for a purpose.

We have been given a brand-new life with which we can make a difference in our world. That is the purpose behind it. And it is our responsibility to seek out all the things that God wants us to accomplish with the gifts He has provided *(Ephesians 2:10)*.

Some translations of the Bible, including the New King James, sometimes use the word *liberty* whereas more modern versions would say *freedom*. So, I want to make sure that such references that are relevant to my purposes in this writing are not overlooked.

Is this not the fast that I have chosen: to loose lose the bonds of wickedness, to undo the heavy burdens, to let the oppressed go free, and that you break every yoke?

(Isaiah 58:6)

In the Old Testament, we find that this is God's response to the Jews who were complaining to Him that they had fasted, but He had not noticed. Sadly, they were focussed on outward appearances again rather than heart issues. In the context here, God points them towards freedom from oppression.

Freedom for those who were effectively being oppressed by the ones who were fasting! True freedom is for all, not a chosen and favoured few at the expense of others. We do not encounter true freedom in the scriptures, of course, until we reach the New Testament and the ministry of Jesus.

Then Jesus said to those Jews who believed Him, "If you abide in My word, you are My disciples indeed. And you shall know the truth, and the truth shall make you free."

Therefore, if the Son makes you free, you shall be free indeed.

(John 8:31-32, 36)

The truth we are to know is a Person *(John 14:6)* not a collection of facts about Him. Knowing Him in increasing measure and beginning to do the things He is calling us into is exercising our freedom in Christ. We find Him through prayer and worship, through personal encounters and through reading the Word of God.

It is that unique combination of Word and Spirit that fuels the Christian life. It enables us to experience true freedom in Him. It is to be part of how those around us can see something of *Christ in us, the Hope of Glory* (Colossians 1:27) and come into freedom themselves.

But the free gift is not like the offence. For if by the one man's offence, many died, much more the grace of God and the gift by the grace of the one Man, Jesus Christ, abounded to many. And the gift is not like that which came through the one who sinned. For the judgment which came from one offence resulted in condemnation, but the free gift which came from many offences resulted in justification.

For if by the one man's offence death reigned through the one, much more those who receive abundance of grace and of the gift of righteousness will reign in life through the One, Jesus Christ. Therefore, as through one man's offence, judgment came to all men, resulting in condemnation, even so through one Man's righteous act the free gift came to all men, resulting in justification of life.

(Romans 5:15-18)

When Adam sinned the whole of mankind was *contaminated* by sin. It was our inheritance, a legacy from him. When Jesus died and rose again, He provided the antidote to this *poison* for the whole of mankind. There is no escape for any of us from what Adam bequeathed to us except through accepting Jesus' bequest.

So, it is available to all but only efficacious for those who actually receive it. He has purchased for us our freedom from slavery to sin. But this gift is offered to us, not foisted upon us. It's that issue of individual choice once again!

This is also an example of what has been called *The Divine Exchange*. Jesus, through the cross, takes a curse from us and exchanges it for a blessing. (Other instances would be life for death; light for darkness; poverty for riches, and so on). Here is another one:

But now that you have been set free from sin and have become slaves of God, the benefit you reap leads to holiness, and the result is eternal life. For the wages of sin is death, but the gift of God is eternal life in Christ Jesus our Lord.

(Romans 6:22-23, NIV)

In 1 Corinthians 1:30 we read that Christ has become *our righteousness, holiness and redemption* by the free gift of God's grace. When He redeems us from sin, therefore, we enter into His righteousness and holiness as if it were our own. We discovered, in Part One, that so many of the characteristics that Jesus displayed during His earthly ministry are also freely available to us when we abide in Him. He reminds us, doesn't He, that we can do nothing apart from Him *(John 15:5)*? It is possible only in the freedom He has purchased for us.

There is therefore now no condemnation to those who are in Christ Jesus, who do not walk according to the flesh, but according to the Spirit. For the law of the Spirit of life in Christ Jesus has made me free from the law of sin and death.

(Romans 8:1-2)

We have the freedom of the Spirit *(2 Corinthians 3:17)* now that we have been set free from the *law* of sin and death by the *law* of the Spirit of Life in Christ Jesus. There has been no person freer on this Earth than Jesus was as the Son of Man during His incarnation.

We are destined to walk in His footsteps. He has made it possible by yet another *Divine Exchange*. However, with this freedom comes responsibility. It is ours to use for good, not to misuse for selfish purposes.

So then, brethren, we are not children of the bondwoman but of the free. Stand fast therefore in the liberty by which Christ has made us free, and do not be entangled again with a yoke of bondage.

(Galatians 4:31-5:1)

I don't really want to go over again the ground that we have already covered. It is easy to see how so many things are linked, or overlap, in scripture. We are set free to live in the Spirit, not to use our freedom (our free will or our freedom to choose if you prefer) to indulge the *flesh*.

For this is the will of God, that by doing good you may put to silence the ignorance of foolish men—as free, yet not using liberty as a cloak for vice, but as bondservants of God. Honour all people. Love the brotherhood. Fear God. Honour the king.

(1 Peter 2:15-17)

Peter emphasises the point just made. You will have noticed that he mentions 'honour' a couple of times. He exhorts us to treat everyone with honour and respect, from the smallest to the greatest (i.e., in human terms). This reminds me again of Danny Silk's book, 'The Culture of Honour'. I have no hesitation in recommending it to you. (See *Philippians 2:3-4* for an example of the biblical basis for this requirement).

Now the Lord is the Spirit; and where the Spirit of the Lord is, there is liberty.

(2 Corinthians 3:17)

The Lord Himself is the One who has bought us and brought us into freedom. Freedom is a glorious quality found in His Presence, both individually and corporately. Whether we are worshipping Him alone in spirit and truth or with others there is a wonderful sense of freedom. Especially so when His tangible Presence can be experienced. When the Spirit moves and His Presence is so real and obvious, the gifts flow and fruit results.

However, freedom is not something we would associate with 'religion'. If a meeting is religious rather than spiritual in nature, people can be bound in cold rituals and rigid formality. I am not pushing what might be called a strictly non-conformist viewpoint here as opposed to a liturgical one.

I am not unaware that some non-conformist meetings can be *religious* and liturgical worship beautifully *spiritual*. As always, the key is His Presence. If He is there, so is freedom, whatever the style of *service*.

The Spirit of the Lord is upon Me because He has anointed Me to preach the gospel to the poor; He has sent Me to heal the broken-hearted, to proclaim liberty to the captives and recovery of sight to the blind, to set at liberty those who are oppressed.

(Luke 4:18, *from* Isaiah 61:1)

In 'First Steps' I wrote about *prisoners* and *captives*, so I don't want to repeat myself here. Suffice it to say that the gospel message combined with Spirit-led ministry can and does heal and set free those who are captive to or bound by habits, addictions, and traumatic issues from the past. It is not unusual for such ministry to involve deliverance.

For you, brethren, have been called to liberty; only do not use liberty as an opportunity for the flesh, but through love serve one another.

(Galatians 5:13)

Freedom without responsibility is anarchy. The responsibility that comes with freedom can have many aspects. One of these is our responsibility towards others. Especially towards those believers who may not live in the same level of freedom as us.

As I have already stated several times, sanctification is a process. It is progressive. We are all at different stages of our life journeys, both in this process and in other respects. Paul illustrates this in connection with food, specifically the eating of food which has been sacrificed to idols.

But beware lest somehow this liberty of yours become a stumbling block to those who are weak. For if anyone sees you who have knowledge eating in an idol's temple, will not the conscience of him who is weak be emboldened to eat those things offered to idols? And because of your knowledge shall the weak brother perish, for whom Christ died? But when you thus sin against the brethren and wound their weak conscience, you sin against Christ. Therefore, if food makes my brother stumble, I will never again eat meat, lest I make my brother stumble.

(1 Corinthians 8:9-13)

We should be free to eat anything for which we have first given thanks to God. The blessing He provides through this can include protection. The truth of this may not yet be evident to every fellow believer. So, it is beholden upon us to respect their weaker conscience in this respect.

They may be troubled by seeing us eat something which they feel duty-bound to avoid (e.g., pork). So, we should not go ahead and eat such food in front of them if it would offend them. Even though we feel completely free, and not outside of the will of God in so doing, we should honour them by abstaining in their presence.

The same principle would apply to any number of things over which opinions differ. Provided, of course, we are not dealing with a fundamental truth of the faith but a lesser matter. We can always seek God for the right time and place to (humbly) enlighten our friends about the level of freedom we enjoy. It is also available to them—when they are ready to receive it.

They promise others freedom, yet they themselves are slaves to corruption, for people are slaves to whatever overcomes them.

(2 Peter 2:19, TPT)

Peter gives us a warning about those who would lead us astray by trying to persuade us to go along with false teachings or practices. These are hypocrites who are not living up to their calling. If we follow their bad example, we risk being led into bondage to something spiritually unhealthy.

We need to be on our guard when we sense a *check* in our spirit. By which I mean a warning from Holy Spirit to our spirit, through our conscience, that we need to be careful.

Because the creation itself also will be delivered from the bondage of corruption into the glorious liberty of the children of God.

(Romans 8:21)

The effects of sin, of the fall, are so pervasive that even the creation has been adversely affected by its contamination. The good news means that there will come a day when creation itself is freed from this captivity. It will be brought into the freedom which is ours by the grace of God. Just as we are now a new creation, so there will be a new heaven and a new Earth.

It is for freedom that Christ has set us free. This glorious freedom is for us to enjoy—to the glory of God. It pleases Him when we use our freedom and gifts, received from Him, to bless others. All of us can hear, read, and learn about our freedom. We should also put it into practice. Put it into action as He guides and directs us to share and extend His Kingdom wherever we go.

But he who looks into the perfect law of liberty and continues in it and is not a forgetful hearer but a doer of the work, this one will be blessed in what he does.

(James 1:25)

The primary purpose of Part Two of this book is to draw attention to ways in which we can pass on to others all that we have been blessed with ourselves. We have been freely given so much by the grace of God. Now we are called to freely pass on what we have received *(Matthew 10:8)*.

The gifts of the spirit, we know, have been given to us for the benefit of others. Bill Johnson teaches that Holy Spirit is *in* us for our sake but *upon* us for the sake of others. We need to be looking outwards rather than gazing at our own navels! Therefore, our calling is to be *doers* of the word, not just hearers or readers of it. Therein lies the danger of passivity, as already mentioned.

In Matthew 10, Jesus commissioned the 12 for a specific mission. He sent them out, with His authority delegated to them, to minister to people in the same ways they had seen Him minister to others.

Later, after His resurrection, He breathed on the apostles and said, "Receive the Holy Spirit" *(John 20:22)*.

In Matthew 28 He gives them what we know as *The Great Commission*. There is a parallel passage in Mark 16 containing a similar instruction. In Acts 2, we find that they receive the anointing, their first infilling of Holy Spirit. This provides the power necessary to fuel their ministries.

Holy Spirit is the water of life, freely offered to us to drink deeply. He alone enables us to *do* the works God has prepared in advance for us to do. To bring all kinds of *freedom* to those around us. Let us not pass up any opportunities He gives us. Neither should we simply wait for them, though, but actively look out for them.

And the Spirit and the bride say, "Come!"
And let him who hears say, "Come!"
And let him who thirsts come. Whoever desires, let him take the water of life freely.

(Revelation 22:17)

6
Blessed by Healing

*And great multitudes followed Him, and He **healed** them all.*

(Matthew 12:15b)

My previous book, published in 2018, was called 'First Steps into Healing'. It carried the sub-title *as part of normal everyday Christian life*. Written from my own personal journey, mostly alongside my wife, Cathy, it was about growing in the knowledge, experience, and practice of healing ministry. My aim was to encourage others to do the same, especially if it would mean stepping out in faith for the very first time.

My general experience predates my own amazing healing from *M.E.* involving deliverance from a spirit of infirmity, in May 2008. However, I concentrated particularly on the period of growth following from that. If you have read that book, I hesitate to risk boring you with too much repetition.

On the other hand, if you have not read that book, I believe it makes sense to provide you with a bit of my/our story from it. I think it serves me well to introduce the subject of healing in the context of this writing.

I became a Christian in May 1971 and was baptised in Holy Spirit during the following year. My early church background was primarily evangelical but there was an introduction to elements of the charismatic from quite early on.

However, the latter did not find much expression beyond praying in tongues until the mid-1980s. This was when I was introduced to words of knowledge in addition to very basic aspects of the prophetic. That coincided with the time I was recruited to join the healing ministry team of my (then) home church.

The team used to meet before services to pray and to seek the Lord for words of knowledge. Those would reveal what He wanted us to pray for with people who came forward at the end of the services. Mostly they were responding to those revelations which were accurate.

As far as I can remember, although I witnessed some deliverance ministry, there were no physical healings. Just (if I can use that word reverently) inner healings, dealing primarily with emotional problems. I heard and read stories/testimonies about physical healing, but I have no firm recollection of being involved with such back in those days.

Cathy and I were married in December 1996 (a second marriage for both of us). Soon afterwards, I went down with some sort of virus or *bug*. I was laid low for a few days, just as you would expect. Sadly, I never seemed to recover my previous energy levels, which gradually deteriorated further.

Of course, I consulted my doctor, who was also a friend from church. Over a period of years, I was subjected to several different medical tests. Finally, when nothing else was revealed, it was concluded that I had *M.E.* (also known as chronic fatigue syndrome). I was told that, although some people seem to recover, there was no cure. I would just have to learn to *manage* the illness.

Well, I was determined to get it prayed for too! In fact, I was prayed for on a few different occasions. Often the Presence of God was obvious, but I was not healed and there was no improvement either. I once went on a healing retreat for a few days and still came home with *M.E.* Not only that but I had also picked up a *bug* from one of the people mentoring me during my stay!

Eventually, by letting go of some responsibilities and only working the designated hours of my employment contract, I could manage to keep going full-time. This still meant that I was often exhausted in the evenings and at weekends.

As time went on, I had to lay aside various church responsibilities and activities also. In addition, I was more susceptible to whatever illness was going around currently. My immune system must have been affected. In 2004, I suffered burn-out, probably brought on by stress.

In 2005, I was afflicted with something called *cough syncopé*. The latter first came to light when I was halfway up the stairs at home. I began a coughing fit, fainted and fell back down the stairs, hitting my head on a radiator at the bottom!

In the early part of 2008, I was probably at my lowest ebb. I was unable to be of much practical help around the home, so Cathy found herself doing almost everything domestically. She also had her very demanding full-time job as a primary school teacher!

She reached the stage where she was confessing to one or two close friends that she was not sure how much longer she could cope with all the demands upon her time and energy. During the Easter holidays that year we decided to spend a couple of weeks in one of our favourite places, Southwold in Suffolk. I was fine during the first week but struggled more with fatigue during the second one.

When we returned home, we picked up an answerphone message from some friends asking if we had been watching the 'Lakeland Revival' on God TV. They recommended that we do just that because many people were being healed, both in the auditorium and whilst watching from home.

We looked in that night and were impressed by the way many people were healed where they sat in response to words of knowledge from the platform. They went forward only to give testimony and to be prayed for afterwards. Written words of many healing testimonies, from people across the world watching at home, were being scrolled across the bottom of the screen throughout the broadcast.

Chronic Fatigue was included in the words of knowledge more than once on the first few nights we watched the programme. However, I did not sense God prompting me to respond. One special night this word of knowledge came up again but, this time, coupled with *spirit of infirmity*. My spirit was clearly stirred by that verbal combination.

I found myself saying immediately to Cathy, "That's for me!"

Todd Bentley, the speaker, asked if any of the words resonated with viewers at home. If so, they should get up, touch their television or computer screens, and God would heal them!

My immediate reaction was, "That's ridiculous! I'm not doing that!"

Instantly, the thought of Namaan the Syrian came to me. If you recall, he was asked to do something he considered *demeaning* in order to be healed. *Ok, Lord, I thought to myself, I've got nothing to lose. I'll do it. If I look foolish there's only Cathy with me, and she's seen that happen before!*

So, I told her I was going to get up and touch the screen—if she came with me. She agreed and, after stepping around both the large coffee table in front of our settee and the front of an armchair located beside the TV, I touched the screen.

Nothing happened!

A thought (or perhaps another revelation) instantly came to me. *Get Cathy to touch the TV, too!* She agreed and, as soon as we both touched it, it was like I was hit by 10,000 volts of electricity! I was thrown backwards through the air, over the front of the armchair, and above the coffee table laden with mugs, etc.

I landed back on the settee, where I proceeded to bounce up and down for what seemed like several minutes. During that time, I sensed (without quite actually seeing it with my physical eyes) something come out of my chest and disappear through the wall opposite. I am convinced it was the spirit of infirmity! Cathy had meanwhile fallen to the floor, in the Spirit, for the very first time.

Over the next few days, I experienced several different proofs that I had been completely healed and set free. I should add that, up to that point, nobody had raised with me, even if they thought it, the possibility that I might be oppressed by a spirit of infirmity. Or any other afflicting spirit for that matter.[1]

Since then, as well as being used by God in a variety of healing ministry situations, we have been privileged to see others set free from *M.E.* The most memorable instance is also recorded in my previous book, so I won't repeat it here. Nor will I recap any of the other testimonies recorded therein.

As time has gone by, we have discovered that Cathy has a particular passion for inner and emotional healing. She is now very involved with the Bethel Sozo ministry. I find myself drawn more towards those needing physical healing.

One quite remarkable aspect of that is skeletal realignment. This came about after being introduced to the ministry of the late Charles and Frances Hunter. They were possibly the first to expand their healing ministry to embrace the involvement of *ordinary* Christians to share the *doing* with them. The latter was also something which inspired us, as *ordinary* Christians, to step up. We also felt moved to enthuse, encourage, and try to teach others to follow this example.

We advocate what we call the *Martini anointing*. Do you remember the old TV advertisement with the strapline, "Anytime, anyplace, anywhere?"

We see healing ministry being just as valid out on the streets and in the supermarkets, etc. It's not meant to be confined within the four walls of church buildings on special occasions. Why should we always expect people to come to *us*?

Back to the skeletal realignment phenomena. Here is a testimony concerning an event that took place after my previous book was written. We were in France again and spent one of our evenings with a home group on the outskirts of Caen. During the teaching part, I happened to mention that we had seen many healings involving skeletal realignment. Even the actual growing out of shorter limbs to match the length of the other arm or leg.

On the following Sunday, we were ministering at the church in Caen with which the home group was linked. There was a time of ministry at the end of the service. A guy who had been at the home group meeting brought forward a young man who had not long since arrived in France from Angola. He was limping and wore what looked like a built-up shoe on his right foot.

He explained that an operation on his right leg, following an injury, had left him with walking difficulties. When he removed his *boot*, it was clear that his foot and ankle were twisted out of their natural shape. There was also an *insert* in his *boot* to make it more comfortable, possibly due to a fallen arch.

We started to pray for the twisted foot, and in due course, it went back into its natural position. It then emerged that, as a side effect of the surgery, he now had one leg shorter than the other. This was why the guy from the home group had brought him out to us. Responding like this to a testimony heard previously often results in God doing the same again.

We checked the discrepancy in lengths between his legs, using a traditional, manual, but non-scientific method which would not be validated by the medical profession. Therefore, we always make that clear to everyone. It may not have medical approval, but it does provide an indication that a difference exists.

In fact, in most cases, the discrepancy is obvious to the naked eye anyway. Also, it is invariably indicated by a limping gait and/or a less-than-upright stance. We prayed and watched as the right leg gradually extended to match the length of the left leg, praise God!

As a lifelong football enthusiast, what I can never forget is when the young man exclaimed, "Now I will be able to play football again!"

He had already stood up, walked normally without pain, and realised he no longer needed his special shoe. Even now, whenever I recount this testimony to anyone, it brings a tear to my eye. (You can't keep an old football enthusiast quiet for long!).

One of the problems for anyone involved in healing ministry to any degree is having to deal with disappointment. This is inevitable when someone we minister to is not healed there and then.

Sometimes the healing simply does not happen at all. Other times it may be gradual with little or no sign of it manifesting at the time. There are also occasions when complete healing comes later after we have moved on. So, we may never get to hear about it.

Whilst in South America on a mission trip our friend, Paul, was asked by a pastor to pray for a lady who seemed (to Paul) to be in a coma. He did so but, seeing nothing happen straightaway, he moved on to minister to others. Six years later he made a return visit to the same church. He was talking to the pastor about some of the amazing things that had happened during his first visit. This included a young man who was healed of AIDS while simply being hugged.

When Paul asked about the elderly lady in a coma, the pastor looked puzzled for a while. Then the penny dropped. It turned out that the lady had not been in a coma but had been dead!

Then the pastor turned around, pointed across the room, and said, "That's her over there!"

There are many reasons why someone is not healed, either instantly or after a short time. During John G Lake's ministry in South Africa, in the very early 1900s, it was discovered that his wife had a revelatory grace gift which proved to be invaluable in such instances. It became the practice to invite such people into a separate room where Jenny Lake would go with them.

There, Holy Spirit would reveal to her why each person had not been healed. It was often a case of them needing to forgive someone before the healing could be released.

If they cooperated, they were ministered to again and invariably healed. If they chose not to cooperate, they were told that, sadly, there was nothing further that could be done for them. They were free to leave—just as they came in.

Cathy had an experience along these lines when we were ministering in Rouen. A lady came forward complaining of tinnitus and a rash on her arm. Cathy prayed for her but nothing much seemed to be happening. She felt prompted to ask the lady if there was someone she needed to forgive.

She said, "No."

Almost immediately she changed her mind and admitted there was someone, actually her ex-husband. Cathy led her in a prayer of forgiveness for him. When the healing ministry resumed, the lady's rash disappeared, as did the tinnitus (almost completely).

But He was wounded for our transgressions, he was bruised for our iniquities; the chastisement for our peace was upon Him, and by His stripes, we ARE healed.

(Isaiah 53:5)

Not everyone in church circles agrees that healing is within the atonement, along with forgiveness and deliverance. Such people would interpret this verse as using *"healed"* as an alternative to forgive. In the New Testament, the Greek word *sozo* can be translated accurately as *salvation*.

However, as highlighted by the literature and website of the Bethel Sozo UK ministry, the same word is variously translated in scripture. According to context, it can mean either *saved* (i.e., forgiven), *healed* or *delivered*. Our salvation can manifest in any or all these ways.

Of course, we are always saved (forgiven) when we are first born again. Not everyone will be, or needs to be, healed, or delivered at that time—although some will.

Peter quotes from this verse in his epistle but with a subtle change of emphasis. This, to my mind at least, confirms the difference between the old and new covenants, prior to and after the death and resurrection of Jesus.

Who Himself bore our sins in His own body on the tree, that we, having died to sins, might live for righteousness—by whose stripes you WERE healed.

(1 Peter 2:24)

As you can see, Peter uses the *past* tense, whereas Isaiah uses the present tense. For Peter, inspired by Holy Spirit, healing has *already* taken place. It was accomplished at the cross on a *once-and-forever* basis. Therefore, it *is* part of the atonement. Unless one prefers the interpretation of *healed* as just another way of saying *saved* or *forgiven*, regardless of context.

If it is not already obvious, let me confirm that I believe that healing, indeed the multiple aspects of *sozo*, are in the atonement. I believe that this is at least part of the reason why Jesus cried, *It is finished,* when He died on the cross.

All that would be needed for every salvation, healing and deliverance was accomplished both in that one moment at Calvary—and throughout time from God's heavenly, Kingdom perspective.

Just as it is God's will for everyone to be saved, so I believe it is His will for *all* to be healed. I consider that to be a simple but complete interpretation of the atonement. To reiterate, in my opinion, it is a *once-and-forever* provision of grace. But that provision is required to be applied experientially in every life.

> *The Lord is not slack concerning His promise, as some count slackness, but is longsuffering toward us, not willing that any should perish but that all should come to repentance.*
>
> (2 Peter 3:9)

Having said that, I must acknowledge it is my experience (and of everyone else except Jesus) that not every person we minister to is healed. By the same token, not everyone to whom the gospel is preached is saved immediately. That always brings disappointment, of course. But we do not give up as some sadly do when they encounter such *mysteries*.

I have already told you that I was miraculously healed of *M.E.* in May 2008. Later, in September 2013, I underwent an operation for a hip replacement. People were praying for my healing right up until the Sunday evening before my operation, scheduled for the next afternoon. We were all expectant, because of what had happened before but, frankly, ended up disappointed.

Our friend, Paul (mentioned earlier) has seen God heal many arthritic knees during his years of healing ministry. Many such healings occurred after he contracted the same infirmity, and he eventually struggled to walk unaided. When I first drafted these words, he was recovering from heart surgery and had suffered other infirmities! Sadly, Paul died last year without ever making a full recovery. Bill Johnson's son, Eric, is deaf. Eric has prayed for several deaf people who have been healed, but he remains deaf.

There is a mystery involved. We rarely receive an answer to the question, "Why, Lord?"

He does not have to explain Himself to us. We still believe that God is good all the time and that it *is* His will to heal. On this side of heaven, we may never get all the answers we seek. But because of who He is, we will continue to trust Him and press on.

When there are no answers, we look at the perfectly innocent Jesus suffering alone on the cross for the sins of the whole world and regain perspective.

One thing to bear in mind, in this context, is the tension between what we want to see happen and what is the will of God at *that* moment. Jesus only did what He saw the Father doing and only said what He heard the Father saying.

His relationship with His Father was perfect, a total oneness of complete intimacy. The Son of Man always knew exactly what He was to do and when.

We would like that to be true of us and we seek it out. But we are still a work in progress in terms of the experiential side of *working out our salvation.*

For now, we see in a mirror, dimly, but then face to face. Now I know in part, but then I shall know just as I also am known.

(1 Corinthians 13:12)

Jesus had such an intimate relationship with Father God that He did not see in a mirror dimly. Neither did He know only in part. As we progress through the adventure of sanctification, it is possible for us to move closer to the position the Son always has. But I don't expect to attain it fully before I see Him face to face and know Him as I am fully known by Him.

And great multitudes followed Him, and He healed them all.

(Matthew 12:15)

There are 37 different accounts of miracles performed by Jesus recorded in the gospels. Most are healings or deliverances, including raising the dead on more than one occasion. Clearly, in the light of what John writes *(see John 20:30 and 21:25),* this is not a comprehensive list. The actual number, from over three years of regular, daily ministry must have been phenomenal!

And remember, Jesus only did what He saw the Father doing, so He healed only those the Father prompted Him to heal. These did not include the crippled man who was laid every day at the Beautiful Gate of the Temple *(see Acts 3).*

Jesus probably passed Him every time He visited the temple when He was in Jerusalem for the various annual Feasts. This man was not healed until after Jesus' ascension. That was when Holy Spirit specifically brought him to the attention of Peter and John.

This tells me that God's *timing* is crucial. Jesus would have had no less love and compassion for this crippled man than He had for anyone else. It is impossible to faithfully and regularly be used to minister healing without having love and compassion for people.

This indicates that love and compassion alone are not enough. There is a right time and place. Why was it more than 10 years before I was healed from M.E.?

I don't know. I must conclude that, for reasons I have yet to discover, May 2008, was God's perfect timing for me.

Consider this carefully. We are motivated solely by love and compassion. We have faith in God's ability. As such, are we less likely to see healing than if we have these things combined with a revelation in our spirit that *this* is God's timing for an individual?

I don't know. It must be possible, but I am keeping an open mind on that one for now. Living with mystery is not always easy but I have found it unavoidable in my Christian experience.

But the manifestation of the Spirit is given to each one for the profit of all: to another gifts of healings healing by the same Spirit...But one and the same Spirit works all these things, distributing to each one individually as He wills.

(1 Corinthians 12:7, 9b, 11)

What have been your thoughts, opinions, and experiences of the healing ministry to date? Whatever your answer is, I want to encourage you to view this gift and ministry in a positive and optimistic light.

Learn to recognise every opportunity that God provides and step out in faith. Minister in the power of Holy Spirit, with the delegated authority of Jesus Christ, and in His Holy Name.

Alongside the prophetic, the healing ministry is a wonderful evangelistic and/or faith-building tool. It facilitates a God encounter for a person who may never have attended a church. They can shut their ears to our evangelistic words. But how can they honestly deny a powerful experience of God touching their bodies, minds, or emotions?

Go for it!

1 For a complete version of the healing story and an amazing follow-up example of freedom when the spirit of infirmity tried to return 12 months later, I am afraid you will have to read 'First Steps' (originally published by Zacc Media, 2018).

7
Blessed by Sonship

Behold what manner of love the Father has bestowed on us,
that we should be called children of God!

(1 John 3:1a)

The Spirit Himself bears witness with our spirit that we are children of God.

(Romans 8:16)

Jesus told a remarkable parable about a prodigal son. However, there are many, like me, who feel its primary emphasis is really upon the gracious and loving father. So, a better title might be 'The Good Father', not least because the father in the tale is obviously Father God. Also *sons* is an inclusive term because His daughters are not excluded from the purpose of the tale.

There are many lessons to be learned from this great story. One of the most important, in my opinion, concerns the matter of our true *identity*. If we don't know who we are (in Christ) how can we possibly live and express ourselves as He has called and equipped us to function in His Kingdom on Earth? Let's take a closer look at Luke 15:11-32.

A certain man had two sons. And the younger of them said to his father, "Father, give me the portion of goods that falls to me."
So, he divided to them his livelihood.

The younger son asked, in advance, for his inheritance. Presumably, he was too greedy to wait for his father's natural demise. Immediately he was also shown to be impatient and self-centred. What a sad indicator for what was about to follow. He was keen to break away from his heritage to plough his own furrow. This reminds us, doesn't it, of man's rebellion and *original sin*?

And not many days after, the younger son gathered all together, journeyed to a far country, and there wasted his possessions with prodigal living. But when he had spent all, there arose a severe famine in that land, and he began to be in want.

He wasted his considerable wealth on all kinds of self-indulgence. None of this would have met with his father's approval nor followed the parental example. His became a sinful, godless existence, without any trace of lasting satisfaction or fulfilment. Again, a picture of unregenerate mankind generally.

Then he went and joined himself to a citizen of that country, and he sent him into his fields to feed swine. And he would gladly have filled his stomach with the pods that the swine ate, and no one gave him anything.

Not ready, willing, or humble enough to acknowledge his mistakes, he tried to make the best of it. I assume that the suggestion of a young Jewish man being reduced to feeding *unclean* pigs is an illustration of his having reached rock bottom.

Sadly, too many of us must sink that low before we are prepared to change our ways. It is an age-old, universal problem, as illustrated by Isaiah in one of the most well-known chapters of his prophetic writing.

All we like sheep have gone astray; we have turned, everyone, to his own way; and the Lord has laid on Him the iniquity of us all.

(Isaiah 53:6)

Finally, the young man made a positive decision. He realised that, even as a servant in his father's household, he would enjoy a much better lifestyle than he currently had.

But when he came to himself, he said, "How many of my father's hired servants have bread enough and to spare, and I perish with hunger! I will arise and go to my father and will say to him, Father, I have sinned against heaven and before you, and I am no longer worthy to be called your son. Make me like one of your hired servants."

He resolved to turn around and go back to his father (repentance). To admit his errant ways (confession). To willingly take on the role of a servant rather than that of a son. He reasoned that what he had done disqualified him from being a son. He had become desperate and humble enough to go *home* to accept a much lower position than he once had. He accepted that it would be a significant improvement in his present circumstances.

It seems that all the time he had been away, his father had been watching out for his return. There was nothing he wanted more than to have his son back in the family fold. What is so amazing is that he ran to his son the moment he saw him.

To do that, because he was wearing long robes, he would have to hitch them up to be able to run without tripping himself up. A respectable Jewish elder of that time and culture would never act in such an undignified way. Such was his joy in seeing his son heading back to him, he laid aside his dignity.

And he arose and came to his father. But when he was still a great way off, his father saw him and had compassion, and ran and fell on his neck and kissed him.

The son, no doubt embarrassed, went straight into his impeccably rehearsed confession speech. He could not believe that his father would be overjoyed about such a prodigal returning home.

And the son said to him, "Father, I have sinned against heaven and in your sight, and am no longer worthy to be called your son."

It was as if the father did not hear any of it. He seemed to ignore it totally. Although I am sure he heard and rejoiced over every word, recognising the genuine sincerity conveyed by the confession. Notice he chose not to respond with recriminations and a superior, *I told you so.*

But the father said to his servants, "Bring out the best robe and put it on him and put a ring on his hand and sandals on his feet. And bring the fatted calf here

and kill it and let us eat and be merry; for this, my son was dead and is alive again; he was lost and is found."
And they began to be merry.

His son may have been happy enough to be a servant. But, to the father, he never ceased to be a son and never would. Dad wanted to celebrate. And this is the response of Heaven over every sinner who repents, confesses, and wants to return to (or enter) the Family and a restored relationship with Father God.

I say to you that likewise there will be more joy in heaven over one sinner who repents than over ninety-nine just persons who need no repentance... Likewise, I say to you, there is joy in the presence of the angels of God over one sinner who repents.

(Luke 15:7, 10)

But not everyone was happy to hear the news and to join in with the celebrations. The older son was obviously a diligent and conscientious worker but there was more than a hint of self-righteousness about him.

Now his older son was in the field. And as he came and drew near to the house, he heard music and dancing. So, he called one of the servants and asked what these things meant.
And he said to him, "Your brother has come, and because he has received him safe and sound, your father has killed the fatted calf."
But he was angry and would not go in. Therefore, his father came out and pleaded with him.

What would be your reaction and mine towards a Christian brother who went astray but saw the error of their ways? Who wanted to be restored to us? As I have mentioned before, there can be too much of a desire to see someone punished first and foremost.

Then, if they pass whatever test we set them to prove the genuineness of their remorse, we will gradually let them return to some semblance of the position or office they once held. The scripture makes it clear that we should treat them with love and compassion—if indeed repentance is expressed and meant. *There, but for the grace of God, go I.*

My beloved friends, if you see a believer who is overtaken with a fault, the one who is in the Spirit should seek to restore him in the Spirit of gentleness. But keep watch over your own heart so that you won't be tempted to exalt yourself over him.

(Galatians 6:1, TPT)

In the parable, the father had no alternative but to go out to the elder son and plead with him to come and welcome his brother back. To join in with the joyous celebrations. The older son may well have been a conscientious and disciplined person, but he was totally lacking in grace.

So, he answered and said to his father, "Lo, these many years I have been serving you; I never transgressed your commandment at any time; and yet you never gave me a young goat, that I might make merry with my friends. But as soon as this son of yours came, who has devoured your livelihood with harlots, you killed the fatted calf for him."

Here we see the conflict between imputed righteousness (ours by the grace of God through faith—(*Ephesians 2:8-9*) and self-righteousness—(*Romans 3:20-22*). Jesus came to save us not to condemn us *(John 3:17, 8:11)*. We do well to remember just how gracious the grace of God towards us is when we fail, and towards others when they fail us (and Him).

And he said to him, "Son, you are always with me, and all that I have is yours. It was right that we should make merry and be glad, for your brother was dead and is alive again, and was lost and is found."

The father reminded the son about what was his and always had been. What was true, even if he had not lived in the light of that privileged position. It was almost as if he was saying, *why do you need to ask me for a fatted calf when the whole farm is yours?* The elder son was in the right place, as it were, but with the wrong attitude. He was a son but had the mentality of a servant.

The younger son, on the other hand, returned to his father willing to be a mere servant, because of his failings. He knew some kind of penalty was not unjustifiable. But he was welcomed back as the son he had never ceased to be regarded as by his father.

No longer do I call you servants, for a servant does not know what his master is doing; but I have called you friends, for all things that I heard from My Father I have made known to you.

(John 15:15)

God-fearing Jews under the old covenant saw themselves in the kind of relationship with God that would be like that of master and servant. They had the Law (the rules). They saw it as their primary goal in life to obey them.
To do whatever God, through the Law and the Prophets, told them to do. Jesus came to change that, beginning with the dramatic transition from servants to friends—and sons.

The Spirit Himself bears witness with our spirit that we are children of God.

(Romans 8:16)

The new covenant sees us blessed ones as children of God, adopted into the heavenly family *(Galatians 4:5, Ephesians 1:5)*. This is our identity in Christ. Ours by grace through faith *(Ephesians 2:8)* in accordance with the will of the Father. Jesus, the Son, has made it possible for us to be His brethren *(Romans 8:29)*. Holy Spirit enables us to cry, *Abba, Father, (Romans 8:15)*.

As Christians, we often say about ourselves that *we are sinners saved by grace*. We can easily forget that, even more importantly, we are a brand-new creation now. The old has gone and the new has come *(2 Corinthians 5:17)*. Therefore, I suggest that it is more accurate to say we **were** *sinners* **now** *saved by grace* I have covered this point already so I will not elaborate on it here.

The question we are left to ask ourselves, then, is this.

"Am I a sinner, a servant, or a son?"

In giving an honest answer, we reveal what our perception of our identity is.

When we **were** *sinners* who repented, He **now** saved us. When we try to please Him as *servants*, He tells us that we are friends. More than that, we are His *sons* (and daughters). We are family. We belong.

May I suggest that we are no longer sinners nor servants but sons who are called and equipped to serve (*do*) in the Family business as His co-workers?

8
Blessed by Seeds Sown

Listen! A farmer went out to sow his seed.
As he was scattering the seed, some fell along the path,
and the birds came and ate it up.
Some fell on rocky places, where it did not have much soil.
It sprang up quickly because the soil was shallow.
But when the sun came up, the plants were scorched,
and they withered because they had no root.
Other seed fell among thorns, which grew up and
choked the plants so that they did not bear grain.
Still, other seed fell on good soil.
It came up, grew, and produced a crop,
some multiplying thirty, some sixty, some a hundred times.

Mark 4: 3-8 (TPT)

This chapter is a reworking of a sermon I once preached that was entitled "Sow and Sow". A typical example of a feeble play on words ('S.O.W' and 'S.O.') that I sometimes find myself indulging in. I know it's sad but, anyway, here goes:

The Parable of the Sower is extremely well known. It features in each of the three synoptic gospels, Matthew, Mark, and Luke. However, it is interesting to me that the three gospel accounts are not exactly identical. There are some subtle differences between them. These are particularly evident in Jesus' recorded interpretations that follow the parables themselves.

I have always tended to understand this parable as showing various ways in which different people respond to hearing the gospel preached for the first time. I was reading Mark's Gospel in the Passion Translation recently when I was really struck by the footnote relating to these verses. This made me look at the parable, and its interpretation, in a different, broader light.

I am not questioning the validity of the traditional interpretation, simply now wondering if it might be incomplete. Parables are often multi-layered: like an onion. Perhaps it is not meant to apply only to non-believers hearing the gospel for the first time. Maybe it also applies to us as believers at any stage of the Christian life we may have reached to date.

Maybe the word is not only sown into the hearts of non-believers to awaken them. Maybe it is also sown into the hearts of believers to challenge, rebuke, restore, encourage, and mature them. What, then, is this sow and sow? Can it really mean that the word is sown to the unbeliever *and* to the believer?

After teaching the parable to his audience, Jesus talked to His disciples. They were curious, having failed to grasp the meaning of it as He spoke.

When he was alone, the 12 and the others around him asked him about the parables. He told them, "The secret of the Kingdom of God has been given to you. But to those on the outside everything is said in parables so that, they may be ever seeing but never perceiving, and ever hearing but never understanding; otherwise, they might turn and be forgiven!"

(Mark 4:10-12, TPT)

The TPT footnote to these verses asks who *those on the outside*, or *the outsiders* are. It suggests that a translation from the original Aramaic would be *backward ones*. Further, when Jesus spoke allegorically it was so that those who didn't *care* to understand Him couldn't understand Him.

But the hungry ones, like His disciples, would be keen to seek out the hidden meaning of His parables. To understand the secrets of God's kingdom realm. It makes the point that this is still the same today. Do you agree?

It is the glory of God to conceal a matter, but the glory of kings is to search out a matter.

(Proverbs 25:2)

Do you and I, as maturing believers, identify ourselves with the hungry ones? As adopted children of God, do we need to be reminded that we are now royal personages in His Kingdom on Earth? We are authorised, now as *insiders*, to search out matters that God keeps hidden from *outsiders*.

Bill Johnson teaches that God doesn't hide something *from* us but *for* us. He illustrates this by talking about an Easter Egg Hunt for children. A common pursuit in the US which is now adopted more widely in the UK. For the very young, it makes sense to (almost) hide the eggs in comparatively obvious, easy to find, places. Whereas older children would be very disappointed not to have a more difficult, but nevertheless achievable, task set for them.

When you and I receive a revelation that is not readily understandable, we need to seek out diligently the meaning of it. I recently read somewhere that: *God is in control, but we are not meant just to lean on a shovel expecting Him to create, supernaturally, a hole in the ground for us!*

There will be times when a contribution, a bit of effort on our part, is expected. What interpretation does Jesus give to this parable? What does it say to or about us, as we look at it from a believer's perspective?

The farmer sows the word. Some people are like seed seeds along the path, where the word is sown. As soon as they hear it, Satan comes and takes away the word that was sown in them. Others, like seed seeds sown on rocky places, hear the word and at once receive it with joy. But since they have no root roots, they last only a short time.

When trouble or persecution comes because of the word, they quickly fall away. Still others, like seed sown among thorns, hear the word; but the worries of this life, the deceitfulness of wealth and the desires for other things come in and choke the word, making it unfruitful. Others, like seed sown on good soil, hear the word, accept it, and produce a crop—some thirty, some sixty, some a hundred times what was sown.

(Mark 4: 14-20, TPT)

The farmer sowing the word is, of course, God speaking words of revelation through the preacher or the evangelist. Even one of us talking to a friend, a neighbour, a work colleague, or a stranger in the street.

But, the other kind of sowing, I suggest, is God speaking to us, as believers, either directly or through any other person. He is giving a word of revelation to our hearts.

It may be given in the form of a parable. We may not have either an instant or complete understanding to be able to receive it fully straightaway. If it is a word or message that does not mean something to us readily, we need to seek out the meaning. Just as one of the *hungry ones* would do.

In looking at the interpretation of this parable in terms of its application to a believer, I must acknowledge my debt to the very interesting footnote to verse 9 in TPT which I quote below.

The four kinds of soils speak of four kinds of hearts: **hard** *hearts,* **hollow** *hearts,* **half** *hearts, and* **whole** *hearts. With the first soil, we see the activity of* **Satan***, with the second, that of the* **flesh***, and with the third, that of the* **world***. Bearing fruit is never a problem with what is sown, but with what soil it falls upon.*

I think we all know it is not true to claim that God doesn't speak to us today. The real issues are:

- Do we always recognise His voice?
- Do we always receive what He says?
- What are we to *do* with what we hear?

In seeking to apply His revelatory Word to our lives, we need to understand that He always speaks to us with a Kingdom purpose in mind.

Looking at Mark 4:15, we see that it refers to *hard* hearts. Hard hearts combined with the activity of Satan. Mark's Gospel is specific about *hearing* the message, whereas Matthew focusses on *understanding* it.

Satan will do his best to make sure that we never *hear* the word of God. If that strategy fails, he doesn't want us to *understand* what we hear. He will not want us to *believe* and *act* upon God's Word to us. We can be sure of that. So, not only do we need to be able to recognise God's voice when He is speaking to us, however He chooses to do it. But also, to recognise the efforts of Satan to deflect us from an understanding of those words.

And we are not meant only to *hear* from God, but also to *do* something because of what we have heard.

But be doers of the word, and not hearers only, deceiving yourselves. For if anyone is a hearer of the word and not a doer, he is like a man observing his natural face in a mirror; for he observes himself, goes away, and immediately forgets what kind of man he was. But he who looks into the perfect law of liberty and continues in it and is not a forgetful hearer but a doer of the work, this one will be blessed in what he does.

James 1:22-25

Let's make sure that our hearts are not hard. That we do not succumb to any of the distractions Satan creates to hold us back from obedient action.

Mark 4:16-17 refers to *hollow* hearts. Hearts that are weakened by the flesh. Before Jesus went through great agonies in the Garden of Gethsemane, He had asked His disciples to support Him in prayer, but they were unable to stay awake to *do* that.

Watch and pray, lest you enter into temptation. The spirit indeed is willing, but the flesh is weak.

Mark 14:38

In their hearts, the disciples wanted to do as He asked, but their flesh was too weak to cooperate. When God speaks to us, we may know in our spirits that we should do as He wants. But we can easily fall back into the ways of the *old man*, the flesh and, in our natural weakness, neglect to obey Him.

God will give us the strength we need, but Satan will tempt us to believe that is not so. A strong spirit will believe and trust God to equip us with everything we need to do His will and to overcome the flesh.

In John 16:33, Jesus tells us that we will indeed have trouble in this world. We may even have to face some persecution for our faith. But Jesus has overcome the world system, and He has taken up residence in us. Truly, in Him, we are fully equipped to do whatever He says, whenever He wants us to do it.

Luke 8:13 provides a slightly different interpretation. Luke refers to a time of testing. Of course, trouble and persecution will provide times of testing. But there could be other, more subtle, ways of testing us, too. For example, at the Last Supper, Jesus prophesied about a particular time of testing coming upon the disciples.

And the Lord said, "Simon, Simon! Indeed, Satan has asked for you (plural)*, that he may sift you* (plural) *as wheat."*

Luke 22:31

Times of testing will come upon us, and not only when we have just received a word of revelation. Troubles in this world are inevitable. So many of our brothers and sisters around the world suffer violent persecution. We may only encounter doubts or a little ridicule, but these will still test our hearts.

When God speaks to us, however He chooses to do it, let us make sure that our hearts are not hollow. Always remember that our spirits are strengthened, in Him. Our resolve need not be weakened by the flesh.

Mark 4:18-19 deals with *half* hearts. Hearts that are distracted by the things of this world. It is easy to be half-hearted when we let worries about material things distract us from the revelatory word of God. And from the more important spiritual matters concerning us.

Look at the birds of the air, for they neither sow nor reap nor gather into barns; yet your heavenly Father feeds them. Are you not of more value than they? Which of you by worrying can add one cubit to his stature?

Matthew 6:26-27

We can be half-hearted if we are more concerned about material wealth than with following Jesus. The rich young man seemed to be intent on religiously obeying all the rules. But his strong attachment to wealth was his underlying problem, his *Achilles heel*. Each of us will almost certainly have something negative to which we are still vulnerable.

Jesus said to him, "If you want to be perfect, go, sell what you have and give to the poor, and you will have treasure in heaven; and come, follow Me."

But when the young man heard that saying, he went away sorrowful, for he had great possessions.

Matthew 19:21

Another example of putting other things first, of having wrong priorities, is prevarication. Of course, I hesitate to mention that!

Then another of His disciples said to Him, "Lord, let me first go and bury my father."
But Jesus said to him, "Follow Me, and let the dead bury their own dead."

Matthew 8:21-22

The TPT notes that this man had probably not just been bereaved. He wanted to delay his full commitment to Jesus *until* his father had died and was buried. A person who has died in that culture, and in that climate, would be buried almost immediately. For me, this brings clarification to what otherwise might seem a hard response from the Lord.

Mark's Gospel says that half-hearted people will be unfruitful. Luke 8:14, however, focuses on maturity.

A mature believer's life bears fruit for the Kingdom because he or she is not half-hearted. I think Matthew 6:33 sums up the problem of distractions that choke the Word of God to us, holding us back from fruitfulness and greater maturity.

But seek first the Kingdom of God and His righteousness, and all these things shall be added to you.

Matthew 6:33

What, then, can be said about the word that falls on *good* soil?

Listen carefully to the words we are given. Hear and receive it fully. If we do not readily understand it, seek out an interpretation. When we have taken it on board, *do* something with or about it. Isn't that what the parable and Jesus' interpretation of it tell us, as believers?

Mark 4:20 references those who accept the word that they have heard. Matthew 13:23, on the other hand, relates to those who hear the word and understand it. Luke's gospel 8:15, NIV gives yet another interpretation. He writes about those who both hear and *retain* the word, then produce a crop by *persevering*.

That means, although fruitfulness may not come easily to them, and may not be immediately apparent, they will press on. Being convinced of the truth, the authenticity, and the importance of what they have just heard.

Accept the word. Come to an understanding of it. Retain it. Persevere with it. And, when the time is right, act upon it. Yes, *do* something with it.

God wants to speak to each one of us on a regular basis. So, are we going to stay alert, always listening expectantly for Him? Sometimes He speaks through the Bible. Sometimes through the prophetic. Sometimes in various other ways. It is His prerogative to choose the method, not ours! But never forget that He always wants the best for us. He will not try to catch us out.

We are called the *light of the world* because Holy Spirit shines within us. He brings enlightenment both to us and through us to others. We are very privileged. We need to be constantly aware of all the privileges we have as His beloved children.

No one lights a lamp and then hides it, covering it over or putting it where no one sees its light. No, he places the lamp on a lampstand, so others benefit from its brightness. Because this revelation lamp now shines within you nothing will be hidden from you—it will all be revealed. Every secret of the kingdom will be unveiled and out in the open, made known by the revelation light.

So, pay careful attention to your hearts as you listen to my teaching, for to those who have open hearts, even more revelation will be given to them until it overflows. And for those who do not listen with open hearts, what little light they imagine themselves to have will be taken away.

Luke 8: 16-18 TPT

Rather than *listen*, Luke 8:18 in the NKJV says, *Therefore take heed how you hear.* Listen with your *spiritual ears*. Hear clearly and receive the Word of

God fully into your heart. Seek it out hungrily if you do not readily understand it. Diligent seeking of Kingdom truths will always lead to finding.

We are not meant to be those with *hard* hearts, who will succumb to the activity of Satan.

We are not meant to be those with *hollow* hearts, who will give in to the weakness of the flesh.

We are not meant to be those with *half* hearts, who are distracted by the things of the world.

We blessed ones are those with *whole hearts* who *hear the word, accept it and produce a crop*. In other words, we *do* something to bear lasting fruit.

And, just like a tiny mustard seed grows into an enormous plant, that crop, that fruitfulness, will be out of all proportion to *what was sown.*

9
Blessed by the Five-fold Ministries

And He Himself (Jesus) *gave some to be apostles, some prophets, some evangelists, and some pastors and teachers, for the equipping of the saints for the work of ministry, for the edifying of the Body of Christ,*

(Ephesians 4:11-12)

I want to share some thoughts with you now on the family of the church. This chapter will focus primarily on those in leadership and/or other prominent roles, either now or in the future. The significant others of us are those who, though we are equally important in the eyes of God, do not (yet) carry such responsibilities.

And He said to them, "The kings of the Gentiles exercise lordship over them, and those who exercise authority over them are called benefactors. But not so among you; on the contrary, he who is greatest among you, let him be as the younger, and he who governs as he who serves. For who is greater, he who sits at the table, or he who serves? Is it not he who sits at the table? Yet I am among you as the One who serves."

(Luke 22:25-27)

Jesus modelled leadership as one who serves, not as one who is authoritarian, or who considers himself to be superior. Even though *He* is obviously superior to us in every way.

Unconditional love will put the interests of another first. Leaders are to be an example to those who follow them. Just as Jesus is the perfect example to all who would be leaders in the church. By the same token, those of us who are not leaders are to honour and respect those who have been called by Him to that office.

And we urge you, brethren, to recognise those who labour among you, and are over you in the Lord and admonish you, and to esteem them very highly in love for their work's sake. Be at peace among yourselves.

(1 Thessalonians 5:12-13)

Each person required to exercise one of the five-fold ministries must be called and equipped by God alone for that very purpose. Holy Spirit anoints them specifically for their role. Very often what they have been anointed and called to do is revealed gradually as they begin to *do* it. Their part is to respond in obedience to His promptings.

Church leaders, at least those who are not threatened by the emergence of other anointed and gifted people, will then recognise and acknowledge the hand of God in the lives of such men and women. They will encourage them to explore all that God is revealing in, about, to and through them. They will even encourage them to progress beyond the point at which they themselves peak.

There are colleges, courses and *how-to* books that offer training for these five ministries. But, unless someone has a definite calling and anointing from God, the effectiveness of such initiatives will be limited.

There are many people who append the prefix *Apostle*, *Prophet* or *Evangelist* to their names, especially when promoting their own ministries. When such titles or designations are self-awarded, I'm afraid my own (dubious) *gift* of cynicism tends to kick in!

There is also a line of teaching that adamantly contends that none of these ministries, or the first two anyway, are relevant for today. It chimes with Cessationist and/or Dispensationalist beliefs. I do not subscribe to either of these views.

The fact that the established church has, for some 1600 years, largely drifted away from its biblical apostolic/prophetic foundation does not override clear biblical statements. Ephesians 2:20 is a prime example.

Now, therefore, you are no longer strangers and foreigners, but fellow citizens with the saints and members of the household of God, having been built on the foundation of the apostles and prophets, Jesus Christ Himself being the chief cornerstone, in whom the whole building, being fitted together, grows into a holy temple in the Lord, in whom you also are being built together for a dwelling place of God in the Spirit.

(Ephesians 2:19-22)

Our traditional denominations do not, for the most part at least, recognise these five ministries in their original form. Or, at least, not always officially. They may have certain authentically Holy Spirit-anointed people operating in these ministries. But they are not necessarily designated as such by some official title.

Mind you, that is probably not such a bad thing. The function is far more important than any title. It doesn't matter what we call them if we recognise them because they are fulfilling a Kingdom job description!

The primary calling of five-fold ministers should never be forgotten. That is to pass on what they have received to the family of the church. I recently came across the following, from N. T. Wright. This is his interpretation of the verses at the beginning of this chapter.

So, these were the gifts that he gave. Some were to be apostles, others prophets, others evangelists, and others pastors and teachers. Their job is to give God's people the equipment they need for their work of service, and so to build up the King's body.

(NTE)

Many have concluded that pastors and teachers are the same person(s) with a joint responsibility. This is how many churches function today. This is so whether the appointed leader has both giftings, in the measure required to lead, or not. Others consider that the construction of the original text establishes them as separate ministries under this heading.

Personally, I am in favour of the latter view. I also feel that *leadership* is a separate gift *(see Romans 12:8 TPT)*. A gifting usually, but not necessarily always, combined with one of the five-fold offices, especially that of an *apostle*.

One can function in one of these roles without having an obvious leadership gifting. Or, even more importantly, someone who is appointed by human choice alone.

Just compare the reigns of Saul and David. The former had every appearance, physically, of being a born leader but failed completely. The latter did not and, but for some isolated failings not glossed over by scripture, was described as a man after God's own heart *(Acts 13:22)*.

There may be some in effective leadership who do not function in one of the five ministries. Nevertheless, they will no doubt operate in one or more of them as giftings, e.g., apostolic, prophetic, evangelistic, pastoral, or didactic.

The offices of apostles, prophets and evangelists are more likely to be either itinerant or for a comparatively short term only in any one location. Normally, I would suggest, the pastor and the teacher would be in position for a longer season, but always as God determines.

However, the latter will be pleased to work alongside those functioning in the other giftings or offices if they want overall biblically balanced leadership for their church family members.

There is a need for spiritual maturity in the church. Paul's letter to the Ephesians is a clear statement that this is achieved by the five-fold ministries functioning in harmonious relationships. The combination of their individual emphases is God's provision for a healthy church.

Apostles

And when it was day, He called His disciples to Himself; and from them, He chose 12 whom He also named apostles.

(Luke 6:13)

Apostle was the first ministry mentioned by Jesus. He chose 12 men and *designated* them apostles. This Greek word had long been used to describe a role in secular society. Jesus chose it as the name to apply to a specific 'office' in His church. What He intended for them to do was very much in keeping with what the secular Greek apostles did, albeit with a specific Kingdom purpose.

The secular function of an apostle (or ambassador) was to bring the culture of his homeland into the region to which he had been appointed. Usually, there would have been an invading, conquering army preceding him. The biblical function of the Christian apostle is to bring Heaven's culture to Earth, just as Jesus did.

Jesus appointed 12 apostles quite early on in His earthly ministry. There are many who consider that there were never intended to be any others. Of course, Judas was one of the original 12 and he was replaced after his death *(Acts 1:26).*

However, if the 12 were the only ones intended to be apostles in the church, not only in the first century AD but through the centuries until Jesus returns, there seems little point in Holy Spirit inspiring Paul to write the words from Ephesians 4 quoted above. In addition, there are scriptures, like the following, which make it quite clear that it was not only the 12 who would be recognised as apostles.

Greet Andronicus and Junia, my countrymen and my fellow prisoners, who are of note among the apostles, who also were in Christ before me.

(Romans 16:7)

The original New Testament apostles were largely pioneers, establishing new churches, recognising and appointing leaders (e.g., those emerging as people with five-fold anointings and/or giftings) and moving on after the work had been established. Such a role would still be important today in new, geographical areas of Kingdom expansion. Incidentally, Junia was almost certainly a woman.

However, there is also a need for them in countries, regions, towns, and villages where there are already established churches. They can build on what has gone before but may be in decline. They can expand upon the current Kingdom influence of those churches.

Their passion will be to see greater manifestations of Kingdom culture by encouraging believers in spiritual gifts and Kingdom values. They may have to be involved in planting new churches. Especially if, sadly, Kingdom culture is not, or no longer, embraced by the existing leaders or congregations in an area.

Paul also makes it clear what it is that provides evidence of apostleship. He did this without ever intending, in my view, to limit the working of signs, wonders and miracles to those recognised as apostles.

I believe he was simply pointing out that we will always find these manifestations occurring in the ministry of a genuine apostle. Neither does it preclude those of us who are not actually apostles from being apostolic on occasion, as the Lord leads us.

Truly the signs of an apostle were accomplished among you with all perseverance, in signs and wonders and mighty deeds.

(2 Corinthians 12:12)

Do you see and experience such evidence in your church family today? Do you appreciate the need to pursue either such manifestations yourself or through others in your church family?

Prophets

I have delivered a message entitled 'Making a Prophet' on a few occasions and this section is largely based on what I have shared in that context.

For prophecy never came by the will of man, but holy men of God spoke as they were moved by the Holy Spirit.

(2 Peter 1:21)

A prophet is someone who hears God's voice and delivers His message to others. People want to hear from God, not from us. Let us make every effort not to disappoint them by imposing our own agenda on what God has revealed to us for them. And always give the glory to Him for the results.

Pursue love, and desire spiritual (gifts), *but especially that you may prophesy.*

(1 Corinthians 14:1)

This verse makes it clear that prophecy is to have a primary place in the life of the church. What can be more important than passing on a word of revelation received from God? No one is excluded from exercising this gift. The only requirement is to eagerly desire it! Indeed, the original Greek can be accurately translated as *lust after* rather than *eagerly desire*!

Beloved, do not believe every spirit, but test the spirits, whether they are of God because many false prophets have gone out into the world.

(1 John 4:1)

We need to be aware that there are both false prophets and false teachers in existence. They just might visit our neck of the woods. This is where the gift of discernment comes in. Some will have this to a higher level than others. They, and the leaders, should *weigh* every word and deal gently with anyone who speaks in error—it may not have been deliberate.

I love Shawn Bolz's qualification, *I am learning to hear from God and sometimes I get it wrong.* Sometimes we will get it wrong, in all or in part. We need to be open to positive correction, have a *teachable spirit*, and humbly learn to grow in our gifting.

In John 10:27, Jesus makes it clear that we can, and are intended to, hear His voice. Hearing from God is our birthright. When we are born again, this privilege is meant to be the norm for us.

His voice is distinguished by love, hope and peace. It is always positive, encouraging, and loving. He would never condemn or belittle us. When we speak out to someone, we should do so with these characteristics of His informing our hearts and voices *(see also 1 Corinthians 14:3)*.

Having then gifts differing according to the grace that is given to us, let us use them: if prophecy, let us prophesy in proportion to our faith.

(Romans 12:6)

It is important never to speak beyond the revelation received from Holy Spirit and for which we have faith to deliver His message. The inspiration comes from Him. So we listen to Him before (and whilst) speaking out into a person's life or situation. We should say only what we hear from Him and not add our own opinion or interpretation.

We should also be aware that, sometimes, the revelation is not something to be passed on. There are times when it is to be retained and used as fuel for prayer for the person concerned. In addition, something highly personal could be revealed in a group setting that would be better retained until it could be shared privately with the individual concerned.

Generally, although a prophet can and will do this, a prophet<u>ic</u> person is not usually involved in predicting the future. Instead, their focus is what has been described well as *calling out the gold in someone*. That means highlighting what God has revealed as good, honourable, and positive about them. Things that they might not be aware of themselves at the time *(1 Corinthians 14:3)*.

Do not neglect the gift that is in you, which was given to you by prophecy with the laying on of the hands of the eldership.

(1 Timothy 4:14)

It is possible to receive the gift of prophecy (and other ministry gifts) through *impartation*. That is, by the laying on of hands and prophetic prayer of another person. Usually, this will be someone who already has the particular office or gifting themselves.

Let two or three prophets speak, and let the others judge. For you can all prophesy one by one, that all may learn, and all may be encouraged. And the spirits of the prophets are subject to the prophets.

(1 Corinthians 14:29, 31-32)

Most of what I have written about prophets and prophecy applies to personal or private opportunities to pass on messages from God to individuals. In this verse, we see principles laid down for the exercise of the gift in a corporate setting. During a church service for example.

We may all be able to prophesy but, if we all try to prophesy at once, chaos would ensue. This will devalue the whole purpose. Is there no time for you to speak during a meeting? Then share your message with a leader afterwards and trust them to pass it on.

And though I have the gift of prophecy, and understand all mysteries and all knowledge...but have not love, I am nothing.

(1 Corinthians 13:2)

To function well a prophet, or a prophetic person, must be motivated by love for the individual or group he or she is ministering to. This makes it a real blessing to be in a church environment in which you can speak out and/or receive a prophetic word at any time. It is so freeing when this has become accepted as the norm in that environment.

A prophet is someone who should be encouraged to help create a prophetic culture. A place where it is expected that God will speak and that people will both actively listen and respond. We just need to be prepared to step out of the 'safety' of our comfort zones if this is a new area for us to move into.

Evangelists

There is a very real sense in which we are all called to be evangelists or, more accurately, to be evangelistic. At the other extreme are those with large international ministries, like the late Billy Graham or Reinhard Bonnke. They are the only ones considered by many to warrant this description.

Yet who are the most effective evangelists, especially today? The ones who tend to exercise their ministries quietly out on the streets, not in massive auditoriums or stadiums. That is not to decry what went on before, simply to suggest that we may now be in a new season.

There will always be exceptions to every *rule*. But it seems to me, this is the way God is moving more and more in our day. How many large evangelistic crusades can we find in the gospels or Acts? You may point to Peter on the day of Pentecost in Acts 2. But that was not an event planned and put together in advance with human organisation. It was a spontaneous move of God that took *all* those present by surprise, including Peter!

On the next day, we who were Paul's companions departed and came to Caesarea, and entered the house of Philip the evangelist, who was one of the seven, and stayed with him. Now this man had four virgin daughters who prophesied.

(Acts 21:8-9)

One of the original 12 apostles was named Philip. But this Philip is the deacon who was appointed, with Stephen and others, to solve a practical problem of food distribution within the early church (Acts 6). He was gifted beyond the abilities required for this first appointment. In due course, he was recognised and became known as an evangelist. This could be equally true of you or me, if we keep ourselves open to what God is saying to us.

But you be watchful in all things, endure afflictions, do the work of an evangelist, fulfil your ministry.

(2 Timothy 4:5)

Timothy was not known as an evangelist but, clearly, he was expected to do evangelist<u>ic</u> things at the very least. In the same way, you and I may not be evangelists, but we never know when we might be called upon by Holy Spirit to be evangelistic during an encounter with someone *(1 Peter 3:15)*.

I know I am not an evangelist, but God has clearly directed me into the ministry of Treasure Hunting[1]. This is an endeavour which includes evangelistic, prophetic, and healing ministry at different times.

For some while, I have found myself facilitating groups of Treasure Hunters. Although not obviously gifted evangelistically, I can contribute more effectively when opportunities for the prophetic or healing arise. It doesn't matter who leads a person to Christ—provided someone does!

Pastors

Many church leaders, across a whole range of denominations, are known as and/or addressed as *pastors*. This is simply because it has become the custom to bestow this title. This is regardless of whether or not the leader concerned has a true pastoral anointing for ministry.

Those denominations for whom *preaching with a view* is a significant part of their pastoral appointment process demonstrate in this way what their priority for a leader is. He, or she, is to be an excellent preacher/teacher, almost regardless of whether or not they have any person-to-person skills. Not all of them excel in this latter regard!

When reading Ephesians 4:11, we find that this is the only time the original Greek word is translated as *pastor*. It is conveyed as *shepherd* every other time it is used, some 16 in all I believe. It is important for sheep to have a shepherd to guide, nurture and protect them from predators. The role of the pastor is similar but, obviously, in a spiritual context.

Then Jesus went about all the cities and villages, teaching in their synagogues, preaching the gospel of the kingdom, and healing every sickness and every disease among the people. But when He saw the multitudes, He was moved with compassion for them, because they were weary and scattered, like sheep having no shepherd.

(Matthew 9:35-36)

Jesus is the true prototype of the New Testament shepherd (pastor). His love and compassion reached a sacrificial level, ultimately, at the cross.

I am the good shepherd. The good shepherd gives His life for the sheep.

(John 10:11)

When the pre-Christian comes under conviction by Holy Spirit, and turns to Jesus, he or she no longer drifts off into their own way. They turn to Him and receive the blessing of a restored relationship with Father God through Him.

For you were like sheep going astray but have now returned to the Shepherd and Overseer of your souls.

(1 Peter 2:25)

The sheep in a shepherd's flock know his voice and respond to no other. They put complete trust in him and follow him wherever he leads. Learning to *hear* the voice of Jesus, to trust, obey and follow His promptings, is an essential ingredient of the normal Christian life of the blessed ones.

My sheep hear My voice, and I know them, and they follow Me. And I give them eternal life, and they shall never perish; neither shall anyone snatch them out of My hand.

(John 10:27-28)

Jesus has ultimate authority, of course, but He has delegated at least some of His undisputed authority to others within His Body, the church. We find the use of such authority in pastors/shepherds who are termed *overseers* by the New Testament writers.

The elders who are among you I exhort, I who am a fellow elder and a witness of the sufferings of Christ, and also a partaker of the glory that will be revealed: Shepherd the flock of God which is among you, serving as overseers, not by compulsion but willingly, not for dishonest gain but eagerly; nor as being lords over those entrusted to you, but being examples to the flock; and when the Chief Shepherd appears, you will receive the crown of glory that does not fade away.

(1 Peter 5:1-4)

Alongside this use of delegated authority is the exhortation to serve, not to dictate, dominate or intimidate. Nor to profit from the use of such a position. Again, Jesus, the One who came to serve not to be served, is the perfect example. People do not respect those who wield a big stick. They follow and obey them out of fear (and not the variety of fear better termed as *awe*).

We find that the words *overseer* and *bishop* can be interchangeable in our English translations of the Bible. Paul lays down certain qualifications for someone who is blessed to have such a position in the church. It is at least debatable just how many of these stringent conditions are met in every successful candidate for such appointments today.

This is a faithful saying: If a man desires the position of a bishop (overseer), he desires a good work. A bishop (overseer) then must be blameless, the husband of one wife, temperate, sober-minded, of good behaviour, hospitable, able to teach; not given to wine, not violent, not greedy for money, but gentle, not quarrelsome, not covetous; one who rules his own house well, having his children in submission with all reverence (for if a man does not know how to rule his own house, how will he take care of the church of God?); not a novice, lest being puffed up with pride he fall into the same condemnation as the devil. Moreover, he must have a good testimony among those who are outside, lest he fall into reproach and the snare of the devil.

(1 Timothy 3:1-7)

Another term relating to an office carrying a degree of authority in the church is found in 1 Timothy 3:8-13 *Likewise, deacons*. Again, someone in this position is required to meet certain specific criteria, much like those expected of bishops/overseers.

Deacon is a translation of the Greek word *diakanos*, and can be interpreted as deacon, minister, or servant. The actual role of a deacon in the church today varies somewhat between denominations. But it seems fair to say that the biblical function of this role is connected to the concept of servanthood.

The *bishop/overseer* role seems to carry a greater degree of authority than the *deacon* as, perhaps, does the *pastor*/shepherd. However, that should not detract from the expectation that every person called to a church office is meant to be one who serves. Even if a deacon may be considered a kind of third-tier appointment, the qualifications are no less exacting.

Therefore, brethren, seek out from among you seven men of good reputation, full of the Holy Spirit and wisdom, whom we may appoint over this business.

(Acts 6:3)

The first deacons were appointed to *serve at tables*. More precisely in a role delegated to them by the apostles to ensure fair treatment for all widows within the church family. These first deacons included Stephen and Philip, of course. The scriptures make it very clear that, in addition, they were both used by God in amazing ways. One became a martyr, the other an evangelist. Both were greatly used in signs and wonders.

Suffice it to say that the roles of bishop/overseer, pastor, and deacon each have a pastoral context. However, those who fulfil these offices, whatever that may mean in greater detail in different church environments, are not thereby limited in the scope to which God may call them to serve Him.

As already indicated, Philip is later described as an *evangelist*. This is a role which he was found already pursuing earlier in Samaria, and then when encountering the Ethiopian official.

Teachers

The words *pastors* and *teachers* are often read together as though both offices are always to be filled by one person. The grammatical construction of our English language does not permit a comma after *pastors* (apart from a form of correction that Microsoft Word hints at). I think that this probably contributes largely to the idea of it always being a dual role.

Those who know these things much better than I do say that the Greek language makes it quite clear that there is a distinction between the two roles in the original biblical texts. It does not help either that, in many denominations, as already said, most church leaders are called *pastors*, but their primary role is invariably that of preacher/teacher.

But the Helper, the Holy Spirit, whom the Father will send in My name, He will teach you all things, and bring to your remembrance all things that I said to you.

(John 14:26)

Holy Spirit is the ultimate teacher of us all, bringing wisdom and revelation to each one, not only through the called and equipped five-fold teacher. A significant *level* of anointing should be readily discernible upon anyone who aspires to be a teacher within the church family. This role carries a very important responsibility for the accurate dissemination of biblical truths.

And the things that you have heard from me among many witnesses, commit these to faithful men who will be able to teach others also.

(2 Timothy 2:2)

Paul indicates to Timothy, I believe, that the teacher anointing can be transferrable. It can be passed on from one to another by impartation, as the Spirit leads. This can either be in the context of a specific role or, in more general terms, the ability given to each one of us to pass on, informally, to another whatever we have already been taught ourselves.

A bishop then must be blameless, the husband of one wife, temperate, sober-minded, of good behaviour, hospitable, able to teach.

(1 Timothy 2:2)

Here we find that at least part of a bishop/overseer's brief is to teach those under his or her care. This may be at a leadership *level* or at a general congregational *level*, depending upon the circumstances. It follows, at least by implication, that the same can be said of the pastor/shepherd. Although more likely for him/her it would be exclusively at the congregational *level*.

For though by this time you ought to be teachers, you need someone to teach you again the first principles of the oracles of God; and you have come to need milk and not solid food.

(Hebrews 5:12)

The letter to the Hebrews is aimed at Christians generally, emphasising that any one of us can find ourselves in the role of teacher, whether temporarily or more permanently. Again, when we pass on to another something we have already been taught, we are *teaching*. Yes, even if it is only over coffee in our homes. Titles don't come into it!

But the anointing which you have received from Him abides in you, and you do not need that anyone teach you; but as the same anointing teaches you concerning all things, and is true, and is not a lie, and just as it has taught you, you will abide in Him.

(1 John 2:27)

All those who are Christians are born again of Holy Spirit and, hopefully, carry the anointing of Holy Spirit baptism. Therefore, the anointing John writes about is an anointing common to everyone, whether realised or not. This confirms that Holy Spirit is the Teacher of us all.

Each of us is able to receive from Him on a one-to-one basis. This may be for purely personal revelation. It may also be for passing on to others. This could be either individually or, if we are called and equipped for a teaching role in the church, corporately.

Preach the word! Be ready in season and out of season. Convince, rebuke, exhort, with all longsuffering and teaching.

(2 Timothy 4:2)

Is Paul encouraging Timothy in the pursuance of his leadership role in the church, or is there more to it than that? I think it is also an encouragement to each one of *us*, whether in leadership or not. We all have informal opportunities to meet with and speak with people in a multitude of situations. There is room for Kingdom activity in each of them if we are *listening* as He leads us.

My brethren, let not many of you become teachers, knowing that we shall receive a stricter judgment. For we all stumble in on many things. If anyone does not stumble in word words, he is a perfect man, able also to bridle the whole body.

(James 3:1-2)

Hopefully, we are agreed that each of us can be a teacher, whether it is in a leadership or other *upfront* capacity. So, here is a word of warning from James that is particularly directed, I believe, to those with some degree of corporate responsibility.

Yes, one must be called and equipped to properly fulfil the role of teacher. But one must also be aware of the great responsibility that comes with such a calling. This explains why there are demanding *pre-conditions* laid down by Paul (and Holy Spirit) for the appointment of people to the office of bishop, pastor/shepherd, or teacher.

But there were also false prophets among the people, even as there will be false teachers among you, who will secretly bring in destructive heresies, even denying the Lord who bought them and bring on themselves swift destruction.

(2 Peter 2:1)

Sadly, we must all be aware of the possibility of false teachers among us. Either that or teaching which is not sound—even if it does not emanate from a false teacher *per se*. The gifts of wisdom and discernment, which are available to every one of us as needed, are required to filter what we hear.

Then we apply what is good and discard what is not *of Him*. It is for church leaders to deal with false teachers, but we must all be aware that they exist and could infiltrate our environment.

Teachers are always to remain *teachable* and to be open to correction when necessary. We can read, in Acts 18, how the truly gifted Apollos was humble enough to be corrected by Priscilla and Aquila. They were companions of and co-workers with Paul during his apostolic ministry in different locations.

The church was originally built on the foundation of apostles and prophets. There have always been evangelists, or people operating evangelistically. What we used to call *witnessing*. Every church seems to have a *pastor*, whatever his or her primary gifting may be. And none of us would grow spiritually without being taught by teachers of the Word.

Are the five-fold ministries active in your own church family today? Is the Ephesians 4 pattern of balanced leadership established there?

Now you are the Body of Christ, and members individually. And God has appointed these in the church: first apostles, second prophets, third teachers, after that, miracles, then gifts of healings healing, helps, administrations, varieties of tongues. Are all apostles? Are all prophets? Are all teachers? Are all workers of miracles? Do all have gifts of healings healing? Do all speak with tongues? Do all interpret? But earnestly desire the best gifts. And yet I show you a more excellent way.

(1 Corinthians 12:27-31

It is interesting that the above passage does not mention either evangelists or pastors. Of course, that doesn't mean that they are not important. We already know, from other scriptures, that they are. But a church functioning in all these giftings would grow anyway (evangelistic) and it would look after its own family members with love and compassion (pastoral), wouldn't it?

And the *more excellent way*? Whatever you do, always do it in the context of unconditional *love*. That is the most important distinguishing mark of a leader who serves well.

1. '*The Ultimate Treasure Hunt*', Kevin Dedmon (Destiny Image Publishers Inc).

10
Blessed by Metamorphosis

But we all, with unveiled face, beholding as in a mirror the glory of the Lord, are being transformed into the same image from glory to glory, just as by the Spirit of the Lord.

(2 Corinthians 3:18)

Some years ago, I came across a cartoon[1] which proved to be the ideal opening for a sermon with the above title that I recently preached at my home church. I adapted the cartoon into a very short story, for my introduction. It went something like this:

Once upon a time, there were two huge, hairy, hungry caterpillars living on a juicy leaf. They were voraciously eating themselves out of house and home. They paused, very briefly, between mouthfuls to look up at the sky. At a particular moment a gorgeous, multi-hued butterfly flew over their heads. They were stunned by its incredible beauty.

Then one caterpillar turned to the other and declared, "You'll never get me up in one of those things!"

This caterpillar demonstrates, hopefully in a humorous way, what living in denial, or in ignorance, of our own destiny can look like. Every caterpillar is designed and destined to be transformed. They are meant to become butterflies. They can't remain caterpillars forever. That is not God's purpose for them.

We should each ask ourselves this question. Do I live in denial or ignorance of my own destiny in Christ? Or do I truly seek to understand and fully embrace God's *whole* purpose in saving me?

Of course, it is a given that salvation is primarily to restore the relationship between mankind and God. And that is not possible without confession, repentance, and forgiveness of sins. But the original word translated as *salvation* means more than simply being forgiven. It means being saved—and healed—and delivered. It also means that we are destined to undergo a process of change, of transformation, as this familiar verse already quoted above reminds us.

But we all, with unveiled faces, beholding as in a mirror the glory of the Lord, are being transformed into the same image from glory to glory, just as by the Spirit of the Lord.

(2 Corinthians 3:18)

I tend to prefer the Passion Translation rendering on this occasion, though.

We can all draw close to him with the veil removed from our faces. And with no veil, we all become like mirrors who brightly reflect the glory of the Lord Jesus. We are being transfigured into his very image as we move from one brighter level of glory to another. And this glorious transfiguration comes from the Lord, who is the Spirit.

(2 Corinthians 3:18, TPT)

The anglicised version of the original Greek word translated as *transformed* (NKJV) or *transfigured* (TPT) is *metamorphosis*. This is why I have used it for my chapter heading.

The Passion's Footnotes tell us that, *The Greek verb* metamorphoō *is the same word used for Jesus' being transfigured on the mountain—and for our transfiguration through the renewing of the thoughts of our minds (see Romans 12:2).*

Metamorphosis is described by the online Oxford Learners' Dictionaries as, *a process in which someone or something changes completely into something different.* It goes on to give *transformation* as a synonym for:

- *the <u>metamorphosis</u> of a caterpillar into a butterfly.*
- *She had undergone an amazing <u>metamorphosis</u> from an awkward schoolgirl into a beautiful woman.*

That certainly accords with the NKJV interpretation. But, perhaps, a more biblical synonym would be *transfiguration*, as the TPT puts it. However, it is our deepening relationship with Jesus that brings it all about, as another Passion footnote underlines.

The source of our transformation comes from Christ's glory, and the destination we are brought to is more glory. The transforming glory is the result of gazing upon the beauty and splendour of Jesus Christ.

This metamorphosis, transformation or transfiguration is a *process*, both for the caterpillar/butterfly and for the blessed ones. We could say that, as non-Christians, we were effectively caterpillars until we began a process of transformation after encountering the beautiful butterfly, who is Jesus.

As his opening address for the 2021 Bethel Sozo Ministry Conference, David West preached a sermon entitled: 'Breakthrough is hidden in a process'. This really resonated with me. Much of what happens to us in the Kingdom is not sudden but is part of an ongoing process. The purpose of the metamorphosis process is to enable us to become more like Jesus.

And I think that, in the Kingdom of God, there are also processes within that process. There are three sub-processes I have in mind. Each of them requires a breakthrough to bring them about. As David said, "Breakthrough is hidden in a process."

1. Conversion   (The Steppingstones Process)
2. Sanctification   (The Individual Christian Maturity Process)
3. Corporate Growth   (The Church Body Maturity Process)

We tend to use the expression, *the moment of conversion*. At least we used to when I was a *boy* Christian! Billy Graham aimed to bring people to the point of making a *decision* in response to his evangelistic addresses. The magazine published by his ministry was entitled *Decision*. Decisions are not always instant. They very often come at the end of a process of learning or deliberation.

I think there is indeed a specific moment in time when we are transferred from the kingdom of darkness into God's Kingdom of Light. But, building up to that moment, there is invariably a process over time, be it long or short.

I'm not implying that there can never be instant conversions. After all, God is Sovereign. Being Sovereign means He can do what He likes, how He likes and when He likes. I'm simply suggesting that, for the most part, it is not the norm. Usually, it takes time. Time to come to the crucial point of *decision*.

I have often used *stepping stones* as an illustration of the conversion process. Many of us become involved in ultimately evangelistic endeavours, like treasure hunting, for example. Sadly, we can too easily put ourselves under pressure to see instant conversions every time we talk to someone.

In the final analysis, conversion is always dependent upon Holy Spirit-inspired conviction. We may say or do something to help the person along. But, ultimately, their *decision* comes as they respond to Him, not directly to us.

Imagine a stream, or a small river, with a row of stepping stones across the full width of it. Imagine that one side of the stream/river represents where the non-believer stands now. Imagine that on the other side of the stream/river lies a destination, the Kingdom of God. The journey, the process of our conversion, involves us moving from one side of it to the other, using the stepping stones.

We may encounter a person when they are yet to move from the opposite bank towards the Kingdom. It may be our privilege to help them from there onto the very first stepping stone. Maybe we will meet them when they are on the last stepping stone, ready to step into the Kingdom of God. Or we may meet them somewhere in the middle, to help them to go maybe just one stage further.

We must learn not to be disappointed if we're not chosen to be involved in their final step. It is an honour to be involved at any stage of the process. That's whether we are there at the moment of *decision* or not. And it is a big mistake to try to hurry someone along too quickly from one step to another. We risk getting ahead of what the Lord knows is best for them at any given moment. *His* timing is always perfect. We should remain in submission to Him.

When they have finally stepped onto the Kingdom bank, the process of *sanctification* begins. By the way, this will run alongside another process—discipleship. It is not enough to become a believer only. *Knowing* Him is to be combined with *doing* things. Jesus taught His disciples and part of the education process involved teaching them to *do* what He did. The practical.

Each of us will have had an individual journey through the conversion process. Equally, each one will also have a unique journey through the sanctification process. Our Kingdom journey, this side of Heaven. Of course, there are bound to be some experiences that are common to most of us. But, overall, your journey and my journey will be as unique as we are.

That is why we should never make unwise comparisons with one another. We will all go through different stages at different times. Some of them will be harder for me than for you—and vice versa.

That's okay! That's normal! What we might call the degrees of difficulty will vary. To some extent, this will be in accord with our unique backstories. Our personal history will have an influence on the extent and speed of our development.

We should never let our past dictate our future, but it will have an influence all the same. I will struggle more in some areas than you because of my unique history. I will find some areas easier than you do because of your uniquely different history.

That is why comparing ourselves with another Christian, or measuring ourselves against someone else, is so unwise. It is also very counterproductive.

There is nothing wrong with *sharing* with each other stories of our individual journeys through the process. But let us not fall into the trap of making unwise comparisons. Or doubting the authenticity of our experience because it differs from theirs.

For the same reasons, we should never be quick to judge someone who has a different perspective from us. Especially if we don't know their history or their various influences. If they *do* need to change an opinion, let us lovingly agree to disagree about what could divide us and let God introduce those changes in His timing.

Jesus is our true judge, our only wise standard of measure. We know we will *all* fall short when we compare ourselves with Him. He alone is entirely perfect. Let us simply look at Him for guidance, for the example we need to follow. He was always loving and compassionate to everyone. Except perhaps towards the hypocritical religious leaders of His time on Earth as the Son of Man!

Consider His interaction with the woman at the well. Or with the woman caught in adultery. With Zacchaeus—the dishonest tax collector. Or with the penitent thief hanging on the cross next to His. There are so many other examples we could examine. We will find Him always loving, always compassionate, always understanding. And always willing to forgive the truly repentant.

The Sanctification Process is designed solely to make us more like Him. Not someone else in our church family or whom we have seen in the media. That process, whatever it may involve, has been individually tailored for you and for me. God knows best.

He takes account of all our little quirks, our individual stories up to that point. What has framed us? What has influenced us? What has hurt us? What has cheered us? What has made us? Yes, our secrets, too. In fact, how we are at any given moment in our lives. He knows it all, and He loves us just the same!

Our responsibility is to let His influence alone be the most effective upon us at all times.

It is possible to view both the Conversion Process and the Sanctification Process as pertaining primarily, if not exclusively, to the individual. That's fair enough, I think. But my third sub-heading is *Corporate* Growth. Or you could call it the church *body* maturity process.

We are individuals called to be part of a Body, the Body of Christ. His Church on Earth. We are individuals called to be part of a holy nation. Of a royal priesthood—together. And together we are called out of darkness into His Kingdom of Light. We are to remain together, in unity. And haven't we, the church generally that is, made a great job of that?!?

There is nothing wrong with diversity. Just look at the myriad varieties within creation. Even among one species like caterpillars/butterflies! We Christians are not meant to be clones of one another.

But we are meant to be together. United in one Body on Earth, growing together. And, down through church history, too often we have made a real mess of it!

Did you know that the phrase *one another* occurs 190 times in the Bible? 90 times in the Old Testament and 100 times in the New Testament to be precise. The following examples are found in Romans alone and are all about being together—in a very positive way:

- Be devoted to one another in love.
- Honour one another above yourselves.
- Live in harmony with one another.
- Stop passing judgment on one another.
- Accept one another.
- You are filled with knowledge and competent to instruct one another.

- Greet one another with a holy kiss.
- Love one another.

Love one another appears in several places throughout the New Testament, of course. There is also this well-known passage in Psalm 133:

"How good and pleasant it is when God's people live together in unity! It is like precious oil poured on the head, running down on the beard, running down on Aaron's beard, down on the collar of his robe. It is as if the dew of Hermon were falling on Mount Zion. For there the Lord bestows his blessing, even life forevermore."

So, this requirement for God's people to dwell together in unity applies to both the old and the new covenants. Under the new covenant, we have less of an excuse for failure because we have the indwelling Holy Spirit. He wants to help us keep that unity, modelled on the perfect unity of the Trinity.

As I draw this chapter to a close, I want us to look at one specific aspect of *the Church Body Maturity Process*. You will recall that I have already touched on it in the previous one.

"And, He Himself gave some to be apostles, some prophets, some evangelists, and some pastors and teachers, for the equipping of the saints for the work of ministry, for the edifying of the Body of Christ till we all come to the unity of the faith and of the knowledge of the Son of God, to a perfect man, to the measure of the stature of the fullness of Christ; that we should no longer be children, tossed to and fro, and carried about with every wind of doctrine, by the trickery of men, in the cunning craftiness of deceitful plotting, but, speaking the truth in love, may grow up in all things into Him who is the head—Christ—from whom the whole body, joined and knit together by what every joint supplies, according to the effective working by which every part does its share, causes growth of the body for the edifying of itself in love."

(Ephesians 4:11-16)

These verses state quite clearly that the goal of the church is to be unity in the faith. Unity in the knowledge of Jesus. Unity in maturity, thereby attaining to the whole measure of the fullness of Christ.

I believe that *unity of the faith* means that, even with the diversity of practices, we can share the same convictions about the most important tenets of our faith. These must never divide us. However, we should show tolerance for the lesser things about which we might differ.

The biggest issue there is *who* decides which are the more or the less important tenets! I would suggest that, if we have unity in the Spirit, He is the one who decides and informs us all.

I believe that in referring to *the knowledge of the Son of God,* Holy Spirit is speaking less of knowing *about* Jesus, and more of knowing Him. In other words, our relationship with Him. A relationship intended to be intimate.

I believe that the *perfect man* or to put it perhaps more helpfully, the *maturity,* Holy Spirit speaks about here is the measure of our progression through the process of sanctification. And not only individually but also collectively.

I believe that His reference to *the measure of the stature of the fullness of Christ* is Holy Spirit emphasising the importance of becoming more and more like Jesus in every way. This comprehensively covers thought, word, and deed.

"I would like to think that my readers would not want to argue with me over the validity of these summarising statements. Even if some would prefer to word them slightly differently."

But *how* do we get there? That's the $64,000 question! (That dates me!).

Paul, in writing to the Ephesian church under the anointing of Holy Spirit, is clear on this. It is through living in and being influenced by, the right sort of church environment.

Jesus *has* gifted His church with the means to this end. He *has* given His church apostolic, prophetic, evangelistic, pastoral, and didactic gifts. These are ministered through the men and women He has called and equipped to fulfil these roles. All in order to achieve *His* perfect purposes, of course.

What concerns me is that, in the church generally, these gifts are not always recognised, let alone employed. How often do we see the release of people with these gifts into the freedom to exercise them? Always in submission to and under the authority of godly leadership.

You are blessed if you are part of a church family that does not have such reservations. A fellowship that seeks to pursue the biblical ideals for ministry and growth, both individually and collectively.

Part of the function of these gifts is to share them with others.

- Apostles are to *equip God's people for works of service* that are apostolic.
- Prophets are to *equip God's people for works of service* that are prophetic.
- Evangelists are to *equip God's people for works of service* that are evangelistic.
- And so on. You get the picture?

Both my last and present home church families have welcomed and released such gifted people. Folk have seen one another consistently exercising the freedom to use the various and varying gifts they have been given.

We want to see this happening more and more, though. Always within the perfect will and purposes of God for us as a Body. I hope you want the same for your own fellowship.

All of this is very much part of an ongoing process. We can legitimately call it metamorphosising. We are changing from one degree of glory to another as we move towards full maturity in Christ. Approaching that great day when we will meet Him face to face.

That is when we long to hear Him say to us, "Well done, good and faithful servant—"

Therefore, we also, since we are surrounded by so great a cloud of witnesses, let us lay aside every weight, and the sin which so easily ensnares us, and let us run with endurance the race that is set before us, looking unto Jesus, the author and finisher of our faith.

(Hebrews 12:1-2a)

Let us all resolve to metamorphose into *butterflies of faith* in God's Kingdom. Let us all diligently pursue our destinies in Christ. Never being tempted to say, "You'll never get me up in one of those things!"

1. I cannot remember the source of this cartoon otherwise I would happily acknowledge it.

Empowered to Do
Postscript 2

"Do not merely listen to the word, and so deceive yourselves. Do what it says. Anyone who listens to the word but does not do what it says is like someone who looks at his face in a mirror and, after looking at himself, goes away and immediately forgets what he looks like.
But whoever looks intently into the perfect law that gives freedom, and continues in it—not forgetting what they have heard, but doing it—they will be blessed in what they do."

(James 1:22-25)

For too many, perhaps, Christianity is just another religion. But religions tend to be characterised by long lists of *dos and don'ts*. These all have to be complied with in order to receive some sort of reward.

Of course, we can also go to the other extreme and determine that a gospel of grace requires us to *do* nothing. We can be easily misunderstood if we suggest that the latter *ain't necessarily so*.

However, we can do this legitimately without overriding what Paul tells us in Ephesians 2. Here he writes about being saved by grace alone, through faith, which itself is a gift of God. When we read on to verse 10, we come to what God has prepared (in advance) for us to *do*. Therefore, it is not a matter of *either/or* but of *both/and*.

What we *do* provides evidence of what we have already received by grace, through faith. John the Baptiser sent his disciples to question Jesus about whether He was truly the Messiah *(see Matthew 11)*. Jesus sent them back to tell John about the things He had *done* as evidence of who He *was*. This would remind John about the prophecy in Isaiah 61—and Jesus' words recorded in Luke 4 about His mission to fulfil that prophecy.

John 14:12 is one of my favourite verses. This makes it perfectly clear that Jesus expects us to *do* the things that He did. And even more! In the Great Commission of Matthew 28 and also in Mark 16, we find the same emphasis. This enforces what Jesus had already commissioned His first disciples to *do*, back in Matthew 10.

The evidence for the authentic ministry of an apostle includes the working of signs, wonders, and miracles *(2 Corinthians 12:12)*. We are not all called to be apostles. But there will be times and seasons when we are enabled and equipped to be *apostolic*.

When my wife, Cathy, and I were exercising our ministry, *Eagles 4031*, I would suggest that there were elements of the *apostolic* in it. Having said that, neither of us would claim to hold the office of Apostle. Our ministry involved us in teaching and demonstrating various spiritual gifts, with an emphasis on healing.

We also focussed on prophecy and word of knowledge, but a little less about the other gifts. The primary aim of our ministry was getting people to *do it*. Once we had moved on, we wanted them to remain participants, not merely spectators. There was no greater reward than to see that happening and we treasure many such memories.

Let us rejoice in who we are, as the blessed ones, by the grace of God. But let us never lose sight of our calling. It is only by *doing*, as well as *being*, that we will enter the fullness of the abundant life that is our destiny in Christ, both now and forever in Heaven.

The Alpha Course hint at a football match in a stadium as an illustration of a typical church problem. It refers to 22 people rushing around, in need of a rest, and 22,000 others, in need of exercise, simply watching them! In too many churches 10% of the congregation does 90% of the *work*, the *doing*! Jesus taught His disciples to *go* and to *do*. All of us blessed ones are His disciples, too.

Remember, Jesus is our perfect example in all things relating to His Kingdom. We have a whole array of spiritual gifts at our disposal. Although these should be allied to spiritual fruit as we exercise them in love. This is how to enjoy a life of abundance and of full freedom in Christ, whatever the prevailing circumstances may be.

Let us rediscover the blessings of healing—if this gift has been neglected. Aware that we are sons who serve a merciful and compassionate God. He has sown seeds in our lives to provoke a positive and fruitful reaction. Recognition of and positive response to the five-fold ministries enables us to learn to become apostolic, prophetic, evangelistic, pastoral, or didactic. All this will help us through the metamorphotic process that God will use to bring us to maturity in Christ.

May God richly bless you in your endeavours to follow His calling upon your life and ministry because He is equipping us all to be *doers* of His Word.

"And as you go, preach, saying, The Kingdom of Heaven is at hand. Heal the sick, cleanse the lepers, raise the dead, cast out demons. Freely you have received, freely give."

(Matthew 10:7-8)

"And Jesus came and spoke to them, saying, "All authority has been given to Me in heaven and on Earth. Go therefore and make disciples of all the nations, baptising them in the name of the Father and of the Son and of the Holy Spirit, teaching them to observe all things that I have commanded you; and lo, I am with you always, even to the end of the age." Amen.

(Matthew 28:18-20)

What men call salvation is simply the first stage of God's plan for our lives, which is to conform us in character and power to the image of Jesus Christ. If we fail to see our relationship with God as such, we will allow too many areas within us to remain unchanged. Pulling down strongholds is the demolition and removal of these old ways of thinking so that the actual Presence of Jesus Christ can be manifested through us.

(Francis Frangipane—
'The Three Battlegrounds')

In July 2018, Dennis and Cathy Acott left their home in Kent to enjoy retirement in Hunstanton, Norfolk. There they joined The Way Christian Fellowship, in due course being invited onto the leadership team. Cathy, in particular, became more actively involved in the Bethel Sozo ministry.

They are passionate about exercising the Christian ministry of healing, both physical and emotional, and seeing the gifts of the Spirit actively employed in the normal daily life of contemporary church fellowships of every stream and denomination.

They no longer travel around to minister as Eagles 4031 but are pleased to maintain the various contacts they made in that capacity. They are still open to the occasional invitation to minister in other churches' events, usually under the banner of D & C.